ISBN 978-1-331-93366-3
PIBN 10256445

1 MONTH OF
FREE
READING

at

www.ForgottenBooks.com

By purchasing this book you are eligible for one month membership to ForgottenBooks.com, giving you unlimited access to our entire collection of over 700,000 titles via our web site and mobile apps.

To claim your free month visit:

www.forgottenbooks.com/free256445

English
Français
Deutsche
Italiano
Español
Português

www.forgottenbooks.com

Mythology Photography **Fiction**
Fishing Christianity **Art** Cooking
Essays Buddhism Freemasonry
Medicine **Biology** Music **Ancient
Egypt** Evolution Carpentry Physics
Dance Geology **Mathematics** Fitness
Shakespeare **Folklore** Yoga Marketing
Confidence Immortality Biographies
Poetry **Psychology** Witchcraft
Electronics Chemistry History **Law**
Accounting **Philosophy** Anthropology
Alchemy Drama Quantum Mechanics
Atheism Sexual Health **Ancient History**
Entrepreneurship Languages Sport
Paleontology Needlework Islam
Metaphysics Investment Archaeology
Parenting Statistics Criminology
Motivational

THE BLACK DEATH

OF

1348 AND 1349

BY

FRANCIS AIDAN GASQUET, D.D.

ABBOT PRESIDENT OF THE ENGLISH BENEDICTINES

SECOND EDITION

LONDON

GEORGE BELL AND SONS

CHISWICK PRESS: CHARLES WHITTINGHAM AND CO.
TOOKS COURT, CHANCERY LANE, LONDON.

PREFACE TO THE SECOND EDITION

THIS essay, published in 1893, has long been out of print, and second-hand copies are difficult to procure, as they very rarely find their way into booksellers' catalogues. For this reason it has been thought well to reprint this account of the greatest plague that has probably ever devastated the world in historic times. Although the subject is necessarily of a doleful and melancholy character, it is of importance in the world's history, both as the account of a universal catastrophe and in its far-reaching effects.

Since the original publication of *The Great Pestilence* additional interest in the subject of bubonic plague has been aroused by the alarming mortality recently caused by it in India, and by the threatened outbreaks in various parts of Europe, where, however, the watchful care of the sanitary authorities has so far enabled them to deal with the sporadic cases which have appeared during the past few years, and to prevent the spread of the terrible scourge.

From the researches made in India and elsewhere into the nature and causes of the disease, many new facts have been established which assist us to understand the story of the great epidemic of the fourteenth century, now commonly known as "The Black Death," which is related in some detail in these pages. The accounts of the ravages of the disease in India, which have appeared in the newspapers, are little less than appalling, and would probably have attracted more attention were it not for the fact that few Europeans have succumbed to a malady which has been so fatal to the natives of the country.

The present bubonic plague in India assumed the nature of an epidemic in the Punjab in October, 1897, and, in spite of the drastic precautions of the sanitary authorities, it so far seems to baffle their endeavours to stamp it out, notwithstanding all the resources of modern science which they possess. In April, 1907, a telegram from Simla announced that the total number of deaths from plague in India during the week ending April 13th was seventy-five thousand; all but five thousand of these having taken place in the United Provinces and the Punjab. At this time the total number of victims from the epidemic in the Punjab alone, during the nine years it had existed, was estimated at about a million and a half.   ·

So far as it can be traced, the origin of the Indian plague, as indeed that of the great pestilence of 1348-9, is China, the great breeding ground of epidemics.   It is supposed to have been imported from Hong Kong to Bombay, and the disease had already made great headway before investigation established the fact that the infection was conveyed by means of the ships' rats.   From January to August, 1903, the estimated mortality in India from plague was 600,000, and in 1904 the total rose to the appalling figure of 938,000. Even this was exceeded in 1905; and it is stated that from 1897 to 1904 the plague claimed three and a quarter millions of victims.

The campaign against the plague-carrying rats has been waged with comparatively little result, owing, in great measure, to the religious suscepti-bilities of the native peoples, and their aversion to leaving their insanitary homes, leading ob-viously to concealment of infection. Moreover, the rat is regarded by the natives as somewhat of a domestic animal. Its destruction is thus resented and its facilities for spreading the disease greatly increased. Curiously enough it would appear that it has long been recognised by the native inhabitants of India that some connection did in fact exist between the rat and the bubonic plague. " When the rats begin to fall it is time for people to leave the houses," is an old and common saying in India; in which sentence was registered the popular belief that an outbreak of plague was preceded by a mortality among the rats. It is now certain that this connection does exist. The special commission appointed in 1905 to examine into this matter has established, by a series of experiments, that bubonic plague is due to the rat-flea, called *pulex cheopis*, which not only carries the plague germ from rat to rat, but is almost certainly the means by which it is communicated to man.

It may be taken for granted, as an established fact, that malarial diseases are produced by the bites of the mosquito, and that sleeping sickness follows from that of a blood-sucking fly which transmits to man the bacilli of the disease. In the same way it is now known that the plague is passed on from the infected rat through the agency of rat-fleas, which, when biting man, impregnate him with the bacillus of the deadly bubonic plague. It has even been suggested as by no means impossible that the plague may at any time be reintroduced into Europe by means of the rat parasite, and modern research has made it certain that want of cleanliness is a fertile cause of disease and its dissemination. In particular, it is proved that the fleas and bugs which exist in the poorer quarters of cities and villages may be the means of communication of many various forms of disease.

As a suggestion to explain the rapid spread of " The Great Pestilence " of 1348-9, these results of modern research are of interest and importance. The houses which sheltered the people in the fourteenth century were only too well calculated to assist the spread of the contagion, if it was carried, as now appears certain, by the agency of blood-sucking parasites. The account of French rural life at this period, given by M. Siméon Luce, and reproduced in Chapter III of this volume, is probably true, in the main, in regard to our own country, and the insanitary state and habitual dirt in which our ancestors lived, would have provided an ideal field for the indefinite multiplication of fleas, and possibly of other plague-bearing insects.

It remains to add that, with one or two minor corrections, and a few additions, the present volume is a reprint of the previous edition.

CONTENTS

CHAPTER I

THE COMMENCEMENT OF THE EPIDEMIC

CHAPTER II

THE EPIDEMIC IN ITALY

CHAPTER III

PROGRESS OF THE PLAGUE IN FRANCE

CHAPTER IV

THE PLAGUE IN OTHER EUROPEAN COUNTRIES

CHAPTER V

THE PLAGUE REACHES ENGLAND

CHAPTER VI

PROGRESS OF THE DISEASE IN LONDON AND THE SOUTH

CHAPTER VII

The Epidemic in Gloucester, Worcester, Warwick, and Oxford

CHAPTER VIII

Story of the Disease in the Rest of England

CHAPTER IX

The Desolation of the Country

CHAPTER X

Some Consequences of the Great Mortality

b

TO THE READER

IN publishing this story of a great and overwhelming calamity, which fell upon England in common with the rest of Europe, in the middle of the fourteenth century, I desire to record my grateful thanks to those who have in any way assisted me in gathering together any material, or in weaving it into a connected narrative. Amongst these many kind friends I may specially name the late Mr. F. Bickley, of the British Museum; Mr. F. J. Baigent, the Rev. Prebendary Hingeston-Randolph, and, above all, Mr. Edmund Bishop, to whom I am greatly indebted for advice, criticism, and ever-patient assistance in revising the proof-sheets.

INTRODUCTION

THE story of the Great Pestilence of 1348-9 has never been fully told. In fact, until comparatively recent times, little attention was paid to an event which, nevertheless, whether viewed in the magnitude of the catastrophe, or in regard to its far-reaching results, is certainly one of the most important in the history of our country.

Judged by the ordinary manuals, the middle of the fourteenth century appears as the time of England's greatest glory. Edward III was at the very height of his renown. The crushing defeat of France at Crecy, in 1346, followed the next year by the taking of Calais, had raised him to the height of his fame. When, wearing the laurels of the most brilliant victory of the age, he landed at Sandwich, on October 14th, 1347, the country, or at least the English courtiers, seemed intoxicated by the success of his arms. "A new sun," says the chronicler Walsingham, " seemed to have arisen over the people, in the perfect peace, in the plenty of all things, and in the glory of such victories. There was hardly a woman of any name who did not possess spoils of Caen, Calais, and other French towns across the sea;" and the English matrons proudly decked themselves with the rich dresses and costly ornaments carried off from foreign households. This was, moreover, the golden era of chivalry, and here and there throughout the country tournaments celebrated with exceptional pomp the establishment of the Order of the Garter, instituted by King Edward to perpetuate the memory of his martial successes. It is little wonder, then, that the Great Pestilence, now known as the "Black Death," coming as it does between Crecy and Poitiers, and at the very time of the creation of the first Knights of the Garter, should seem to fall aside from the general narrative as though something apart from, and not consonant with, the natural course of events.

It is accordingly no matter for wonder that a classic like Hume, in common with our older writers on English history, should have dismissed the calamity in a few lines; but a reader may well feel surprise at finding that the late Mr. J. R. Green, who saw deeper into causes and effects than his predecessors, deals with the great epidemic in a scanty notice only as a mere episode in his account of the agricultural changes in the fourteenth century. Although he speaks generally of the death of one-half the population through the disease, he evidently has not realised the enormous effects, social and religious, which are directly traceable to the catastrophe.

Excellent articles, indeed, such as those from the pen of Professor Seebohm and Dr. Jessopp, and chance pages in books on political and social economy, like those of the late Professor Thorold Rogers and Dr. Cunningham, have done much in our time to draw attention to the importance of the subject. Still, so far as I am aware, no writer has yet treated the plague as a whole, or, indeed, has utilised the material available for forming a fairly accurate estimate of its ravages. The collections for the present study had been entirely made when a book on the *Epidemics in Britain*, by Dr. Creighton, was announced, and, as a consequence, the work was set aside. On the appearance of Dr. Creighton's volume, however, it was found that, whilst treating this pestilence at considerable length as a portion of his general subject, not merely had it not entered into his design to utilise the great bulk of material to be found in the various records of the period, but the author had dealt with the matter from a wholly different point of view.

It is proper, therefore, to state why a detailed treatment of a subject, in itself so uninviting, is here undertaken. The pestilence of 1348-9, for its own sake, must necessarily be treated by the professional writer as an item in the general series of epidemics; but there are many reasons why it has never been dealt with in detail from the mere point of view of the historian. Yet an adequate realisation of its effects is of the first importance for the right understanding of the history of England in the later Middle Ages. The "Black Death" inflicted what can only be called a wound deep in the social body, and produced nothing less than a revolution of feeling and practice, especially of religious feeling and practice. Unless this is understood, from the very circumstances of the case, we shall go astray in our interpretation of the later history of England. In truth, this great pestilence was a turning-point in the national life. It formed the real close of the Mediaeval period and the beginning of our Modern age. It produced a break with the past, and was the dawn of a new era. The sudden sweeping away of the population and the consequent scarcity of labourers, raised, it is well recognised, new and extravagant expectations in the minds of the lower classes; or, to use a modern expression, labour began then to understand its value and assert its power.

But there is another and yet more important result of the pestilence which, it would seem, is not sufficiently recognised. To most people, looking back into the past, the history of the Church during the Middle Ages in England appears one continuous and stately progress. It is much nearer to the truth to say that in 1351 the whole ecclesiastical system was wholly disorganised, or, indeed, more than half ruined, and that everything had to be built up anew. As regards education, the effect of the catastrophe on the body of the clergy was prejudicial beyond the power of calculation. To secure the most necessary public ministrations of the rites of religion the most inadequately-prepared subjects had to be accepted, and even these could be obtained only in insufficient numbers. The immediate effect on the people was a religious paralysis. Instead of turning men to God the scourge turned them to despair, and this not only in England, but in all parts of Europe. Writers of every nation describe the same dissoluteness of manners consequent upon the epidemic. In time the religious sense and feeling revived, but in many respects it took a new tone, and its manifestations ran in new channels.

If the change is to be described in brief, I should say that the religion of Englishmen, as it now manifested itself on the recovery of religion, and as it existed from that time to the Reformation, was characterised by a devotional and more self-reflective cast than previously. This is evidenced in particular by the rise of a whole school of spiritual writers, the beginnings of which had been already manifested in the writings of Hampole, himself a victim of the plague. It was subsequently developed by such writers as Walter Hilton and the authors of a mass of anonymous tracts, still in manuscript, which, in so far as they have attracted notice at all, have been commonly set down under the general designation of *Wycliffite*. The reason for this misleading classification is not difficult to understand. Finding on the one hand that these tracts are pervaded by a deeply religious spirit, and on the other being convinced that the religion of those days was little better than a mere formalism, the few persons who have hitherto paid attention to the subject have not hesitated to attribute them to the " religious revival of the Lollards," and were naturally unable to believe them to be inspired by the teaching of " a Church shrivelled into a self-seeking secular priesthood."[1] The reader, who has a practical and personal experience of the tone, spirit, and teaching of works of Catholic piety, will, however, at once recognise that these tracts are perfectly Catholic in tone, spirit, and doctrine, and differ essentially from those of men inspired by the teaching of Wycliffe.

The new religious spirit found outward expression in

[1] Green, *Short History of the English People*, p. 216.

the multitude of guilds which sprang into existence at this time, in the remarkable and almost, as it may seem to some, extravagant development of certain pious practices, in the singular spread of a more personal devotion to the Blessed Sacrament, to the Blessed Virgin, to the Five Wounds, to the Holy Name, and other such manifestations of a more tender or more familiar piety. Even the very adornment and enrichment of the churches, so distinctive of this period, bears witness to the change. At the close of the fourteenth century and during the course of the fifteenth the supply of ornaments, furniture, plate, statues painted or in highly decked " coats," with which the churches were literally encumbered as time went on, proved a striking contrast to the comparative simplicity which characterised former days, as witnessed by a comparison of inventories. Moreover, the source of all this wealth and elaboration is another indication of the change that had come over the country. Benefactions to the Church are no longer contributed entirely, or at least chiefly, by the great nobles, but they are now the gifts of the burgher folk and middle classes, and this very profusion corresponds, according to the ideas and feelings of those days, to the abundant material comfort which from the early years of the last century to the present has specially characterised the English homes of modern times. In fact, the fifteenth century witnessed the beginnings of a great middle-class movement, which can be distinctly traced to the effect of the great pestilence, and which, whether for good or for evil, was checked by the change of religion in the sixteenth century.

It is sufficient here to have indicated in the most general way the change which took place in the religious life of the English people and the new tendencies which manifested themselves. If the later religious history of the country is to be understood it is necessary to take this catastrophe, social and religious, as a starting-point, and to bring home to the mind the part the Black Death really played in the national history.

Merely to report what is said of England would tend to raise in the mind of the reader a certain incredulity. A short and rapid review has accordingly been made of the progress of the pestilence from Eastern Europe to these Western shores, and by this means the very distressing unanimity, even to definite forms of language, of writers who recorded events hundreds and even thousands of miles apart, brings home the reality of the catastrophe with irresistible force. The story, so far as England is concerned, is told at greater length, and the progress of the disease is followed as it swept from south to north and passed on to higher latitudes. The state of the country after the pestilence was over is then briefly described, and attention is called to some of the immediate results of the great plague, especially as bearing upon the Church life of the country.

THE BLACK DEATH

CHAPTER I

THE COMMENCEMENT OF THE EPIDEMIC

THE Great Pestilence, which first reached Europe in the autumn of 1347, is said to have originated in the East some three or four years previously. So far as actual history goes, however, the progress of the disease can be traced only from the ports of the Black Sea and possibly from those of the Mediterranean, to which traders along the main roads of commerce with Asiatic countries brought their merchandise for conveyance to the Western world. Reports at the time spoke of great earthquakes and other physical disturbances as having taken place in the far East, and these were said to have been accompanied by peculiar conditions of the atmosphere, and followed by a great mortality among the teeming populations of India and China. Pope Clement VI was informed that the pestilence then raging at Avignon had had its origin in the East, and that, in the countries included under that vague name, the infection had spread so rapidly, and had proved to be so deadly, that the victims were calculated at the enormous, and no doubt exaggerated, number of nearly four-and-twenty millions.

B

A Prague chronicle speaks of the epidemic in the kingdoms of China, India, and Persia, and the contemporary historian, Matteo Villani, reports its conveyance to Europe by Italian traders, who had fled before it from the ports on the eastern shores of the Black Sea. The same authority corroborates, by the testimony of one who had been an eye-witness in Asia, the reports of certain Genoese merchants as to earthquakes devastating the continent and pestilential fogs covering the land. "A venerable friar minor of Florence, now a bishop, declared," so says Villani, "that he was then in that part of the country at the city of Lamech, where by the violence of the shock part of the temple of Mahomet was thrown down."[1]

A quotation from Hecker's "Epidemics of the Middle Ages" will be a sufficient summary of what was reported of the plague in eastern countries before its arrival in Europe. "Cairo lost daily, when the plague was raging with its greatest violence, from 10 to 15,000, being as many as, in modern times, great plagues have carried off during their whole course. In China more than thirteen millions are said to have died, and this is in correspondence with the certainly exaggerated accounts from the rest of Asia. India was depopulated. Tartary, Mesopotamia, Syria, Armenia were covered with dead bodies; the Kurds fled in vain to the mountains. In Caramania and Cæsarea none were left alive. On the roads, in the camps, in the caravansaries unburied bodies were alone to be seen. . . . In Aleppo 500 died daily; 22,000 people and most of the animals were carried off in Gaza within six weeks. Cyprus lost almost all its inhabitants; and ships without crews were often seen in the Mediter-

[1] Muratori, *Rerum Italicarum Scriptores*, xiv, col. 14.

ranean, as afterwards in the North Sea, driving about and spreading the plague wherever they went ashore."[1]

There can be little doubt that the contagion was first spread by means of the great trade routes of the East. The lines of commerce of European countries with India, China, and Asiatic countries generally are first definitely described in 1321 by Marino Sanudo, a Venetian, in a work addressed to Pope John XXI, not thirty years before the outbreak of the pestilence.[2] His object was to indicate the difficulties and dangers which then beset the traffic of the mercantile world with the East. In so doing he pointed out that the ancient centre of all trade with the far East was Bagdad. To and from this great depôt of Oriental merchandise all the caravan routes led; but, at the time when Sanudo wrote, the incursion of barbarian hordes into Central Asia had rendered trade along these roads difficult and unsafe. Two trading tracts are in particular named by the author as the chief lines of communication. One ran from Bagdad over the plains of Mesopotamia and Syria to Lycia,[3] where the goods were purchased by the Italian merchants. This, the best known route, was the shortest by which the produce of China and India could be conveyed to the European markets; but in the fourteenth century it was the most perilous. The second route also started from Bagdad, and having followed the Tigris to its sources in Armenia, passed on, either to Trebizond and other ports

[1] *The Epidemics of the Middle Ages*, translated by B. G. Babington (Sydenham Society), p. 21.

[2] Marinus Sanutus, *Liber secretorum Fidelium crucis super Terrae Sanctae recuperatione et conversatione*, in Bongars, *Gesta Dei per Francos*, vol. ii.

[3] The most southern part of Asiatic Turkey.

of the Black Sea, or taking the road from the Caspian, upon the other side of the Caucasus, passed to the Genoese and other flourishing Italian settlements in the Crimea.

A third route was, however, according to Sanudo, the most used in his day because the least dangerous. By it the produce of eastern lands was brought to Alexandria, whence, after having been heavily taxed by the Sultan, it was transported to Europe. Merchandise coming to Italy and other countries by this route from India was, according to the same authority, shipped from two ports of the peninsula, which he calls Mahabar[1] and Cambeth.[2] Thence it was conveyed to ports in the Persian Gulf, to the river Tigris, or to Aden, at the entrance of the Red Sea. From this last point a journey of nine days across the desert brought the caravans to a city called Chus[3] on the Nile. Fifteen days more of river carriage, however, was required before the produce of the Eastern marts reached Cairo, or Babylon, as it was called by mediaeval writers. From Cairo it was conveyed to Alexandria by canal.

These were the three chief routes by which communication between Asiatic countries and Europe was kept up, and the markets of the Western world supplied with the spices, gums, and silks of the East. It is more than probable that the great pestilence was conveyed to Europe by the trading caravans coming from the East by all these roads and by other similar lines of

[1] Probably Mahe, on the Malabar coast.
[2] Now Cambay, in the Baroda Dominion to the north of Bombay.
[3] Otherwise Kus, now Koos, in Upper Egypt, not far from Thebes.

commerce. In the country along one of the trade routes, by which caravans reached the Italian ports established on the Crimea, it is certain that the plague was raging with great virulence in 1346, the year before its appearance in Europe. Moreover, Gabriele de' Mussi, a notary of Piacenza, and an eye-witness of the first outbreak of the plague in Upper Italy, has described the way in which the infection was conveyed in the ships of traders from Caffa,[1] a Genoese settlement in the Crimea. This account will be found in the next chapter; and here it is only necessary to report what he gathered from the survivors about the outbreak of the plague among the Tartar tribes and its appearance at Caffa.[2]

"In the year 1346," he writes, "in eastern parts an immense number of Tartars and Saracens fell victims to

[1] Sometimes known as S. Feodosia. This port was by the beginning of the fourteenth century a most important trading settlement of Genoese merchants. In 1316 Pope John XXII issued a Bull making it the cathedral city of an extensive diocese. By the time of the outbreak of the great plague it had become the centre of almost all commerce between Asia and Europe (*Cf.* M. G. Canale, *Della Crimea, del suo commercio et dei suoi dominatori*, i, p. 208 *et seq.*

[2] The account of Gabriele de' Mussi, called *Ystoria de morbo seu mortalitate qui fuit a.* 1348, was first printed by Henschel, in Haeser's *Archiv für gesammte Medicin* (Jena), ii, 26-59. The editor claims that De' Mussi was actually present at Caffa during the Tartar siege, and came to Europe in the plague-stricken ships which conveyed the infection to Italy. Signor Tononi, who in 1884 reprinted the *Ystoria* in the *Giornale Ligustico* (Genoa), vol. x (1883), p. 139 *seqq.*, has proved by the acts of the notaries of Piacenza that De' Mussi never quitted the city at this time, and his realistic narrative must have been consequently derived from the accounts of others. From the same source Tononi has shown that De' Mussi acted as notary between A.D. 1300 and 1356, and was consequently born probably somewhere about 1280. He died in the first half of the year 1356.

a mysterious and sudden death. In these regions vast districts, numerous provinces, magnificent kingdoms, cities, castles, and villages, peopled by a great multitude, were suddenly attacked by the mortality, and in a brief space were depopulated. A place in the East called Tana, situated in a northerly direction from Constantinople and under the rule of the Tartars, to which Italian merchants much resorted, was besieged by a vast horde of Tartars and was in a short time taken." [1] The Christian merchants violently expelled from the city were then received for the protection of their persons and property within the walls of Caffa, which the Genoese had built in that country.

"The Tartars followed these fugitive Italian merchants, and, surrounding the city of Caffa, besieged it likewise.[2] Completely encircled by this vast army of enemies, the inhabitants were hardly able to obtain the necessaries of life, and their only hope lay in the fleet which brought them provisions. Suddenly 'the death,' as it was called, broke out in the Tartar host, and thousands were daily carried off by the disease, as if 'arrows from heaven were striking at them and beating down their pride.'

"At first the Tartars were paralysed with fear at the ravages of the disease, and at the prospect that sooner or later all must fall victims to it. Then they turned their vengeance on the besieged, and in the hope of

---

[1] Tana was the port on the north-western shore of the sea of Azov, which was then known as the sea of Tana. The port is now Azov.

[2] De' Mussi says the siege lasted "three years." Tononi shows that this is clearly a mistake, and adduces it as additional evidence that the author was not himself at Caffa.

communicating the infection to their Christian enemies, by the aid of the engines of war, they projected the bodies of the dead over the walls into the city. The Christian defenders, however, held their ground, and committed as many of these plague-infected bodies as possible to the waters of the sea.

"Soon, as might be supposed, the air became tainted and the wells of water poisoned, and in this way the disease spread so rapidly in the city that few of the inhabitants had strength sufficient to fly from it."[1]

The further account of Gabriele de' Mussi describing how a ship from Caffa conveyed the infection to Genoa, from which it spread to other districts and cities of Italy, must be deferred to the next chapter. Here a short space may be usefully devoted to a consideration of the disease itself, which proved so destructive to human life in every European country in the years 1348-1350. And, in the first place, it may be well to state that the name *Black Death*, by which the great pestilence is now generally known, not only in England, but elsewhere, is of comparatively modern origin.[2] In no contemporary account of the epidemic is it called by that ominous title; at the time people spoke of it as "the pestilence," "the great mortality," "the death," "the plague of Florence," etc., and, apparently, not until some centuries later was it given the name of "the Black Death." This it seems to have first received in Denmark or Sweden, although it is doubtful whether the *atra mors* of Pontanus is equivalent to the English *Black Death*.[3] It is hard to resist

[1] Gabriele de' Mussi, *Ystoria de Morbo*, in Haeser, *ut supra*.
[2] K. Lechner, *Das grosse Sterben in Deutschland* (Innsbrück, Wagner, 1884), p. 8.
[3] J. J. Pontanus *Rerum Danicarum Historia* (1631), p. 476.

the impression that in England, at least, it was used as the recognised name for the epidemic of 1349 only after the pestilence of the seventeenth century had assumed to itself the title of the *Great Plague*. Whether the name *Black Death* was first adopted to express the universal state of mourning to which the disease reduced the people of all countries, or to mark the special characteristic symptoms of this epidemic, is, under the circumstances of its late origin, unimportant to determine.

The epidemic would appear to have been some form of the ordinary Eastern or bubonic plague. Together, however, with the usual characteristic marks of the common plague, there were certain peculiar and very marked symptoms, which, although not universal, are recorded very generally in European countries.

In its common form the disease showed itself in swellings and carbuncles under the arm and in the groin. These were either few and large—being at times as large as a hen's egg—or smaller and distributed over the body of the sufferer. In this the disease does not appear to have been different from the ordinary bubonic plague, which ravaged Europe during many centuries, and which is perhaps best known in England as so destructive to human life in the great plague of London in 1665. In this ordinary form it still exists in Eastern countries, and its origin is commonly traced to the method of burying the dead there in vogue.

The special symptoms characteristic of the plague of 1348-9 were four in number:

(1) Gangrenous inflammation of the throat and lungs;

(2) Violent pains in the region of the chest;

(3) The vomiting and spitting of blood; and

(4) The pestilential odour coming from the bodies and breath of the sick.

In almost every detailed account by contemporary writers these characteristics are noted. And, although not all who were stricken with the disease manifested it in this special form, it is clear that, not only were many, and indeed vast numbers, carried off by rapid corruption of the lungs and blood-spitting, without any signs of swellings or carbuncles, but also that the disease was at the time regarded as most deadly and fatal in this special form. " From the carbuncles and glandular swellings," says a contemporary writer, " many recovered; from the blood-spitting none."[1] Matteo Villani, one of the most exact writers about this plague at Florence, says that the sick "who began to vomit blood quickly died;"[2] whilst Gui de Chauliac, the Pope's physician at Avignon, who watched the course of the disease there and left the most valuable medical account of his observations, says that the epidemic was of two kinds. The first was marked by "constant fever and blood-spitting, and from this the patient died in three days;" the second was the well-known and less fatal bubonic plague.

The characteristic symptoms of this epidemic, noted in numerous contemporary accounts, appear to be identical with those of the disease known as malignant pus-

---

[1] See Lechner, *Das grosse Sterben*, p. 15. De' Mussi gives the same account.

[2] "Chi cominciavano a sputare sangue, morivano chi di subito." The contemporary chronicle of Parma by the Dominican John de Cornazano also notes the same: "Et fuit talis quod aliqui sani, si spuebant sanguinem, subito ibi moriebantur, nec erat ullum remedium" (*Monumenta historica ad provincias Parmensem et Placentinam pertinentia*, vol. v, p. 386).

tule of the lung; and it would appear probable that this outbreak of the plague must be distinguished from every other of which there is any record. " I express my profound conviction," writes an eminent French physician, " that the Black Death stands apart from all those which preceded or followed it. It ought to be classed among the great and new popular maladies." [1]

Be that as it may, the disease, as will be subsequently seen in the accounts of those who lived at the time, showed itself in various ways. Some were struck suddenly, and died within a few hours; others fell into a deep sleep, from which they could not be roused; whilst others, again, were racked with a sleepless fever, and tormented with a burning thirst. The usual course of the sickness, when it first made its appearance, was from three to five days; but towards the close of the epidemic the recovery of those suffering from the carbuncular swellings was extended, as in the case of ordinary Eastern plague, over many months. [1]

[1] Anglada, *Étude sur les Maladies Éteintes* (Paris, 1869), p. 416. The idea that this peculiar malady was altogether novel in character is confirmed by its specially malignant nature. According to a well-recognised law, new epidemics are always most violent and fatal. The depopulation of the Fiji Islands by the measles is an instance of the way in which a comparatively mild disease may in its first attack upon a people prove terribly destructive. It is commonly thought that it has been the action of some new disease whereby the races which built the great prehistoric cities of Africa and America have been completely swept away.

[2] The following account of an outbreak of disease somewhat similar to the " Black Death " appeared in the *British Medical Journal* of 5th November, 1892: "An official report of the Governor-General of Turkestan, which has recently been published in St. Petersburg, states that that province has been severely visited by an epidemic of ' Black Death,' which followed upon the footsteps

Such is a brief account of the disease which devastated the world in the middle of the fourteenth century. Before following the course of the epidemic in Italy, to which it was conveyed, as De' Mussi relates, from the Crimea, some account of its ravages in Constantinople and in Sicily may be given. From the Crimea Constantinople lay upon the highway to the west. Italian ships crossing the Black Sea would naturally touch at this city, then the great centre of communication between the Eastern and Western Worlds. From the relation of De' Mussi it appears that Caffa, the plague-stricken

of cholera. On September 10 (22) it appeared suddenly at Askabad, and in six days it killed 1,303 persons in a population of 30,000. ' Black Death ' has long been known in Western Asia as a scourge more deadly than the cholera or the plague. It comes suddenly, sweeping over a whole district like a pestilential simoon, striking down animals as well as men, and vanishes as suddenly as it came, before there is time to ascertain its nature or its mode of diffusion. The visit here referred to was no exception to this rule. After raging in Askabad for six days the epidemic ceased, leaving no trace of its presence but the corpses of its victims. These putrified so rapidly that no proper post-mortem could be made. The Governor-General gives some details as to the symptoms and course of the disease, which, though interesting as far as they go, do not throw much light on its pathology. The attack begins with rigors of intense severity, the patient shivering literally from head to foot; the rigors occur every five minutes for about an hour. Next an unendurable feeling of heat is complained of; the arteries become tense, and the pulse more and more rapid, while the temperature steadily rises. Unfortunately no thermometric readings or other precise data are given. Neither diarrhœa nor vomiting has been observed. Convulsions alternate with syncopal attacks, and the patients suffer intense pain. Suddenly the extremities become stiff and cold, and in from 10 to 20 minutes the patient sinks into a comatose condition, which speedily ends in death. Immediately after he has ceased to breathe large black bullæ form on the body, and quickly spread over its surface. Decomposition takes place in a few minutes."

Genoese city in the Crimea, besieged by the Tartars, was
in communication by ship with countries from which it
received supplies. To Constantinople, therefore, it seems
not unlikely that the dreaded disease was conveyed by
a ship coming from this plague centre in the Crimea. An
account of the pestilence at the Imperial city has come
from the pen of the Emperor John Cantacuzene, who
was an eye-witness of what he reports. And although
he adopted the language of Thucydides, about the
plague of Athens, to describe his own experiences at
Constantinople, he could hardly have done so had the
description not been fairly faithful to the reality. " The
epidemic which then (1347) raged in northern Scythia,"
he writes, "traversed almost the entire sea-coasts,
whence it was carried over the world. For it invaded
not only Pontus, Thrace, and Macedonia, but Greece,
Italy, the Islands, Egypt, Lybia, Judea, Syria, and
almost the entire universe."

The disease according to his account was incurable.
Neither regularity of life nor bodily strength was any
preservation against it. The strong and the weak were
equally struck down; and death spared not those of
whom care was taken, any more than the poor, destitute
of all help. No other illness of any sort showed itself in
this year; all sickness took the form of the prevalent
disease. Medical science recognised that it was power-
less before the foe. The course of the malady was not in
all cases the same. Some people died suddenly, others
during the course of a day, and some after but an hour's
suffering. In the case of those who lingered for two or
three days the attack commenced with a violent fever.
Soon the poison mounted to the brain, and the sufferer
lost the use of speech, became insensible to what was

taking place about him, and appeared sunk in a deep sleep. If by chance he came to himself and tried to speak, his tongue refused to move, and only a few inarticulate sounds could be uttered, as the nerves had been paralysed; then he died suddenly.

Others who fell sick under the disease were attacked first, not in the head, but in the lungs. The organs of respiration became quickly inflamed, sharp pains were experienced in the chest, blood was vomited, and the breath became fetid. The throat and tongue, burnt up by the excessive fever, became black and congested with blood. " Those who drank copiously experienced no more relief than those who drank but little."

Then, after describing the terrible sleeplessness a d restlessness of some sufferers, and the plague spots which broke out over the body in most cases, the Emperor proceeds: " The few who recovered had no second attack, or at least not of a serious nature." Even some of those who manifested all the symptoms recovered against every expectation. It is certain that no efficacious remedy has been discovered. What had been useful to one appeared a real poison to another. People who nursed the sick took their malady, and on this account the deaths multiplied to such an extent that many houses remained deserted, after all who had lived in them—even the domestic animals—had been carried off by the plague.

The profound discouragement of the sick was specially sad to behold. On the first symptoms of the attack men lost all hope of recovery, and gave themselves up as lost. This moral prostration quickly made them worse and accelerated the hour of their death.

It is impossible in words to give an idea of this malady. All that can be said is that it had nothing in common with the ills to which man is naturally subject, and that it was a chastisement sent by God Himself. By this belief many turned to better things and resolved to change their lives. I do not speak only of those who were swept away by the epidemic, but of those also who recovered and endeavoured to correct their vicious tendencies and devote themselves to the practice of virtue. A large number, too, before they were attacked distributed their goods to the poor, and there were none so insensible or hard-hearted when attacked as not to show a profound sorrow for their faults so as to appear before the judgment seat of God with the best chances of salvation.

"Amongst the innumerable victims of the epidemic in Constantinople must be reckoned Andronicus, the Emperor's son, who died the third day. This young man was not only remarkable for his personal appearance, but was endowed in the highest degree with those qualities which form the chief adornment of youth; and everything about him testified that he would have followed nobly in the footsteps of his ancestors."

From Constantinople the Italian trading ships passed on towards their own country, everywhere spreading the terrible contagion. Their destinations were Genoa and Venice, as De' Mussi relates; but as the same authority says: "The sailors, as if accompanied by evil spirits, as soon as they approached the land, were death to those with whom they mingled." Thus the advent of the plague can be traced in the ports of the Adriatic in the autumn of 1347, and there can be little doubt that it was due to the arrival of ships bound from the East to Venice. Of the islands of the ocean, and particularly of Sicily, De' Mussi speaks as having been affected by the ships that were bound from the Crimea to Genoa. Of the plague in Sicily there exists a particular account by one who must have been a contemporary of the events he describes.[1] "A most deadly pestilence," he says, "sprang up over the entire island. It happened that in the month of October, in the year of our Lord, 1347, about the beginning of the month, twelve Genoese ships, flying from the divine vengeance which our Lord for their sins had sent upon them, put into the port of Messina, bringing with them such a sickness clinging to their very bones that, did anyone speak to them, he was directly struck with a mortal sickness from which there was no escape." After detailing the terrible symptoms and describing the rapid spread of the infection, how the mere breath of the strangers poisoned those who conversed with them, how to touch or meddle with anything that belonged to them was to contract the fatal malady, he continues: "Seeing what a calamity of sudden death had come to them by the arrival of the Genoese, the people of Messina drove them in all haste from their city and port. But the sickness remained and a terrible mortality ensued. The one thought in the mind of all was how to avoid the infection. The father abandoned the sick son; magistrates and notaries refused to come and make the wills of the dying; even the priests to hear their confessions. The care of those stricken fell to the Friars Minor, the Dominicans and members of other orders, whose convents were in consequence soon emptied of their inhabitants. Corpses were abandoned in empty houses, and there was none to give them Christian burial. The houses of the dead were left open and unguarded with their jewels, money, and valuables; if anyone wished to enter, there

[1] A Franciscan friar, Michael Platiensis (of Piazza).

was no one to prevent him. The great pestilence came so suddenly that there was no time to organise any measures of protection; from the very beginning the officials were too few, and soon there were none. The population deserted the city in crowds; fearing even to stay in the environs, they camped out in the open air in the vineyards, whilst some managed to put up at least a temporary shelter for their families. Others, again, trusting in the protection of the virgin, blessed Agatha, sought refuge in Catania, whither the Queen of Sicily had gone, and where she directed her son, Don Frederick, to join her. The Messinese, in the month of November, persuaded the Patriarch [1] Archbishop of Catania to allow the relics of the Saint to be taken to their city, but the people refused to permit them to leave their ancient resting-place. Processions and pilgrimages were organised to beg God's favour. Still the pestilence raged and with greater fury. Everyone was in too great a terror to aid his neighbour. Flight profited nothing, for the sickness, already contracted and clinging to the fugitives, was only carried wherever they sought refuge. Of those who fled some fell on the roads and dragged themselves to die in the fields, the woods, or the valleys. Those who reached Catania breathed their last in the hospitals. At the demand of the terrified populace the Patriarch forbade, under pain of excommunication, the burial of any of these Messina refugees within the city, and their bodies were all thrown into deep pits outside the walls.

"What shall I say more?" adds the historian. "So wicked and timid were the Catanians that they refused

[1] The Archbishop was a member of the Order of St. Francis, and had been created Patriarch of Antioch.

even to speak to any from Messina, or to have anything
to do with them, but quickly fled at their approach.
Had it not been for secret shelter afforded by some of
their fellow citizens, resident in the town, the unfortunate
refugees would have been left destitute of all human
aid." The contagion, however, was already spread, and
the plague soon became rife. The same scenes were
enacted at Catania as before in Messina. The Patriarch,
desiring to provide for the souls of the people, gave to
the priests, even the youngest, all the faculties he himself possessed, both episcopal and patriarchal, for ab-
solving sins. "The pestilence raged in the city from
October, 1347, to April, 1348, and the Patriarch himself,
Gerard Otho, of the Order of St. Francis, fell a victim
to his duty, and was one of the last to be carried off by
the disease. Duke John, who had sought security by
avoiding every infected house and person, died of the
disease at the same time. The plague was spread in the
same way from Messina throughout Sicily; Syracuse,
Girgenti, Sciacca, and Trapani were successively attacked;
in particular it raged in the district of Trapani, in the
extreme west of the island, which," says the writer, "has
remained almost without population." [1]

Having briefly noticed the origin of the great pestilence which ravaged Europe in the fourteenth century, and
its progress towards Italy, the story of Gabriele de' Mussi
may again be taken up at the point where he describes
the flight of the Genoese traders from the Crimea. The
narrative has so far anticipated his account only by giving
the history of the epidemic in Constantinople and Sicily.

[1] Gregorio (R.), *Bibliotheca Scriptorum qui res in Sicilia gestas
retulere*, tom. i, p. 562 *seqq*. The historian wrote probably not later
than A.D. 1361.

CHAPTER II

THE EPIDEMIC IN ITALY

THE great sickness reached Italy in the early days of 1348. The report at Avignon at the time was that three plague-stricken vessels had put into the port of Genoa in January, whilst from another source it would appear that at the same time another ship brought the contagion from the East to Venice. From these two places the epidemic quickly spread over the entire country. What happened in the early days of this frightful scourge is best told in the actual words of Gabriele de' Mussi, who possessed special means of knowledge, and who has until quite recently been looked upon, but incorrectly, as a passenger by one of the very vessels which brought the plague from the Crimea to Genoa. The history of the progress of the plague may be gathered from the pages of the detailed ‚chronicles, which at that time recorded the principal events in the various large and prosperous cities of the Italian peninsula, as well as from the well-known account of the straits to which Florence was reduced by the sickness, given in the introduction to the " Decameron " of Boccaccio.

On reviewing in detail the testimonies from every land relating to this great calamity, it is impossible to overlook the sameness of the terms in which writers the most diverse in character, and in places far distant from one another, describe what passed before their eyes. It has already been remarked that the imperial historian, John Cantacuzene, in recounting the horrors of the plague in Constantinople, has borrowed from Thucydides. But the same ideas, the very same words, suggest themselves involuntarily to one and all. The simple monastic annalist of the half-buried cloister in Engelberg, the more courtly chronicler of St. Denis, the notary who writes with the dryness and technicalities of his profession, but displays withal a weakness for rhetoric and gossip, *littérateurs* like Boccaccio, whose *forte* is narrative, or like Petrarch, delighting in a show of words, the business-like town chronicler of an Italian city, and the author who aspires to the rank of historian, the physician whose interest is professional, even the scribbler who takes this strange theme as the subject for his jingling verse, all speak with such complete oneness of expression that it would almost seem that each had copied his neighbour, and that there is here a fine theme for the scientific amusement known as " investigation of sources." It is only when we come to examine the whole body of evidence that there is borne in upon the mind a realisation of the nature of a calamity which, spreading everywhere, was everywhere the same in its horrors, becoming thus nothing less than a world-wide tragedy, and it is seen that even the phrases of the rhetorician can do no more than rise to the terrible reality of fact.

First in importance, as well as in order of time, comes the testimony of De' Mussi, the substance of which is here given. It so happened that when the ships left Caffa—some bound for Genoa, some for Venice, and some to other parts of the Christian world—a few of the sailors were already infected by the fatal disease. One sick man was enough to infect the whole household, and the corpse as it was carried to the grave brought death to its bearers. "Tell, O Sicily, and ye, the many islands of the sea, the judgments of God. Confess, O Genoa, what thou hast done, since we of Genoa and Venice are compelled to make God's chastisement manifest. Alas! our ships enter the port, but of a thousand sailors hardly ten are spared. We reach our homes; our kindred and our neighbours come from all parts to visit us. Woe to us, for we cast at them the darts of death! Whilst we spoke to them, whilst they embraced us and kissed us, we scattered the poison from our lips. Going back to their homes, they in turn soon infected their whole families, who in three days succumbed, and were buried in one common grave. Priests and doctors visiting the sick returned from their duties ill, and soon were numbered with the dead. O, death! cruel, bitter, impious death! which thus breaks the bonds of affection and divides father and mother, brother and sister, son and wife. Lamenting our misery, we feared to fly, yet we dared not remain."

The terror increased when it was found that even the effects and clothes of the dead were capable of communicating the disease. This was seen in the case of four soldiers at a place near Genoa. Returning to their camp they carried back with them a woollen bed-covering they had found in a house at Rivarolo, on the sea-coast, where the sickness had swept away the entire population. The night following the four slept under the coverlet, and in the morning all were found to be dead. At Genoa the plague spared hardly a seventh part of the population. At Venice it is said that more than seventy died out of every hundred, and out of four-and-twenty excellent doctors twenty were soon carried off by the sickness.

"But as an inhabitant I am asked to write more of Piacenza so that it may be known what happened there in the year 1348. Some Genoese who fled from the plague raging in their city betook themselves hither. They rested at Bobbio, and there sold the merchandise they had brought with them. The purchaser and their host, together with all his family and many neighbours, were quickly stricken with the sickness and died. One of these, wishing to make his will, called a notary, his confessor, and the necessary witnesses. The next day all these were buried together. So greatly did the calamity increase that nearly all the inhabitants of Bobbio soon fell a prey to the sickness, and there remained in the town only the dead.

"In the spring of 1348 another Genoese infected with the plague came to Piacenza. He sought out his friend Fulchino della Croce, who took him into his house. Almost immediately afterwards he died, and the said Fulchino was also quickly carried off with his entire family and many of his neighbours. In a brief space the plague was rife throughout the city. I know not where to begin: everywhere there was weeping and mourning. So great was the mortality that men hardly dared to breathe. The dead were without number, and those who still lived gave themselves up as lost, and prepared for the tomb.

"The cemeteries failing, it was necessary to dig trenches to receive the bodies of the dead. It frequently happened that a husband and wife, a father and son, a mother and daughter—nay, whole families—were cast together in the same pit.

"It was the same in the neighbouring towns and villages. One Oberto di Sasso, who had come one day from an infected place to the church of the Friars Minor to make his will, called thither a notary, witnesses, and neighbours. All these, together with others, to the number of more than sixty, died within a short space of time. Also the religious man, Friar Sifredo de' Bardi, of the convent and order of Preachers, a man of prudence and great learning, who had visited our Lord's sepulchre, died with twenty-three other members of his order and convent. Also the learned and virtuous Friar Bertolin Coxadocha, of Piacenza, of the order of Minorites, with four-and-twenty members of his community, was carried off. So too of the convent of Augustinian Hermits— seven; of the Carmelites—seven; of the Servites of Mary—four, and more than sixty dignitaries and rectors of churches in the city and district of Piacenza died. Of nobles, too, many; of young people a vast number."

De' Mussi then proceeds to give examples of the scenes daily passing before his eyes in the plague-stricken cities of northern Italy. The sick man lay languishing alone in his house and no one came near him. Those most dear to him, regardless of the ties of kindred or affection, withdrew themselves to a distance; the doctor did not come to him, and even the priest with fear and trembling administered the Sacraments of the Church. Men and women, racked with the consuming fever, pleaded—but in vain—for a draught of water, and uselessly raved for someone to watch at their bedside. The father or the wife would not touch the corpse of child or husband to prepare it for the grave, or follow it thither. No prayer was said, nor solemn office sung, nor bell tolled for the funeral of even the noblest citizen;

but by day and night the corpses were borne to the common plague-pit without rite or ceremony. The doors of the houses now desolate and empty remained closed, and no one cared, nor, indeed, dared to enter.

Such is the picture of the effect of the malady and the terrible mortality caused by it drawn by one who seems to have seen its first introduction into Italy, and who certainly had the best opportunity of early observing its rapid progress. It might, perhaps, be thought that his description of the horrors of the infected cities was over-coloured and the creation of his imagination. But in the details it bears on the surface the stamp of truth, and in its chief characteristics it is confirmed by too many independent witnesses in other parts of Italy, and even in Europe generally, to leave a doubt that it corresponded to the literal reality.

What happened at Florence is well-known through the graphic description of Boccaccio. So terrible was the mortality in that prosperous city that the very outbreak became for a time known in Europe as the " Pestilence of Florence." In the spring of the previous year (1347) a severe famine had been experienced, and some 94,000 people had been in receipt of State relief, whilst about 4,000 are supposed to have perished of starvation in the city[1] and its neighbourhood. The people, enfeebled by previous hardships, would naturally fall a prey more easily to the poison of the epidemic. In April, 1348, the dreaded infection began to show itself. " To cure the malady," writes Boccaccio, " neither medical knowledge nor the power of drugs was of any avail, whether because the disease was in its own nature

[1] Sismondi, *Histoire des Républiques Italiennes du Moyen Age*, vi, p. 11.

mortal, or that the physicians (the number of whom—
taking quacks and women pretenders into account—
was grown very great) could form no just idea of the
cause, nor consequently ground a true method of cure;
of those attacked few or none escaped, but they generally died the third day from the first appearance of the
symptoms, without a fever or other form of illness mani-
festing itself. The disease was communicated by the
sick to those in health and seemed daily to gain head
and increase in violence, just as fire will do by casting
fresh fuel on it. The contagion was communicated not
only by conversation with those sick, but also by approaching them too closely, or even by merely handling
their clothes or anything they had previously touched.

"What I am going to relate is certainly marvellous,
and, had I not seen it with my own eyes, and were there
not many witnesses to attest its truth besides myself, I
should not venture to recount it, whatever the credit of
persons who had informed me of it. Such, I say, was the
deadly character of the pestilential matter, that it passed
the infection not only from man to man; but, what is
more wonderful, and has been often proved, anything
belonging to those sick with the disease, if touched by
any other creature, would certainly affect and even kill
it in a short space of time. One instance of this kind I
took special note of, namely, the rags of a poor man just
dead having been thrown into the street, two hogs came
by at the time and began to root amongst them, shaking
them in their jaws. In less than an hour they fell down
and died on the spot.

"Strange were the devices resorted to by the survivors
to secure their safety. Divers as were the means, there
was one feature common to all, selfish and uncharitable

as it was—the avoidance of the sick, and of everything that had been near them; men thought only of themselves.

"Some held it was best to lead a temperate life and to avoid every excess. These making up parties together, and shutting themselves up from the rest of the world, ate and drank moderately of the best, diverting themselves with music and such other entertainments as they might have at home, and never listening to news from without which might make them uneasy. Others maintained that free living was a better preservative, and would gratify every passion and appetite. They would drink and revel incessantly in tavern after tavern, or in those private houses which, frequently found deserted by the owners, were therefore open to anyone; but they yet studiously avoided, with all their irregularity, coming near the infected. And such at that time was the public distress that the laws, human and divine, were not regarded, for the officers to put them in force being either dead, sick, or without assistants, everyone did just as he pleased."

Another class of people chose a middle course. They neither restricted themselves to the diet of the former nor gave way to the intemperance of the latter; but eating and drinking what their appetites required, they went about everywhere with scents and nosegays to smell at, since they looked upon the whole atmosphere as tainted with the effluvia arising from the dead bodies.

"Others, again, of a more callous disposition, declared, as perhaps the safest course in the extremity, that the only remedy was in flight. Persuaded, therefore, of this, and thinking only of themselves, great numbers of men and women left the city, their goods, their house, and kindred, and fled into the country parts; as if the wrath of God had been restricted to a visitation of those only within the city walls, and hence none should remain in the doomed place.

"But different as were the courses pursued, the sickness fell upon all these classes without distinction; neither did all of any class die, nor did all escape; and they who first set the example of forsaking others now languished themselves where there was no one to take pity on them. I pass by the little regard that citizens and distant relations showed one to the other, for the terror was such that brother even fled from brother, wife from husband, nay, the parent from her own child. The sick could obtain help only from the few who still obeyed the law of charity, or from hired servants who demanded extravagant wages and were fit for little else than to hand what was asked for, and to note when the patient died. Even such paid helpers were scarce; and their desire of gain frequently cost them their lives. The rich passed out of this world without a single person to aid them; few had the tears of friends at their departure. The corpse was attended to the grave only by fellows hired for the purpose, who would put the bier on their shoulders and hurry with it to the nearest church, where it was consigned to the tomb without any ceremony whatever, and wherever there was room.

"With regard to the lower classes, and, indeed, in the case of many of the middle rank of life, the scenes enacted were sadder still. They fell sick by thousands, and, having no one whatever to attend them, most of them died. Some breathed their last in the streets, others shut up in their own houses, when the effluvia which came from their corpses was the first intimation of their deaths. An arrangement was now made for the neighbours, assisted by such bearers as they could get, to clear the houses, and every morning to lay the bodies of the dead at their doors. Thence the corpses were carried to the grave on a bier, two or three at a time. There was no one to follow, none to shed tears, for things had come to such a pass that men's lives were no more thought of than those of beasts. Even friends would laugh and make themselves merry, and women had learned to consider their own lives before everything else.

" Consecrated ground no longer sufficed, and it became necessary to dig trenches, into which the bodies were put by hundreds, laid in rows as goods packed in a ship; a little earth was cast upon each successive layer until the pits were filled to the top. The adjacent country presented the same picture as the city; the poor distressed labourers and their families, without physicians, and without help, languished on the highways, in the fields, in their own cottages, dying like cattle rather than human beings. The country people, like the citizens, grew dissolute in their manners and careless of everything. They supposed that each day might be their last; and they took no care nor thought how to improve their substance, or even to utilise it for present support. The flocks and herds, when driven from their homes, would wander unwatched through the forsaken harvest fields, and were left to return of their own accord, if they would, at the approach of night."

Between March and the July following it was estimated that upwards of a hundred thousand souls had perished in the city alone.

" What magnificent dwellings," the writer continues, " what stately palaces, were then rendered desolate, even to the last inhabitant! How many noble families became extinct! What riches, what vast possessions were left with no known heir to inherit them! What numbers of both sexes, in the prime and vigour of youth, whom in the morning Galen, Hippocrates, or Æsculapius himself, would have declared in perfect health, after dining heartily with their friends here, have supped with their departed friends in another world." [1]

It might perhaps be suspected that this description of Boccaccio as to the terrible nature of the plague in Florence was either a fancy picture of his imagination or intended merely as a rhetorical introduction to the tales told in the *Decameron*, with only a slender foundation of fact. Unfortunately other authorities are forthcoming to confirm the graphic relation of the Florentine poet in all its details. Amongst others who were carried off by the pestilence in Florence was the renowned historian, Giovanni Villani. His work was taken up by his brother Matteo, who commences his annals with an account of the epidemic. So terrible did the destruction of human life appear to him that he tells his readers that no greater catastrophe had fallen on the world since the universal Deluge. According to his testimony, it involved the whole of the Italian peninsula, with the exception of Milan and some Alpine districts of northern Lombardy. In each place visited by the scourge it lasted five months, and everywhere Christian parents abandoned their children and kinsfolk, in as callous a way as " might perhaps be expected from infidels and savages." As regards Florence, whilst some few devoted themselves to the care of the sick, many fled from the plague-stricken city. The epidemic raged there from

[1] The *Decameron*, Introduction.

April till September, 1348, and it is the opinion of Villani that three out of every five persons in the city and neighbourhood fell victims to it. As to the effect of the scourge on the survivors, the historian records that whilst it would naturally have been expected that men, impressed by so terrible a chastisement, would have become better, the very contrary was the fact. Work too, was given over, and "men gave themselves up to the enjoyment of the worldly riches to which they had succeeded." Idleness, dissolute morals, sins of gluttony, banquets, revels in taverns, unbridled luxury, fickleness in dress and constant changes according to whim, such were the characteristic marks of the well-to-do Italian citizens when the plague had passed. And the poor, also, Villani states, became idle and unwilling to work, considering that when so many had been carried off by the pestilence there could not but be an abundance for those whom Providence had spared.[1]

The same story is told in all the contemporary chronicles of Italian cities. At Pisa the terrible mortality lasted till September, 1348, and there were few families that did not reckon two or three of their members among the dead. Many names are said to have been completely wiped off from the roll of the living. At least a hundred each week were carried to the grave in the city, whilst those who had been bold enough to watch at the death-bed of a relation or friend appealed in vain to passers-by to aid them to bury the corpse. "Help us to bear this body to the pit," they cried, "so that we in our turn may deserve to find some to carry us." The awful suddenness of the death often inflicted by the scourge is noted by the author of the *Chronicle of Pisa* in common with

[1] Muratori, *Scriptores* xiv, coll. 11-15.

nearly every writer of this period. Men who in the morning were apparently well had before evening been carried to the grave.[1]

A Paduan chronicler, writing at the time, notes that one sick man as a rule infected the house in which he lay, so that once the sickness entered into a dwelling all were seized by it, "even the animals." To Padua a stranger brought the sickness, and in a brief space the whole city was suffering from it. Hardly a third of the population was left after the scourge had passed.[2] At Siena, according to Di Tura, a contemporary chronicler, the plague commenced in April and lasted till October, 1348. All who could fled from the stricken city. In May, July, and August so many died that neither position nor money availed to procure porters to carry the dead to the public pits. "And I, Agniolo di Tura," writes this author, "carried with my own hands my five little sons to the pit; and what I did many others did likewise." All expected death, and people generally said, and believed, that the end of the world had certainly come. In Siena and its neighbourhood, according to Di Tura, about 80,000 people were thought to have died in these seven months.[3]

At Orvieto the plague began in May. Some 500 died in a very short space of time, many of them suddenly; the shops remained closed, and business and work was

---

[1] Muratori, *Scriptores*, xv, 1021.   [2] *Ibid.*, xii, 926.

[3] *Ibid.*, xv, 123. At this period the population at Siena was more than 100,000, and it had been determined to proceed with the building of the vast Cathedral according to the designs of Lando Orefice. The work was hardly undertaken when the plague of 1348 broke out in the city. The operations were suspended, and the money which had been collected for the purpose was devoted to necessary public works" (G. Gigli, *Diario Sanese*, ii, 428).

at a standstill. Here it ran its usual five months' course, and finished in September, when many families were found to have become extinct.[1] At Rimini it was noticed that the poor were the first to be attacked and the chief sufferers. The sickness first showed itself on May 15th, 1348, and only died out in the following December, when, according to the computation of the chronicler, two out of three of the inhabitants had been swept away.[2]

An anonymous contemporary Italian writer describes the sickness as a " swift and sharp fever, with blood-spitting, carbuncle or fistula." Only the few, he says, recovered when once stricken with the disease. The sick visibly infected with their corruption the healthy, even by talking with them; for from this mere convers-ing with the sick an infinite number of men and women died and are buried. "And here," says the writer, " I can give my testimony. A certain man bled me, and the blood flowing touched his face. On that same day he was taken ill, and the next he died; and by the mercy of God I have escaped. I note this because, as by mere communication with the sick the plague infected mortally the healthy, the father afterwards avoided his stricken son, the brother his brother, the wife her husband, and so in each case the man in health studiously avoided the sick. Priests and doctors even fled in fear from those ill, and all avoided the dead. In many places and houses when an inmate died the rest quickly, one after another, expired. And so great was the overwhelming number of the dead that it was necessary to open new cemeteries in every place. In Venice there were almost 100,000 dead, and so great was the multitude of corpses everywhere

---

[1] Muratori, *Scriptores*, xv, 653. [2] *Ibid.*, 902.

that few attended any funeral or dirge.   This pestilence did not cease in the land from February till the feast of All Saints (November 1st, 1348), and the offices of the dead were chanted only by the voices of boys; which boys, without learning, and by rote only, sang the office walking through the streets." The writer then notices the general dissoluteness which ensued after the disease, and its effect in lowering the standard of probity and morals.[1]

To the terrible accounts given by De' Mussi of the state of plague-stricken Genoa and Piacenza, and that of Boccaccio, of the ravages of the pestilence in the city of Florence, may be well added the eloquent letters of the poet Petrarch, in which he laments the overwhelming catastrophe, as he experienced it in the town of Parma. Here, as in so many other places, the inhabitants vainly endeavoured to prevent the entry of the disease by forbidding all intercourse with the suffering cities of Florence, Venice, Genoa, and Pisa. The measures taken to isolate Parma appear to have been, at least, for a time, successful, as the dreaded plague apparently did not make its appearance till the beginning of June, 1348.[2] But in the six months during which it lasted it desolated the entire neighbourhood. In Parma and Reggio many thousands, estimated roundly at 40,000, were carried off by it.[3] Petrarch was at this period a canon of the cathedral of Parma, and had made the acquaintance at Avignon of Laura, who quickly became the object of his admiration as a typical Christian mother of a family, and

---

[1] Muratori, *Scriptores*, xvi, 286.

[2] A. Pezzana, *Storia della città di Parma*, vol. i, p. 12.

Historiae Parmensis Fragmenta, in Muratori, *Scriptores*, xii, 746.

as a fitting subject to inspire his poetic muse. Laura died at Avignon, one of the many who fell victims to the great pestilence which was then raging in that city. The letter written by a friend named Louis to inform Petrarch of this death found him at Parma on May 19th, 1348.[1] A month later the poet wrote to Avignon in the most heart-broken language to his brother, a religious at Monrieux, and the only survivor of a convent of five-and-thirty.[2] "My brother! my brother! my brother," he wrote. "A new beginning to a letter, though used by Marcus Tullius fourteen hundred years ago. Alas! my beloved brother, what shall I say? How shall I begin? Whither shall I turn? On all sides is sorrow; everywhere is fear. I would, my brother, that I had never been born, or, at least, had died before these times. How will posterity believe that there has been a time when without the lightnings of heaven or the fires of earth, without wars or other visible slaughter, not this or that part of the earth, but well-nigh the whole globe, has remained without inhabitants.

"When has any such thing been ever heard or seen; in what annals has it ever been read that houses were left vacant, cities deserted, the country neglected, the fields too small for the dead, and a fearful and universal solitude over the whole earth? Consult your historians, they are silent; question your doctors, they are dumb; seek an answer from your philosophers, they shrug their shoulders and frown, and with their fingers to their lips bid you be silent.

"Will posterity ever believe these things when we, who see, can scarcely credit them? We should think we were

---

[1] T. Michelet, *Histoire de France*, iv, p. 238.
[2] A. Philippe, *Histoire de la Peste Noire* (Paris, 1853), p. 103.

dreaming if we did not with our eyes, when we walk abroad, see the city in mourning with funerals, and returning to our home, find it empty, and thus know that what we lament is real.

" Oh, happy people of the future, who have not known these miseries and perchance will class our testimony with the fables. We have, indeed, deserved these (punishments) and even greater; but our forefathers also have deserved them, and may our posterity not also merit the same."

Then, after saying that the universal misery is enough to make one think that God has ceased to have a care for His creatures, and putting this thought aside as blasphemy, the writer continues: "But whatever the causes and however hidden, the effects are manifest. To turn from public to private sorrows; the first part of the second year is passed since I returned to Italy. I do not ask you to look back any further; count these few days, and think what we were and what we are. Where are now our pleasant friends? Where the loved faces? Where their cheering words? Where their sweet and gentle conversation? We were surrounded by a crowd of intimates, now we are almost alone."

Speaking of one special friend, Paganinus of Milan, Petrarch writes: " He was suddenly seized in the evening by the pestilential sickness. After supping with friends he spent some time in conversation with me, in the enjoyment of our common friendship and in talking over our affairs. He passed the night bravely in the last agony, and in the morning was carried off by a swift death. And, that no horror should be wanting, in three days his sons and all his family had followed him to the tomb."[1]

[1] *Epistolae Familiares* (ed. 1601), lib. viii, pp. 290-303.

In other towns of Italy the same tragedy, as told in the words of Boccaccio and Petrarch, was being enacted during the early spring and the summer months of 1348. At Venice, where the pestilence obtained an early foothold, and the position of which rendered it particularly susceptible to infection, the mortality was so great that it was represented by the round numbers of 100,000 souls.[1]

Signor Cecchetti's researches into the history of the medical faculty at Venice at this period furnish many interesting details as to the spread of the sickness. Although surgeons were not allowed by law to practise medicine, so great was the need during the prevalence of the dread mortality that one surgeon, Andrea di Padova, was allowed to have saved the lives of more than a hundred people by his timely assistance.[3] In the fourteenth century Venice was troubled by the plague some fifteen times, but that of 1348 was " the great epidemic "—" the horrible mortality "—to the chroniclers of the time. For a long period after, public and other documents make it the excuse for all kinds of irregularities.[4] The diplomas of merit bestowed upon doctors who remained faithful to their posts by the authorities of Venice speak of death following upon the first infection within a very short space of time. So depopulated was the city that it might be said no one was left in it. Many doctors fled, others shut themselves in their houses. Artisans and even youths undertook the duties of physicians, and helped numbers to recover.[5]

---

[1] Muratori, *Scriptores*, xii, 926.

[3] See his article *La Medicina in Venezia nel* 1300 in *Archivio Veneto*, tom. xxv, p. 361, *seqq.*

[3] P. 369.   [4] *Ibid.*, 377.   [5] *Ibid.*

On Sunday, March 30th, 1348, the Great Council of Venice chose a commission of three to watch over the public safety. These a few days later ordered deep pits to be made in one of the islands to receive the bodies of those who died in the hospitals and of the poor; and to convey them thither, ships were appointed to be always in waiting.

The rich fled from the place; officials could not be found, and the Great Council was so reduced that the legal number for transacting business could not be got together. Notaries died in great numbers, and the prisons were thrown open.[1] When the epidemic had ceased the Senate had great difficulty in finding three doctors for the city. On January 12th, 1349, Marco Leon, a capable physician, and a native of Venice, who was in practice at Perugia, offered to return to his own city "since," as he says, "it has pleased God by the terrible mortality to leave our native place so destitute of upright and capable doctors that it may be said not one has been left."[2]

An instance of the mortality in Italy may be cited from the records of one religious Order. In 1347 the Olivetans made Blessed Bernard Ptolomey their Abbot General for life. In the following year, 1348, the Order lost eighty, more than half its members, by the plague. Amongst those who perished was their new-made General.[3]

Details of a similar nature might be multiplied from the contemporary Italian records. What has been here

[1] Cecchetti, *La Medicina in Venezia nel* 1300 in *Archivio Veneto,* tom. xxv, p. 378.
[2] *Ibid.,* p. 379.
[3] S. Lancelloto, *Historia Olivetana,* p. 22.

given, however, will enable the reader to form some estimate of the nature of the terrible disease and of the extent of the universal devastation of the Italian peninsula. The annals relate that in every city, castle, and town death and desolation reigned supreme. In most places, as in Pisa, for example, law and order became things of the past; the administration of justice was impossible; criminals of every kind did what they best pleased,[1] and for a considerable time after the plague had passed the Courts of Law were occupied in disputes over the possessions of the dead. When the wave of pestilence had rolled on to other lands there came in its wake famine and general distress in Italy, but strangely accompanied with the lavish expenditure of those who considered that, where so many had died, there should be enough and to spare of worldly goods for such as were left. The land lay uncultivated and the harvest was unreaped. Provisions and other necessaries of life became dear. Markets ceased to be held, and cities and towns devoid of inhabitants were spectacles of decay and desolation. It is said, and there does not appear to be reason to doubt the statement, in view of the many contemporary accounts of the disaster, that at least one half of the general population of Italy were swept away by the scourge. This relation of the horrors of the year 1348 in Italy may be closed by the account left us of some students from Bohemia, who at this time journeyed back to their country from Bologna.

"At this time," says a chronicle of Prague, "some students, coming from Bologna into Bohemia, saw that in most of the cities and castles they passed through few

---

[1] Roncioni, *Istorie Pisane* in *Archivio Storico Italiano*, iv. 808.

remained alive, and in some all were dead. In many houses also those who had escaped with their lives were so weakened by the sickness that one could not give another a draught of water, nor help him in any way, and so passed their time in great affliction and distress. Priests, too, ministering the sacraments, and doctors medicines, to the sick were infected by them and died, and so many passed out of this life without confession or the sacraments of the Church, as the priests were dead. There were generally made great, broad and deep pits in which the bodies of the dead were buried. In many places, too, the air was more infected and more deadly than poisoned food, from the corruption of the corpses, since there was no one left to bury them. Of the foresaid students, moreover, only one returned to Bohemia, and his companions all died on the journey." [1]

[1] *Chronicon Pragense*, ed. Loserth in *Fontes rerum Austriacarum*, *Scriptores*, vol. i, p. 395.

CHAPTER III

PROGRESS OF THE PLAGUE IN FRANCE

ALMOST simultaneously with the outbreak of the pestilence in Italy it obtained a foothold in the South of France. According to a contemporary account, written at Avignon in 1348, the disease was brought into Marseilles by one of the three Genoese ships, which had been compelled to leave the port of Genoa when the inhabitants discovered that by their means the dreaded plague had already commenced its ravages in their city. It would consequently appear most likely that the mortality began in Marseilles somewhere about the first days of January, 1348, although one account places the commencement of the sickness as early as All Saints' Day (November 1) 1347.[1] The number of deaths in this great southern port of France fully equalled that of the populous cities of Italy. In a month the sickness is said to have carried off 57,000 of the inhabitants of Marseilles and its neighbourhood.[2] One chronicle says that "the Bishop, with the entire chapter of the cathedral, and nearly all the friars, Preachers and Minorites, together with two-thirds of the inhabitants, perished" at this time; and adds that upon the sea might be seen ships, laden with merchandise, driven about hither and thither

---

[1] Labbe, *Nova Bibliotheca Manuscriptorum*, i, p. 343.
[2] C. Anglada, *Étude sur les Maladies Éteintes*, p. 432.

39

by the waves, the steersman and every sailor having been carried off by the disease.[1] Another, speaking of Marseilles after the pestilence had passed, says that " so many died that it remained like an uninhabited place."[2] It is of interest to record that amongst the survivors there was an English doctor, William Grisant, of Merton College, Oxford. He had studied medicine at the then celebrated school of Montpellier, and was in practice at Marseilles during the visitation of the great plague of 1348, dying two years later, in 1350.[3]

At Montpellier the ravages were, if possible, even greater. Of the twelve magistrates, or consuls, ten died, and in the numerous monasteries scarcely one religious was spared. The Dominicans here were very numerous, numbering some 140 members, and of these seven only are said to have been left alive.[4] Simon de Covino, a doctor, of Paris, who probably witnessed the course of the disease at Montpellier, wrote an account of his experiences in a poetical form in 1350. The moral of his verse is the same as Boccaccio's, and the chief interest lies in the fact that, like the Italian poet, Covino was an eye-witness of what he relates, whilst his medical training makes his testimony as to the chief characteristics of the disease specially important. The name he gives to the malady is the *pestis inguinaria*, or bubonic plague

[1] Matthias Nuewenburgensis in Boehmer, *Fontes rerum Germanicarum*, iv, p. 261.

[2] Henricus Rebdorfensis, *Ibid.*, p. 560. Another account speaks of Marseilles remaining afterwards almost " depopulated," and of "thousands dying in the adjoining towns " (*Chronicon Pragense*, in *Fontes rerum Austriacarum Scriptores*, i, p. 395).

[3] J. Astruc, *Histoire de la Faculté de Médecine de Montpellier* (Montpellier, 1862), p. 184.

[4] Anglada, *ut supra*, p. 432.

of the East. He describes a burning pain, beginning under the arms, or in the groin, and extending to the regions of the heart. A mortal fever then spread to the vital parts; the heart, lungs, and breathing passages were chiefly affected, the strength fell quickly, and the person so stricken was unable to fight any length of time against the poison.

One very singular effect of the disease is noted by the author: "The pestilence," he asserts, "stamped itself upon the entire population. Faces became pale, and the doom which threatened the people was marked upon their foreheads. It was only necessary to look into the countenances of men and women to read there recorded the blow which was about to fall; a marked pallor announced the approach of the enemy, and before the fatal day the sentence of death was written unmistakably on the face of the victims. No climate appeared to have any effect upon the strange malady. It appeared to be stayed neither by heat nor cold. High and healthy situations were as much subject to it as damp and low places. It spread during the colder season of winter as rapidly as in the heat of the summer months."

About the contagious nature of the epidemic there could be no doubt. "It has been proved," wrote Covino, "that when it once entered a house scarcely one of those who dwelt in it escaped." The contagion was so great that one sick person, so to speak, would "infect the whole world." A touch, even a breath, was sufficient to transmit the malady." Those who were obliged to render ordinary assistance to the sick fell victims. "It happened also that priests, those sacred physicians of souls, were seized by the plague whilst administering spiritual aid; and often by a single touch, or a single breath of the plague-stricken, they perished even before the sick person they had come to assist." Clothes were justly regarded as infected, and even the furniture of houses attacked was suspected. At Montpellier, at the time of the visitation, the writer says there were more doctors than elsewhere, but hardly one escaped the infection, and this even although it was recognised that medical skill was of little or no avail.

According to the experience of this Montpellier doctor the mortality was greatest amongst the poor, because their hard lives and their poverty rendered them more susceptible to the deadly infection, and their condition did not enable them to combat it with the chances of success possessed by the well-to-do classes. As to the extent of the mortality, he says "that the number of those swept away was greater than those left alive; cities are now (*i.e.*, 1350) depopulated, thousands of houses are locked up, thousands stand with their doors wide open, their owners and those who dwelt in them having been swept away." Lastly, the writer bears testimony to the baneful effect the scourge had upon the morals of those who had been spared. Such visitations, he thinks, must always exercise the most lowering influence upon the general virtue of the world.[1]

From Marseilles the epidemic quickly spread northwards up the Rhone valley, and in a westerly direction through Languedoc. Montpellier, too, quickly passed on the infection. It commenced at Narbonne in the first week of Lent, 1348, and is said to have carried off 30,000 of the inhabitants. Indeed, so fearful was the visitation,

[1] *Opuscule relatif à la peste de* 1348, *composé par un contemporain* in *Bibliothèque de l'École des Chartes*, 1e Sér., ii, pp. 201-243.

that this ancient city is reported never to have recovered from the desolation it caused.[1]

At Arles, which was attacked very shortly after the disease had gained a footing on French soil, most of the inhabitants perished.[2] It reached Avignon as early as January, 1348. In this city Pope Clement VI, then in the sixth year of his pontificate, held his court. Before the arrival of the dreaded visitant was publicly recognised sixty-six religious of the convent of Carmelites had been carried off, and in the first three days 1,800 people are reported to have died. In the seven months during which the scourge lasted the vast roll of the dead in the territory of Avignon had mounted up to 150,000 persons, amongst whom was the friend of Petrarch, Laura de Noves, who died on Good Friday, March 27th, 1348.[3] Even in England at the time the excessive mortality at Avignon was noted and remarked upon.[4] Great numbers of Jews are said to have been carried off because of the unsanitary conditions in which they lived, and an equally great number of Spaniards resident in the city, whose propensity for good living rendered them most susceptible to the infection.[5]

The alarming mortality quickly caused a panic. "For such terror," writes an author of the lives of the Popes at Avignon, "took possession of nearly everyone, that as soon as the ulcer or boil appeared on anyone he was deserted by all, no matter how nearly they might be

---

[1] Martin, *Histoire de France* (4th ed.), v, p. 109.

[2] Phillippe, *Histoire de la Peste Noire*, p. 103.

[3] Anglada, *Maladies Éteintes*, p. 431.

[4] Higden, *Polychronicon* (ed. Rolls Series), viii, p. 344.

[5] L. Michon, *Documents inédits sur la grande peste de* 1348 (Paris, 1860), p. 22.

related to him. For the father left his son, the son his father, on his sick bed. In any house when a person became sick with the infirmity and died it generally happened that all others there were attacked and quickly followed him to the grave; yea, even the animals in the place, such as dogs, cats, cocks, and hens also died. Hence those who had strength fled for fear of what had taken place, and, as a consequence, many who might otherwise have recovered perished through want of care. Many, too, who were seized with the sickness, being considered certain to die and without any hope of recovery, were carried off at once to the pit and buried. And in this way many were buried alive."

The same writer notices the charity of the Pope at this terrible time, in causing doctors to visit and assist the sick poor. " And since the ordinary cemeteries did not suffice to hold the bodies of the dead, the Pope purchased a large field and caused it to be consecrated as a cemetery where anyone might be buried. And here an infinite number of people were then interred." [1]

The most important and particular account of the pestilence at Avignon, however, is that of a certain Canon of the Low Countries, who wrote at the time from the city to his friends in Bruges. He was in the train of a Cardinal on a visit to the Roman Curia when the plague broke out. " The disease," he writes, " is threefold in its infection; that is to say, firstly, men suffer in their lungs and breathing, and whoever have these corrupted, or even slightly attacked, cannot by any means escape nor live beyond two days. Examinations have been

---

[1] Baluze, *Vitae Paparum Avenionensium*, i, p. 254. In a second life of Clement VII (p. 274) it is said that vast pits were dug in the public cemetery, where the dead were buried " ut pecora gregatim."

made by doctors in many cities of Italy, and also in
Avignon, by order of the Pope, in order to discover the
origin of this disease. Many dead bodies have been thus
opened and dissected, and it is found that all who have
died thus suddenly have had their lungs infected and
have spat blood. The contagious nature of the disease
is indeed the most terrible of all the terrors (of the
time), for when anyone who is infected by it dies, all
who see him in his sickness, or visit him, or do any
business with him, or even carry him to the grave,
quickly follow him thither, and there is no known means
of protection.

"There is another form of the sickness, however, at
present running its course concurrently with the first;
that is, certain aposthumes appear under both arms, and
by these also people quickly die. A third form of the
disease—like the two former, running its course at this
same time with them—is that from which people of both
sexes suffer from aposthumes in the groin. This, likewise, is quickly fatal. The sickness has already grown
to such proportions that, from fear of contagion, no
doctor will visit a sick man, even if the invalid would
gladly give him everything he possessed; neither does a
father visit his son, nor a mother her daughter, nor a
brother his brother, nor a son his father, nor a friend his
friend, nor an acquaintance his acquaintance, nor, in
fact, does anyone go to another, no matter how closely
he may be allied to him by blood, unless he is prepared
to die with him or quickly to follow after him. Still, a
large number of persons have died merely through their
affection for others; for they might have escaped had
they not, moved by piety and Christian charity, visited
the sick at the time.

"To put the matter shortly, one-half, or more than a half, of the people at Avignon are already dead. Within the walls of the city there are now more than 7,000 houses shut up; in these no one is living, and all who have inhabited them are departed; the suburbs hardly contain any people at all. A field near 'Our Lady of Miracles' has been bought by the Pope and consecrated as a cemetery. In this, from the 13th of March,[1] 11,000 corpses have been buried. This number does not include those interred in the cemetery of the hospital of St. Anthony, in cemeteries belonging to the religious bodies, and in the many others which exist in Avignon. Nor must I be silent about the neighbouring parts, for at Marseilles all the gates of the city, with the exception of two small ones, are now closed, for there four-fifths of the inhabitants are dead.

"The like account I can give of all the cities and towns of Provence. Already the sickness has crossed the Rhone, and ravaged many cities and villages as far as Toulouse, and it ever increases in violence as it proceeds. On account of this great mortality there is such a fear of death that people do not dare even to speak with anyone whose relative has died, because it is frequently remarked that in a family where one dies nearly all the relations follow him, and this is commonly believed among the people. Neither are the sick now served by their kindred, except as dogs would be; food is put near the bed for them to eat and drink, and then those still in health fly and leave the house. When a man dies some rough countrymen, called *gavoti*, come to the house, and, after receiving a sufficiently large

[1] The writer was sending his letter on April 27th, 1348, so that the period would have been about six weeks.

reward, carry the corpse to the grave. Neither relatives nor friends go to the sick, nor do priests even hear their confessions nor give them the Sacraments; but everyone whilst still in health looks after himself. It daily happens that some rich man dying is borne to the grave by these ruffians without lights, and without a soul to follow him, except these hired mourners. When a corpse is carried by all fly through the streets and get into their houses. Nor do these said wretched *gavoti*, strong as they are, escape; but most of them after a time become infected by this contagion and die. All the poor who were wont to receive bread from the rich are dead; that is to say, briefly, where daily in ordinary times there were distributed sixty-four measures of wheat for bread, fifty loaves being made from each measure, now only one measure is given away, and sometimes even a half is found to be sufficient.

" And it is said that altogether in three months—that is from January 25th to the present day (April 27th)— 62,000 bodies have been buried in Avignon. The Pope, however, about the middle of March last past, after mature deliberation, gave plenary absolution till Easter, as far as the keys of the Church extended, to all those who, having confessed and being contrite, should happen to die of the sickness. He ordered likewise devout processions, singing the Litanies, to be made on certain days each week, and to these, it is said, people sometimes come from the neighbouring districts to the number of 2,000; amongst them many of both sexes are barefooted, some are in sackcloth, some with ashes, walking with tears, and tearing their hair, and beating themselves with scourges even to the drawing of blood. The Pope was personally present at some of these processions,

but they were then within the precincts of his palace.
What will be the end, or whence all this has had its
beginning, God alone knows.

"Some wretched men have been caught with certain
dust, and, whether justly or unjustly God only knows,
they are accused of having poisoned the water, and men
in fear do not drink the water from wells; for this many
have been burnt and daily are burnt.

"Fish, even sea fish, is commonly not eaten, as people
say they have been infected by the bad air. Moreover,
people do not eat, nor even touch spices, which have not
been kept a year, since they fear they may have lately
arrived in the aforesaid ships. And, indeed, it has many
times been observed that those who have eaten these new
spices and even some kinds of sea fish have suddenly
been taken ill.

"I write this to you, my friends, that you may know
the dangers in which we live. And if you desire to
preserve yourselves, the best advice is to eat and drink
temperately, to avoid cold, not to commit excess of any
kind, and, above all, to converse little with others, at
this time especially, except with the few whose breath
is sweet. But it is best to remain at home until this
epidemic has passed

"Know, also, that the Pope has lately left Avignon, as
is reported, and has gone to the castle called Stella, near
Valence on the Rhone, two leagues off, to remain there
till times change. The Curia, however, preferred to remain at Avignon, (but) vacations have been proclaimed
till the feast of St. Michael. All the auditors, advocates,
and procurators have either left, intend to leave immediately, or are dead. I am in the hands of God, to whom
I commend myself. My master will follow the Pope, so

they say, and I with him, for there are some castles near the airy mountains where the mortality has not yet appeared, and it is thought that the best chance is there. To choose and to do what is best may the Omnipotent and merciful God grant us all. Amen."[1]

From another source some corroboration of the mortality, described by the writer of this letter, can be obtained. The 11,000, stated by the anonymous canon to have been buried in the Pope's new cemetery from March 13th to April 27th may appear excessive; still more, the 62,000 reported to have died in the three months between the first outbreak, on January 25th, and the date when the letter was written. The statements of the writer are, however, so circumstantial and given with such detail, that, allowing for the tendency in all such catastrophes to exaggerate rather than minimise the number of the victims, it is probable that his estimate of the terrible destruction of life at Avignon and in the neighbourhood is substantially accurate. Writing, as he does, on the Sunday after Easter, 1348, he evidently points to the time of Lent as the period during which the epidemic was at its height. This is borne out by a statement in a German chronicle, which says: "In Venice, in the whole of Italy and Provence, especially in the cities on the sea-coast, there died countless numbers. And at Avignon, where the Roman Curia then was, in the first three days after mid-Lent Sunday, 1,400 people were computed to have been buried."[2] Mid-Lent Sunday, in 1348, fell upon March 30th, and, consequently, according to this authority, on the last

---

[1] *Breve Chronicon clerici anonymi*, in De Smet, *Recueil des Chroniques de Flandre*, iii, pp. 14-18.

[2] Henricus Rebdorfensis, in Boehmer, *Fontes*, iv, p. 560.

day of March and the first two days of April the death-
rate was over 450 a day.

No account of the plague at Avignon would be complete without some notice of Gui de Chauliac, and some
quotations from the work he has left to posterity upon
this particular outbreak. De Chauliac was the medical
attendant of Pope Clement VI. He devoted himself to
the service of the sick during the time of the epidemic,
and, although he himself caught the infection, his life was
happily spared to the service of others, and to enable
him to write an account of the sickness. The mortality,
he says, commenced in the month of January, 1348, and
lasted for the space of seven months. " It was of two
kinds; the first lasted two months, with constant fever
and blood-spitting, and of this people died in three days.

" The second lasted for the rest of the time. In this,
together with constant fever, there were external carbuncles, or buboes, under the arm or in the groin, and
the disease ran its course in five days. The contagion
was so great (especially when there was blood-spitting)
that not only by remaining (with the sick), but even by
looking (at them) people seemed to take it; so much so,
that many died without any to serve them, and were
buried without priests to pray over their graves.

" A father did not visit his son, nor the son his father.
Charity was dead. The mortality was so great that it
left hardly a fourth part of the population. Even the
doctors did not dare to visit the sick from fear of infection, and when they did visit them they attempted
nothing to heal them, and thus almost all those who
were taken ill died, except towards the end of the
epidemic, when some few recovered."

" As for me, to avoid infamy, I did not dare to absent

myself, but still I was in continual fear." Towards the end of the sickness de Chauliac took the infection, and was in great danger for six weeks, but in the end recovered.[1]

It was according to the advice of this same Gui de Chauliac that Pope Clement VI isolated himself and kept large fires always alight in his apartments, just as Pope Nicholas IV had done in a previous epidemic. In the whole district of Provence the mortality appears to have been very great. In the Lent of 1348 no fewer than 358 Dominicans are said to have died.[2] Even by the close of the November of this year the terror of the time had not passed away from Avignon and the Papal Court. Writing to King Louis of Hungary, on the 23rd of that month, the Pope excused himself for not having sent before, "as the deadly plague, which has devastated these and other parts of the world by an unknown and terrible mortality, has not only, by God's will, carried off some of our brethren, but caused others to fly from the Roman Curia to avoid death."[3]

In the early summer of the same year, 1348, just as the plague was lessening its ravages at Avignon, the Pope addressed a letter to the General Chapter of the Friars Minor then being held at Verona. He laments the misery into which the world has been plunged, chiefly "by the mortal sickness which is carrying off from us old and young, rich and poor, in one common, sudden and unforeseen death." He urges them to unite in prayer that the plague may cease, and grants special indulgences "to such among you as, during this Chapter, or whilst returning to your homes, may chance to

---

[1] Anglada, *Maladies Éteintes*, pp. 413-14.
[2] Barnes, *History of Edward III.*, p. 435.
[3] Thiener, *Monumenta Historica Hungariae*, i, p. 767.

die." [1] Of these Franciscans it is said that, in Italy alone, 30,000 died in this sickness.

From its first entry into France in the early days of 1348, the plague was ever spreading far and wide. The letter from Avignon, already given, speaks of the ravages of the mortality in the whole of Provence, and of its having, before the end of April, reached Toulouse on its journey westward. In the August of this year (1348) Bordeaux was apparently suffering from it, since in that month the Princess Joan, daughter of Edward III, who was on her way to be married to Pedro, son of the King of Castille, died suddenly in that city.

In a northerly direction the epidemic spread with equal virulence. At Lyons evidence of the pestilence is afforded by an inscription preserved in the town museum. It relates to the construction of a chapel in 1352 by a citizen, " Michael Pancsus," in which Mass should be said for the souls of several members of his family " who died in the time of the mortality, 1348." [2] The anonymous cleric of Bruges, who preserved the Avignon letter, writing probably at the time, gives the following account of its progress: " In the year of our Lord 1348, that plague, epidemic, and mortality, which we have mentioned before, by the will of God has not ceased; but from day to day grows and descends upon other parts. For in Burgundy, Normandy, and elsewhere it has consumed, and is consuming, many thousands of men, animals, and sheep." [3]

---

[1] Wadding, *Annales Minorum*, viii, p. 25 (ed. 1723).

[2] Olivier de la Haye, *Poëme sur la grande peste de* 1348. Introduction par G. Guigue, p. xviii, *note*.

[3] *Breve Chronicon* in De Smet, *Recueil des Chroniques de Flandre*, iii, p. 19.

It arrived in Normandy probably about the feast of St. James (25th July), 1348. A contemporary note in a manuscript, which certainly came from the Abbey of Foucarmont, gives the following account: "In the year of grace 1348, about the feast of St. James, the great mortality entered into Normandy. And it came into Gascony, and Poitou, and Brittany, and then passed into Picardy. And it was so horrible that in the towns it attacked more than two-thirds of the population died. And a father did not dare to go and visit his son, nor a brother his sister, and people could not be found to nurse one another, because, when the person breathed the breath of another he could not escape. It came to such a pass that no one could be found even to carry the corpses (to the tomb). People said that the end of the world had come."[1] In another manuscript, M. Delisle has found a further note, or portion of a note, referring to the terrible nature of the malady in Normandy. It never entered a city or town without carrying off the greater part of the inhabitants. "And in that time the mortality was so great among the people of Normandy that those in Picardy mocked them."[2]

Paris was, of course, visited by the disease. Apparently, it was some time in the early summer of 1348 when it first manifested itself. In the chronicle of St. Denis it is recorded that "in the year of grace 1348 the said mortality commenced in the Kingdom of France and lasted about a year and a half, more or less. In this way there died in Paris, one day with another, 800 persons. . . . In the space of the said year and a half, as some declare, the number of the dead in Paris rose to

[1] Delisle, *Cabinet des Manuscrits*, i, p. 532.
[2] *Ibid.* Here the note abruptly finishes.

more than 50,000, and in the town of St. Denis the number was as high as 16,000."[1] The chronicle of the Carmelites at Rheims places the total of deaths in Paris at the larger number of 80,000,[2] amongst whom were two Queens, Joan of Navarre, daughter of Louis X, and Joan of Burgundy, wife of King Philip of Valois.

The most circumstantial account of the plague in France at the time when the capital was attacked is given in the continuation of the chronicle of William of Nangis, which was written probably before 1368. " In the same year " (1348), it says, "both in Paris in the kingdom of France, and not less, as is reported, in different parts of the world, and also in the following year, there was so great a mortality of people of both sexes, and of the young rather than the old, that they could hardly be buried. Further they were ill scarcely more than two or three days, and some often died suddenly, so that a man to-day in good health, to-morrow was carried a corpse to the grave. Lumps suddenly appeared under the arm-pits or in the groin, and the appearance of these was an infallible sign of death. This sickness, or pestilence, was called by the doctors the epidemic. And the multitude of people who died in the years 1348 and 1349, was so large that nothing like it was ever heard, read of, or witnessed in past ages. And the said death and sickness often sprung from the imagination, or from the society and (consequent) contagion of another, for a healthy man visiting one sick hardly ever escaped death. So that in many towns, small and great, priests retired through fear, leaving the administration of the Sacraments to religious, who were

---

[1] H. Martin, *Histoire de France*, v, p. 111.
[2] Marlot, *Histoire de Reims*, iv, p. 63.

more bold. Briefly, in many places, there did not remain two alive out of every twenty.

"So great was the mortality in the Hotel-Dieu of Paris that for a long time more than fifty corpses were carried away from it each day in carts to be buried.[1] And the devout sisters of the Hotel-Dieu, not fearing death, worked piously and humbly, not out of regard for any worldly honour. A great number of these said sisters were very frequently summoned to their reward by death, and rest in peace with Christ, as is piously believed."

After saying that the plague had passed through Gascony and Spain, the chronicler speaks of it as going "from town to town, village to village, from house to house, and even from person to person; and coming into the country of France, passed into Germany, where, however, it was less severe than amongst us."

"It lasted in France," the writer says, "the greater part of 1348 and 1349, and afterwards there were to be seen many towns, country places, and houses in good cities remaining empty and without inhabitants."

The writer concludes by declaring that nature soon began to make up for losses. "But, alas! the world by this renovation is not changed for the better. For people were afterwards more avaricious and grasping, even when they possessed more of the goods of this world, than before. They were more covetous, vexing them-

---

[1] All copies of this chronicle give "*quingente*," and it has usually been stated that the number so buried each day was 500. M. Géraud, who edited the work for the Société de l'Histoire de France, suggests that it is a mistake for 50, and quotes two MSS., in which in the margin the following note is found: "L corps par jour a l'Hostel-Dieu de Paris." As this reading is more probable it has been adopted above.

selves by contentious quarrels, strifes, and law suits."
Moreover, all things were much dearer; furniture, food,
merchandise of all sorts, doubled in price, and servants
would work only for higher wages. "Charity, too, from
that time began to grow cold, and wickedness with its
attendant, ignorance, was rampant, and few were found
who could or would teach children the rudiments of
grammar in houses, cities, or villages."[1]

Whilst the plague was at its height King Philip VI
requested the medical faculty of Paris to consult together and to report upon the best methods by which
the deadly nature of the disease could be combated. The
result of their consultation was published, probably in
June, 1348.[2] Unfortunately, adhering closely to the text
of the question addressed to them, their reply does not
furnish any historical details. They broadly state their
views as to the probable origin of the epidemic, and
confine themselves to suggestions as to its treatment,
and to the means by which contagion is to be avoided.
They are clear as to the infectious nature of the disease,
and earnest in their recommendations that all who were
able should have nothing to do with the sick. "It is
chiefly the people of one house, and above all those of
the same family, who are close together," they say, "who
die, for they are always near to those who are sick. We
advise them to depart, for it is in this way that a great
number have been infected by the plague."[3]

Meanwhile the epidemic was spreading northward.

---

[1] *Continuatio Chronici Guillelmi di Nangiaco, éd.* pour la Société
de l'Histoire de France par H. Géraud, ii, pp. 211-217.

[2] They speak in the document of " the 17th of the ensuing month
of July."

[3] Michon, *Documents inédits sur la Peste Noire*, p. 22.

At Amiens, where 17,000 are said to have been carried off by the sickness, it seems probable that the malady was not at its height before the summer of the following year, 1349. The wave of pestilence from Paris seems to have divided. One stream swept on through Normandy towards the coast, which it probably reached, in the regions round Calais, about July or August of the year 1348. The other stream, checked probably by the autumn and winter, made its way more slowly towards Belgium and Holland.

In the June of 1349 the King granted a petition from the Mayor of Amiens for a new cemetery. In the document the plague in the city is described as having been then so terrible that the cemeteries are full, and no more corpses could safely be buried in them. "The mortality in the said town," says the King's letter, "is so marvellously great that people are dying there suddenly, as quickly, as from one evening to the following morning, and often even quicker than that."[1] This was in June, 1349, and already by September of the same year the authorities were called upon to deal with a combination of workmen at a tannery to secure for themselves excessive wages "to the great hurt of the people at large." The promptness of the action of the Mayor, and the tone of the proclamation establishing a rate of wages, is a sufficient proof that the crisis was regarded as serious.[2] This trouble at Amiens is an indication of difficulties which will be seen to have existed elsewhere in France, in Germany, and in England, which had their origin in the dearth of labourers after the scourge had passed.

[1] Thierry, *Recueil des Monuments inédits de l'Histoire du Tiers Etat*, i, p. 544.
[2] *Ibid.*, p. 546.

The account of the ravages of this great pestilence in France, as well as its course in the city of Tournay, where it commenced in August, 1349, is well given in the chronicle of Gilles Li Muisis, Abbot of St. Martin's, Tournay, who was a contemporary of the events he describes. "It is impossible," he says, "to credit the mortality throughout the whole country. Travellers, merchants, pilgrims, and others who have passed through it declare that they have found cattle wandering without herdsmen in fields, towns, and waste lands; that they have seen barns and wine-cellars standing wide open, houses empty, and few people to be found anywhere. So much so that in many towns, cities and villages, where there had been before 20,000 people, scarcely 2,000 are left; and in many cities and country places, where there had been 1,500 people, hardly 100 remain. And in many different lands (*multis climatibus*), both lands and fields are lying uncultivated. I have heard these things from a certain knight well skilled in the law, who was one of the members of the Paris Parliament. He was sent, together with a certain Bishop, by Philip, the most illustrious King of France, to the King of Aragon, and on his return journey passed through Avignon. Both there and in Paris, as he told me, he was informed of the foresaid things by many people worthy of credit."

After speaking of the evidence given by a pilgrim to Santiago, Li Muisis proceeds to relate his own experiences in Tournay in the summer of 1349. This he does in verse and prose. The poem, after speaking of the manifestation of God's anger, describes the plague beginning in the East and passing through France into Flanders. Like other writers, Li Muisis declares that he hesitates to say what he has seen and heard, because posterity will hardly credit what he would relate.[1] The reports of all travellers and merchants as to the terrible state of the country generally give one and the same sad story of universal death and distress. The particulars as to the plague in Tournay, the writer's own city, may best be given from his prose account.

John de Pratis, the Bishop of Tournay, was one of the first to be carried off by the sickness. He had gone away for change of air, and on Corpus Christi Day, June 11th, 1349, he carried the blessed Sacrament in the procession at Arras. He left that city the next day for Cambray, but died the day after almost suddenly.[2] He was buried at Tournay; and "time passed on," says our author, to the beginning of August, up to which no other person of authority died in Tournay. But after the feast of St. John the plague began in the parish of St. Piat, in the quarter of Merdenchor, and afterwards in other parishes. Every day the bodies of the dead were borne to the churches, now five, now ten, now fifteen, and in the parish of St. Brice sometimes twenty or thirty. In all parish churches the curates, parish clerks, and sextons to get their fees, rang morning, evening, and night the passing bells, and by this the whole people of the city, both men and women, began to be filled with fear.

The officials of the town consequently seeing that the Dean and Chapter, and the clerics generally, did not

> "Certe dicere timeo
> Quae vidi et quae video
> De ista pestilentia."

[2] Gams, *Series Episcoporum*, gives 13th June, 1349, as the day of his death.

care to remedy this matter, since it was in their interest
it should go on, as they made profit out of it, having
taken counsel together, issued certain orders. Men and
women who, although not married, were living together
as man and wife, were commanded either to marry or
forthwith to separate. The bodies of the dead were to
be buried immediately in graves at least six feet deep.
There was to be no tolling of any bells at funerals. The
corpse was not to be taken to the church, but at the
service only a pall was to be spread on the ground, whilst
after the service there was to be no gathering together
at the houses of the deceased. Further, all work after
noon on Saturdays and during the entire Sunday was
prohibited, as also was the playing of dice and making
use of profane oaths.

These ordinances having lasted for a time, and the
sickness still further increasing, it was proclaimed on
St. Matthew's Day (September 24th) that there should
be no more ringing of bells, that not more than two
were to meet for any funeral service, and that no one
was to dress in black. This action of the city authorities,
the writer declares to have been most beneficial. In his
own knowledge, he says, many who had hitherto been
living in a state of concubinage were married, that the
practice of swearing notably diminished, and that dice
were so little used that the manufacturers turned " the
square-shaped dice " into " round objects on which people
told their *Pater Nosters*."

I have tried, says our author, to write what I know,
"and let future generations believe that in Tournay
there was a marvellous mortality. I heard from many
about Christmas time who professed to know it as a
fact that more than 25,000 persons had died in Tournay,

and it was strange that the mortality was especially great among the chief people and the rich. Of those who used wine and kept away from the tainted air and visiting the sick few or none died. But those visiting and frequenting the houses of the sick either became grievously ill or died. Deaths were more numerous about the market places and in poor narrow streets than in broader and more spacious areas. And whenever one or two people died in any house, at once, or at least in a short space of time, the rest of the household were carried off. So much so, that very often in one home ten or more ended their lives together, and in many houses the dogs and even cats died. Hence no one, whether rich, in moderate circumstances, or poor, was secure, but everyone from day to day waited on the will of the Lord. And certainly great was the number of curates and chaplains hearing confessions and administering the Sacraments, and even of parish clerks visiting the sick with them, who died."

In the parishes across the river, the mortality was as great as in Tournay itself. Although death as a rule came so suddenly, still the people for the most part were able to receive the Sacraments. The rapidity of the disease, remarked upon by Petrarch and Boccaccio in Italy, is also spoken of in the same terms by the Abbot of St. Martin's. People that one had seen apparently well and had spoken to one evening were reported dead next day. He specially remarks upon the mortality among the clergy visiting the sick,[1] and speaks of the creation of two new cemeteries outside the walls of the

---

[1]   " Quia de sacerdotibus
Infirmos visitantibus
Quamplurimi defecerunt."

town. One was in a field near the Leper House *De Valle*,
the other at the religious house of the Crutched Friars.
Strange to say, Li Muisis speaks of the disfavour with
which this necessary precaution of establishing new
grave-yards was regarded. People, he says, grumbled
because they were no longer allowed to be buried in
their own family vaults. The town authorities, however,
were firm, and as the pestilence increased deep pits were
dug in these two common burying places, and into them
numbers of bodies were constantly being thrown and
covered up with a slight layer of earth.[1]

It has been supposed by many that the accounts
given by contemporary writers of the excessive mortality
throughout the countries of Europe must be greatly
exaggerated, and that the population in the middle of
the fourteenth century was not sufficiently large to allow
of the number of deaths. On the one hand it is evident
that in the majority of cases the round figures stated
can be at most nothing more than a rough approxima-
tion of the actual deaths, and that the natural tendency
of those who have witnessed a catastrophe as great and
as universal as that of the plague of 1348 and subsequent years, is to magnify, rather than to diminish,
the disaster. On the other hand, whilst allowing that in
most cases the actual figures are little more than guesses
at the truth, and can only be taken as evidence of the
belief of the age in the magnitude of the mortality, it
must be admitted that Italy, France, and other countries
of Europe were at the time more teeming with population than is perhaps usually understood.

[1] *Chronicon majus Ægidii Li Muisis, abbatis Sti. Martini
Tornacensis*, in De Smet, *Recueil des Chroniques de Flandre*, ii,
pp. 279-281 and 361-382.

M. Siméon Luce has made a special study of the conditions of French popular life at this period,[1] and the conclusions at which he has arrived may be here usefully stated in brief. It has been proved by the labours of French antiquaries that the general population of France before the great pestilence of 1348-1349, and the hundred years' war with England, was equal to what it is in the present century. Numerous villages were scattered over the face of the country, every trace of which has now disappeared. The houses, or rather huts, in which the population of rural France lived were very seldom framed of any kind of masonry, but were for the most part merely four mud, or clay, walls, and sometimes wickerwork lined, and the interstices filled in, with hay and straw. As a rule there was but one storey, although some, chiefly taverns and places of that class, had an upper floor. The roof was thatched or covered with wood or stone; windows were the exception, and where they did exist they were mere slits in the clay walls closed with wooden shutters. Even the coarse opaque glass then made was beyond the means of the ordinary peasant and farmer, whilst just about this time even a rich bourgeois of Paris recommended the filling of windows with waxen cloth or parchment. The doors were fastened with wooden latches, and over them, according to the general arrangement, a shutter of wood was fixed which was generally left open for air, light, and to allow the smoke of the brushwood fire to pass out of the living room. It will be readily understood how the condition of life in houses such as these would not be such as to put much obstacle to the spread of an epidemic in the rural districts; whilst if such tenements

[1] S. Luce, *Bertrand du Guesclin*, i, ch. 3.

were vacant even for a short time they would readily
fall into decay and would present the spectacle of ruin
and desolation spoken of by so many writers of the
period as caused by the great pestilence.

The furniture of these houses was simple, but very
much what it is now in small country houses. The inventories of the period show that most houses had vessels
of copper, tin and glass, and that there were few who
did not possess some articles of silver. The people for
the most part lived on a soup of bread and meal; but even
by the fourteenth century white bread was by no means
unknown. The principal meat was pork fed in the
forests, but most cottages possessed a spit upon which
fowls, previously larded, were occasionally roasted. Of
condiments, mustard was the chief, and it was much, if
not universally, used. Even in the humblest houses a
cloth would be spread on the table at meals. For drink
there was the wine of the country, and in Normandy
cider was plentiful. With the drink, especially in taverns
which were exceedingly numerous, a little ginger would
generally be mixed. In dress fur of various kinds was
much used, and, by the time of this pestilence, in France
the use of the linen shirt as an undergarment had become almost universal. The sleeping places were dark,
airless recesses, in which the people, having divested
themselves of all clothing, rested upon straw mattresses,
or sometimes on feather beds. Contrary to the opinion
entertained by persons of repute there is evidence to
show that bathing was common and much used, especially among the lower classes, and that even small villages
had their public bath places.

This sketch of the epidemic in these regions may be
concluded by one or two instances of the agrarian diffi-

culties which followed upon it. On August 16th, 1349, the Emperor Charles IV issued an order to the tenants of the Abbey of St. Trond, in the diocese of Liège, to return to their obedience. The document says that the holders of the Abbey lands and other dependents are now demanding their own terms and claiming liberty to do what they like, with the result that the Abbot and monastery are so distressed in temporal matters that absolute ruin is impending.[1] The second instance is that of the Abbey of St. John at Laon. A document, addressed by the French King Charles to the Abbot and convent, says that the monastery is so decayed in revenues that it is impossible to keep up the fitting and proper services of the Church. And although the letter was not written till nearly the close of the century—1392-3—the cause assigned for this poverty and decay is " the great mortality which took place about the year 1349," by which the tithes and other revenues were destroyed.

And to quote but one more example: " On 5th July, 1352, relief was granted to the inhabitants of the town of Arras because by reason of the wars, and because of the mortality which has been universal in the world, the said city is so greatly decayed, both as to buildings and people, as also in revenues and temporal goods, that it is on the high road to (absolute) desolation."[2]

---

[1] Piot, *Cartulaire de l'abbaye de Saint-Trond*, i, 507.

[2] Lechner, *Das grosse Sterben in Deutschland*, p. 93. For the diminution of the population in France, cf. *Le Budget et la Population de la France sous Philippe de Valois*, A. M. de Boislisle, 1875.

CHAPTER IV

THE PLAGUE IN OTHER EUROPEAN COUNTRIES

IN following the great pestilence through Europe, according to the historical sequence of events, its course in England should be now described. Inasmuch, however, as the story of the ravages caused by the disease in England will be told in greater detail, it may conveniently be left till the last. Here a brief account may be interposed of the mortality in other European countries, although it will take the reader to the year 1351.

From Sicily, Sardinia, and Corsica the plague was carried to the Balearic Islands. The three streams of infection met with destructive force at Majorca. The historian Zurita declares that in less than a month 15,000 persons had perished on the island. Another writer estimates the total loss of life during the epidemic at double that number, and some ancient records have been quoted as stating that in the island eight out of every ten people must have died, a proportion, of course, exaggerated, but sufficient to show local tradition as to the extent of the misfortune. In the monasteries and convents, according to this authority, not one religious was left; and the Dominicans are said to have been obliged to recruit their numbers by enrolling quite young children.[1]

The scourge fell upon Spain in the early part of the year 1348. It is supposed to have first appeared at

---

[1] Philippe, *Histoire de la Peste Noire*, p. 54.

Almeira, and in Barcelona whole quarters of the city were depopulated and rendered desolate by it. In May, 1348, it was already raging in Valencia, and by midsummer 300 persons a day are reported to have been buried in the city. At Saragossa, where Pedro IV then was, the malady was at its height in September. The people here, as elsewhere, became hardened, and charity died out in the presence of the terrors of death. They fled from the sick, leaving them to die alone, and abandoned the corpses of the dead in the streets. Most of the cities and villages of Spain suffered more or less severely, and the sickness appears to have lingered longer here than in most other countries. The new Queen of Aragon had been one of the earliest victims; Alfonso XI was one of the last. In March, 1350, he was laying siege to Gibraltar, when the plague broke out suddenly with great violence amongst his troops. He refused to retire, as his officers desired him to do, and fell a victim to the epidemic on Good Friday, March 26th, 1350.[1]

An interesting account of Northern Spain during the plague is given in the chronicle of Li Muisis, Abbot of St. Martin's, Tournay, from which much was cited in the previous chapter. The writer says that he learnt the details from "a pilgrim, who, in going to St. James' (of Compostella), passed by Notre Dame de Roc Amadour'[2] and by Toulouse, because by reason of the wars he could not travel the usual way." This pilgrim to Compostella, in the middle of the fourteenth century, would consequently have crossed the Pyrenees by one of the passes

---

[1] Philippe, *Histoire de la Peste Noire*, pp. 54-56.
[2] This was a place of pilgrimage on the Amadour, not far from Toulouse.

into Navarre, and so travelled along the north of Spain
to Santiago. Having performed his pilgrimage, Li Muisis
informs us that he returned through Galicia, and "with his
companion, reached a town named Salvaterra," probably
the place now called Salvatierra, situated below the
Pyrenees, and just above the Sierra de la Pena. This
town, as the traveller reported, " was so depopulated by
the mortality that not one person out of ten had been
left alive. The city itself was fairly large. The said
pilgrim related," says Li Muisis, " that after supping with
the host (who, with two daughters and one servant, had
alone so far survived of his entire family, and who was
not then conscious of any sickness upon him), he settled
with him for his entertainment, intending to start on his
journey at daybreak, and went to bed. Next morning
rising and wanting something from those with whom
they had supped, the travellers could make no one hear.
Then they learnt from an old woman they found in bed
that the host, his two daughters, and servant had died in
the night. On hearing this the pilgrims made all haste
to leave the place."[1]

From North Italy the pestilence soon spread to the
country across the Adriatic, if indeed it had not already
been infected independently, as seems more than probable, by ships from the East. The port of Ragusa, in
Dalmatia, is said to have been attacked as early as
January 13th, 1348, and more than 7,000 are reported as
having been swept away by it. A letter sent in April to
the authorities " condoles with them on the terrible
mortality, by which the population had been so greatly
diminished."[2] At Spalatro, on March 22nd, 1348, the

---

[1] *Chronicon majus Ægidii Li Muisis*, ii, 280.
[2] Lechner, *Das grosse Sterben in Deutschland*, p. 21.

Archbishop Dominic de Lucaris died of the disease, and it is known to have raged for some months in the city. An anonymous chronicler of Spalatro in the fifteenth century, who professed to take his account of this period from ancient records, declares that it is impossible to picture " the terrors and miseries of these unhappy days." To add to the horror of the situation, as he declares, wolves and other wild animals came down from the mountains and fell upon the plague-stricken city and boldly attacked the survivors. The same writer notes the rapidity with which the disease carried off those it attacked. According to him, when swellings or carbuncles appeared on any part of the body, all hope of saving the life of the patient was abandoned. As a rule, those stricken in this way died in three or at most four days, and so great was the general mortality that bodies were left lying unburied in the streets, because there were none to carry them to the grave.[1]

Further north again, Sebenico, through intercourse with which, very possibly, the plague was carried into Hungary, was attacked in the spring of the same year, 1348. By the 8th of May the Count of Sebenico had written a description of the wretched condition and state of the city, by reason of the great mortality in those parts, through which it had been left almost without inhabitants.[2] Istria, on August 27th, 1348, was declared in a Venetian State paper to have suffered greatly. The people left, especially in the city of Pola, were very few, so many having been swept away " by the late pestilence."[3]

From Venice the epidemic spread northwards into

---

[1] Farlati, *Illyricum Sacrum*, iii, p. 324.
[2] Lechner, *ut sup.*, p. 22.　　　　　　　　　[3] *Ibid.*

Austria and Hungary. Attacking on its way Padua and Verona, it passed up the valley of the Etsch and was already at Trent on June 2nd, 1348. Thence it spread quickly through Botzen up the Brenner Pass, in the Tyrolese Alps, and was at Muhldorf on the Inn, in Bavaria on June 29th, 1348.[1] Here it seems to have lasted for a considerable time. One chronicler, writing of the subsequent year, 1349, says "that from the feast of St. Michael, 1348, there perished in Muhldorf 1,400 of the better class of inhabitants."[2] Another, speaking of the plague generally, says "that it raged so terribly in Carinthia, Austria, and Bavaria that many cities were depopulated, and in some towns which it visited many families were destroyed so completely that not a member was found to have survived."[3]

In November of the same year, 1348, the epidemic is found in Styria, at Neuberg, in the valley of the Mürz. The Neuberg Chronicle, giving an account of it, says, "Since this deadly pestilence raged everywhere, cities became desolate which up to this had been populous. Their inhabitants were swept off in such numbers that such as were left, with closed gates, strenuously watched that no one should steal the property of those departed." After speaking of Venice, it continues, "The pest in its wanderings came to Carinthia, and then so completely took possession of Styria, that people, rendered desperate, walked about as if mad."

"From so many sick pestilential odours proceeded, infecting those visiting and serving them, and very frequently it happened that when one died in a house all,

---

[1] Lechner, *ut sup.*, p. 23.
[2] *Annales Matseenses* in *Mon. Germ.*, ix, 829.
[3] *Annales Mellicenses, Ibid.*, p. 513.

one after the other, were carried off. So certain was this that no one could be found to stop in the houses of the sick, and relations, as if in the natural course of events, seem to die all together. As a consequence of this overwhelming visitation, cattle were left to wander in the fields without guardians, for no one thought of troubling himself about the future; and wolves coming down from the mountains to attack them, against their instincts, and as if frightened by something unseen, quickly fled into the wilds again. Property, too, both moveable and immoveable, which sick people leave by will, is carefully avoided by all, as if it were sure to be infected. The sickness . . . declined about the feast of St. Martin (November 11th), 1348, and at Neuberg it had carried off many monks and inhabitants."[1]

It is necessary to return once again to North Italy, from which another wave of pestilence rolled on to Switzerland. The contemporary—but not very accurate—notary of Novara, Peter Azarius, speaks to the fact of the plague being at Momo, Gallarete, Varese, and Bellinzona,[2] on the great highway over the Alps through the St. Gothard Pass, and all in the immediate neighbourhood of his home. What Azarius says from personal experience of this terrible time is of interest. He had left his house at Novara for fear of the disease, and resting for a while in the town of Tortona, he occupied himself in philosophising upon the misfortunes which had fallen upon Lombardy, and the strange unchristian neglect of the sick he could hardly help noticing. " I have seen," he says, "a rich man perish, who, even by offering an

---

[1] *Continuatio Novimontensis, ibid.*, p. 675.
[2] *Chronicon*, in Muratori, xvi, 361. He places the event under the year 1347.

immense sum of money, could get no one to help him.
Through fear of the infection I have seen a father not
caring for his son, nor a son for his father, nor a brother
for a brother, nor a friend for his friend, nor a neighbour
for his neighbour. And what was worse than this, I have
seen a family, although one of high position, miserably
perish, not being able to get any help or assistance.
Medicine being useless, the strong and the young, men
and women, were struck down in a moment, and all the
infected were so shunned that none dared even to enter
their houses."[1]

From the pass of St. Gothard the epidemic passed
down the Rhine Valley, and before the close of 1348 was
in the neighbourhood of Dissentis; whilst by May, 1349,
the district round about the monastery of Pfäffers, half
way between the pass of St. Gothard and Lake Constance, had been attacked. Shortly afterwards the country
near the celebrated Abbey of St. Gall was likewise
greatly afflicted.[2]

Meanwhile another wave of pestilence passed into
Switzerland from the side of France. Avignon had been
attacked, as it has been shown, in the early part of
1348, and thence the infection was carried up the Rhone
Valley to the Lake of Geneva. Thence one stream
passed in a north-easterly direction over Switzerland,
and a second followed the course of the river Rhone.
By the 17th of March, 1349, the plague was at Ruswyl,
in the neighbourhood of Lucerne, having passed through
Berne on its way.[3] At Lucerne alone, 3,000 people are
said to have died of the disease. It must have remained
about the neighbourhood of this lake for some months,

---

[1] *Chronicon*, in Muratori, xvi, 298.
[2] Lechner, *ut sup.*, p. 27.   [3] *Ibid.*

for it was not until September, 1349, that it is known to have manifested its presence in the high and healthy valley of Engelberg. "This year (1349)," says the chronicler of the Abbey of Engelberg, "the pestilence or mortality was great, and, indeed most great, in this valley, so that more than twenty houses were left empty without an inhabitant. In the same year, from the feast of Our Lady's nativity, September 8th, to the feast of the Epiphany, 116 of our nuns died in the cloister. One of the first to die was the Superior Catherine; about the middle (of the epidemic) the venerable Mother Beatrix, Countess of Arberg, formerly Superior; and on the morrow of Holy Innocents, Mechtilde of Wolfenschiessen, the new Superior likewise passed away. And of our own numbers (there died) two priests and five scholars."[1] Basle was attacked, and is said to have lost some 14,000 people about the middle of the year; Zurich about September 11th; and Constance some time during the winter.

It is unnecessary to follow the wanderings of the great mortality in detail further through Europe. The annals of almost every country prove incontestably that most places were in turn visited, and more or less depopulated, by the epidemic. By April 4th, 1349, it was reported in Venice that the pestilence was raging in Hungary, and by June 7th the King could declare "that by Divine mercy it had now ceased in our kingdom." It must consequently have commenced in the country in the early part of the year, although there is evidence that it was still to be found in some parts in October of the same year. Poland was attacked about the same time as Hungary. Here it is said many of the

[1] *Annales Engelbergenses* in *Mon. Germ.*, xvii, 281.

nobility died. There seemed no help for the daily misfortunes. The sickness rendered desolate not alone numberless houses, but even towns and villages.[1]

It has been already pointed out that the pestilence had reached Neuberg, in Styria, by the autumn of the year 1348. It was only the following year, about the feast of St. John the Baptist, June 24th, 1349, that such a plague as never before was either heard or seen was raging in Vienna.

It commenced seemingly about Easter time, and lasted till St. Michael's, and a third part of the population was carried off by it.[2] Each day there died 500 or 600, and one day 960.[3] The dead were buried in trenches, each of which, according to one chronicle, contained some 6,000 corpses. The parish of St. Stephen lost 54 ecclesiastics during the course of the epidemic, and when it passed some 70 families were found to be entirely extinct, whilst the property of many more had passed into the hands of very distant relations.

Another account declares that in the city and neighbourhood barely a third of the population survived. " Because of the odour, and horror inspired by the dead bodies, burials in the church cemeteries were not allowed; but as soon as life was extinct the corpses were carried out of the city to a common burial-place (called) 'God's acre.' There the deep and broad pits were quickly filled to the top with the dead. And this plague lasted from Pentecost to St. Michael's; and not alone in Vienna, but in the surrounding country it raged with great fury. It spared not the monks and the nuns,

---

[1] Dlugoss, *Historia Polonica*, in Philippe, *ut sup.*, p. 94.

[2] *Kalendarium Zwetlense*, in *Mon. Germ.*, ix, 692.

[3] *Annales Matseenses, Ibid.*, 829.

for in (the Cistercian Abbey of) Heiligenkreuz 53 religious at the same time passed out of this life." [1]

In Bohemia the winter cold apparently put a stop to the sickness at its commencement "The mortality commenced to be severe in Bohemia, but the recent cold and snow stayed it." However, "in the year 1350 the plague again devastated various countries, and then in Bohemia likewise it was to be found." [2]

The wave of pestilence which passed up the Rhine Valley and attacked Basle passed on to Colmar, and appeared in Strasburg in July, 1349. [3] At the end of the same year, about December 18th, it had reached Cologne. "In the first year of archbishop William von Gennep (who succeeded to the See of that city on the above date) there was," says the chronicle, "a great pestilence in Cologne and its neighbourhood." [4]

Meanwhile the wave had divided lower down the valley of the Rhine, for in the summer of 1349 the plague was raging at Frankfort. "In that year," writes Caspar Camentz, "from the feast of St. Mary Magdalene (July 22nd) to the feast of the Purification following (February 2nd, 1350) the universal pestilence was at Frankfort. In the space of 72 days more than 2,000 people died. Every second hour they were buried without bell, priest, or candle. On one day 35 were buried at one time." [5]

During 1349 and 1350 the pestilence was rife in the towns and country places of Prussia. In the latter year

---

[1] *Continuatio Novimontensis*, in *Mon. Germ.*, ix, 675.

[2] *Chronicon Pragense*, ed. Loserth (in *Fontes rerum Austriacarum, Scriptores*, t. viii) p. 603.

[3] Lechner, *ut sup.*, p. 35.   [4] *Ibid.*, p. 38.

[5] Boehmer, *Fontes rerum Germ.*, iv, 434.

it attacked Bremen in the far north, and in the following
year the authorities of the city took a census of the
numbers that had been carried off by it. " In the year of
our Lord 1350," the account says, "the plague had gone
round the world and had visited Bremen, and the Council
determined to take the number of the dead, and it was
found that of known and named people there were
(entered on the list) in the parish of St. Mary 1,816;
in that of St. Martin, 1,415; in St. Anschar's, 1,922;
and in St. Stephen's, 1,813; moreover, numberless people
had died in the fields beyond the walls and in cemeteries,
the number of whom, as known and described, reached
almost 7,000.[1]

From Flanders, where the pestilence was at Tournay
in December, 1349, as before reported, the epidemic
spread into Holland. Here in the following year its progress was marked by the same great mortality, especially
among those who lived together in monasteries and convents. "At this time," writes the chronicler, "the plague
raged in Holland as furiously as has ever been seen.
People died walking in the streets. In the Monastery of
Fleurchamps 80 died, including monks and lay brethren.
In the Abbey of Foswert, which was a double monastery
for men and women, 207 died, including monks, nuns,
lay brethren, and lay sisters."[2]

This brief review of the progress of the plague in
Europe will be sufficient to show that the mortality and
consequent distress were universal. The northern countries of Denmark, Norway, and Sweden received the
infection from England. As will be seen subsequently,

---

[1] Hoeniger (R.), *Der schwarze Tod in Deutschland* (Berlin, 1882),
p. 26.

[2] Philippe, *ut sup.*, p. 124. •

the northern parts of England were troubled with the epidemic in the late summer and autumn of 1349, and either from a port on the eastern coast, or from London, the plague was brought over in a ship. Lagerbring, a Swedish historian of repute, says that a ship with a cargo of woollen cloth sailed out of the port of London early in the summer of 1349.[1] The plague had been very great in the English capital, and all the crew died whilst the ship was at sea. Driven about by the winds and currents the fatal bark was cast on the shore at Bergen, in Norway. The epidemic spread quickly over the entire country. The Archbishop of Drontheim and all his Chapter, with one single exception, died, and the survivor was nominated Archbishop. Most of his suffragans were also carried off.[2] Several families who had fled from Bergen to avoid the infection died in the mountains to which they had retired.

Another Swedish historian states that in the country of West-Gotland alone 466 priests were swept away by the plague. In that district there were then about 479 churches, many of which were served by more than one priest, so that the number given may not be altogether improbable.[3] It is stated that in Norway there long

---

[1] *Historia*, iii, 406.

[2] Finn Jonsson, *Hist. eccl. Islandiae*, ii, p. 198, says that most of the Bishops died, and that Ormus, Bishop of Holar, in Iceland, who happened then to be in Norway, *solus fere evasit.* It appears that the archbishopric of Nidaros, or Drontheim, at that time comprised seven Sees. Changes appear in six of these at this time, including Drontheim and Bergen ; and of Solomon, Bishop of Oslo, it is said that "he was the only Bishop who survived the plague" (Gams, *Series Episcoporum*, 336). The same account is given in the monastic chronicles of Iceland (*Flateyjarbok*, iii, p. 562).

[3] Henric Jacob Sirers, *Historisk Beskrifning om then Pesten*, p. 23.

existed what were called *Find-dale*—wildernesses—in which were unmistakable traces of cultivation, and after the plague there is evidence of a state of exhaustion and a dearth of inhabitants, which lasted for several generations, so that forests grew where there had once been churches and villages.

Some interesting particulars may be gathered about the town of Wisby, on the Isle of Gotland. The annals of the Franciscan convent note that the plague raged in 1350. In the necrology of the same house are entered the names of a great number of friars and many novices who died in this fatal year, and the comparison of one portion of the necrology with another, in which the names are collected into groups, shows that the worst time at Wisby was in July, August, and September, 1350.[1] In all, twenty-four friars, a very large proportion of the convent, appear to have been carried off by the epidemic. In the Cathedral of Wisby five sepulchral slabs are still preserved with the date 1350, whilst of such memorials as have escaped destruction not more than a single one remains for any other year.

The King of Sweden, Magnus II, in 1350 addressed letters patent to his people, wherein he says that "God for the sins of man has struck the world with this great punishment of sudden death. By it most of the people in the land to the west of our country (*i.e.*, Norway) are dead. It is now ravaging in Norway and Holland, and is approaching our kingdom of Sweden." The king

[1] Langebeck, *Scriptores rerum Danicarum*, vi, 564. I am indebted for much assistance in all that regards the plague in the north of Europe to Dr. Lindstrom, of the Riksmusei, Stockholm. He kindly examined for me the original MS. of the Franciscan Necrology at Wisby.

therefore summons them to abstain on every Friday from all food but bread and water, or "at most to take only bread and ale," to walk with bare feet to their parish churches, and to go in procession round about the cemeteries attached to them, carrying with them the holy relics.

In the capital of Sweden, when the plague burst upon the country, it is recorded that "the streets were strewn with corpses," and among the victims are named Hacon and Knut, two brothers of the king.

Denmark and Schleswig Holstein suffered from the pestilence at the same time as Norway and Sweden. In one chronicle it is called "a most grievous plague of buboes;" in another it is recorded that in the year 1350 "a great plague and sudden death raged both in the case of men and in that of cattle."[1] The accounts of the Bishopric of Roskild, on the Isle of Zealand, about the year 1370, or twenty years after this plague had passed, show the state of universal desolation to which the country was reduced. Lands are described as lying idle and uncultivated, villages and houses desolate and uninhabited. Property that formerly used to bring in four marks, or 48 "pund," now produced only 18 "pund." The same story is repeated on almost every page throughout these long accounts.[2]

A few words only need now be said of the desolation which everywhere throughout Europe was naturally the consequence of the great pestilence. Of North Italy John of Parma writes that "at the time (1348) labourers could not be got, and the harvest remained on the fields, since there was none to gather it in."[3] Twenty years

---

[1] Langebeck, *ut sup.*, i, 307, 395.   [2] *Ibid.*, vii, p. 2, *et seqq.*
[3] Pezzana, *Storia di Parma*, i, 52.

after the pestilence, in 1372, it is said of Mayence that
" it is indubitable and notorious that because of the
terrible character of the pestilence and mortality which
suddenly swept away labourers, copyholders (*parciarios*)
and farmers, even the most robust, labourers are to-day
few and rare, for which reason many fields remain uncultivated and deserted."[1]   Again, in 1359, Henry,
Bishop of Constance, impropriated to the monastery of
St. Gall, in Switzerland, the Church of Marbach and
others, to enable the abbey "to keep up its hospitality,
bestow alms, and fulfil its other duties," and he assigns
as a reason why it cannot now do this "that by the epidemic or mortality of people, which by permission of
God has existed in these parts, the number of farmers
and other retainers of both sexes of this abbey, belonging by law of service to the said monastery, which has
passed from this life to the Lord (has been so great)
that many of the possessions of this monastery have remained, on account of the said death, uncultivated, and
no proper return comes from them."[2]

[1] Henricus de Hervordia, *Chronicon* ed. Potthast, 274.
[2] Lechner, *ut sup.*, p. 73.

CHAPTER V

THE PLAGUE REACHES ENGLAND

THE plague first attacked England in the autumn of 1348. It has already been pointed out that Northern France was suffering under the scourge in the summer of that year, and that in August the pestilence had visited Normandy and was found at Calais, then in possession of the English. Probably, also, at this time, Jersey and Guernsey, with which England was in constant communication, were decimated by the disease. So greatly did these islands suffer that the King's taxes, usually raised upon the fishing industries, could not be levied. "By reason," writes the English King to John Mautravers, the Governor, "of the mortality among the people and fishing folk of these islands, which here as elsewhere has been so great, our rent for the fishing, which has been yearly paid us, cannot be now obtained without the impoverishing and excessive oppression of those fishermen still left." [1]

Rumours of the coming scourge reached England in the early summer. On August 17th, 1348, the Bishop of Bath and Wells, Ralph of Shrewsbury, sent letters through his diocese ordering "processions and stations every Friday, in each collegiate, regular, and parish church, to beg God to protect the people from the

[1] Originalia Roll, 24 Ed. III, m. 2.

G

pestilence which had come from the East into the neighbouring kingdom," and granting an indulgence of forty
days to all who, being in a state of grace, should give
alms, fast or pray, in order, if possible, to avert God's
anger.[1]

The "neighbouring kingdom" spoken of by the Bishop
in his letter may be taken almost certainly to refer to
France. From Calais it is probable that the pestilence
was brought into England in certain ships conveying
some who were anxious to escape from it. Most of the
contemporary accounts agree in naming the coast of
Dorsetshire as the part first infected. Thus Galfrid le
Baker, a contemporary, says "it came first to a seaport
in Dorsetshire, and then into the country, which it
almost deprived of inhabitants, and from thence it
passed into Devon and Somerset to Bristol."[2] Two or
three of the chronicles, also, more particular than the
rest, name Melcombe Regis as the memorable spot
where the epidemic first showed itself in England. "In
the year of our Lord 1348, about the feast of the Translation of St. Thomas (July 7th)," writes the author of
the chronicle known as the *Eulogium Historiarum*, who
was a monk of Malmesbury at this time, "the cruel pestilence, terrible to all future ages, came from parts over
the sea to the south coast of England, into a port called
Melcombe, in Dorsetshire. This (plague) sweeping over
the southern districts, destroyed numberless people in
Dorset, Devon, and Somerset."[3] So, too, a continuation

---

[1] B. Mus., Harl. MS. 6965, f. 132.
[2] *Chronicon Galfridi le Baker*, ed. Sir E. M. Thompson, p. 98.
Eulogium Historiarum (ed. Rolls series), iii, p. 213. It seems
not at all improbable that this account was written whilst the plague
was still confined to the West of England.

of Trivet's chronicle, taken down to the death of Edward III by a canon of Bridlington, who was thus probably a contemporary of the event, says that "the great plague came into England to the southern districts, beginning by some (ships) putting in from the sea into a town called Melcombe." [1]

Melcombe Regis, or Weymouth, was at that time a port of considerable importance. In 1347-8, for example, it furnished Edward III, for his siege of Calais, with 20 ships and 264 mariners; whilst Bristol sent only 22 ships and 608 sailors, and even London but 25 boats and 662 men. [2] This fact is of interest, not merely as showing the importance of Melcombe Regis as a port on the southern coast, but as evidence actually connecting the place at this very period with Calais, and, doubtless, with other coast towns of France. It is not at all improbable that by the return of some of the Melcombe boats from Calais, the epidemic may have been conveyed into the town. No evidence is known to exist as to the mortality in the port itself; but an item of information as to the effect of the disease in the neighbourhood is afforded at a subsequent period. Three years after the plague had passed, the King, by his letters patent, forbade any of the inhabitants of the island of Portland to leave their homes there, or, indeed, to sell any of their crops out of the district, "because," he says, "as we have learnt, the island of Portland, in the county of Dorset, has been so depopulated in the time of the late pestilence that the inhabitants remaining are not sufficiently numerous to protect it against our foreign enemies." [3]

[1] Harl. MS. 688, f. 361.
[2] Hutchins, *History of Dorset* (3rd ed.), ii, p. 422.
[3] Rot. Pat., 26 Ed. III, pars 3, m. 5.

The actual date when the pestilence first showed itself
in Dorsetshire has been considered somewhat doubtful.
The earliest day suggested is that assigned by the monk
of Malmesbury in his *Eulogium Historiarum,* who names
July 7th (1348) as the time when it commenced at Melcombe Regis. The latest date is that given by Knighton,
the sub-contemporary canon of Leicester, who mentions
generally that it began in the autumn of the year 1348.
One chronicle gives July 25th, and two others August 1st,
whilst another merely names August as the month.
Under these circumstances, and in view of the fact that
its arrival in England was apparently unknown to the
Bishop of Bath and Wells, who was then in his diocese,
in the middle of August, it seems more than likely that
the terrible scourge did not make itself felt in the West
of England until after the middle of that month and not
later than its end.

The early commencement of the disease is borne out
by a document in the archives of the Dean and Chapter
of Canterbury. Archbishop Strafford died on St. Bartholomew's Eve, August 23rd, 1348, and before the end
of September the Prior of Canterbury, acting with archiepiscopal power during the vacancy, addressed a mandate to the Bishop of London, as the Dean of the College
of Bishops, to issue directions to the suffragans of Canterbury to hold public processions in their respective
dioceses to pray God's aid against " the mortality " which
was already assuming alarming proportions.[1]

The summer and autumn of 1348 were abnormally wet
in England, and the chronicles record that from St. John
the Baptist's Day (June 24th) to Christmas it rained

[1] *Historical Manuscripts Commission, Eighth Report,* App.,
p. 338.

either by night or by day with hardly an exception. In such a season, naturally unhealthy, the sickness, of its own nature most deadly, found every condition suitable for its rapid development.

Starting from Melcombe Regis, the wave of contagion spread itself very quickly over Dorset, Devon, and Somerset, with the other counties comprised in the dioceses of Salisbury, Exeter, and Wells. " It passed," writes Robert of Avesbury, the contemporary Registrar of the Court of Canterbury, " most rapidly from place to place, swiftly killing ere mid-day many who in the morning had been well, and without respect of persons (some few rich people excepted), not permitting those destined to die to live more than three, or at most four, days. On the same day twenty, forty, sixty, and very often more corpses were committed to the same grave."[1] In fact, over the West of England during the late autumn of 1348 and the first months of the following year the words of the old play must have had only too true an application:

> One news straight came huddling on another
> Of death, and death, and death."

In dealing with a case of this kind a first object is to control as far as possible, by means of definite statistics, the general and vague statements of chroniclers and other contemporary writers; whilst in the absence of such statistics lies one of the great difficulties in dealing with the history of the Middle Ages. Owing partly to the troublesome and intricate nature of the subject, as well as to the poverty of the material and the inherent dryness of such matters, modern writers have made little

[1] *De Gestis Edwardi III.* (ed. Rolls series), p. 406.

advance to a more correct knowledge of the population of European countries in those ages. Much, however, might be done. As usual, the ecclesiastical documents form the surest basis for any calculation, and the episcopal registers enable us to arrive at actual numbers. Accordingly, in the present inquiry, these registers are of the highest importance, and it is necessary constantly to recur to them, as they furnish the only means of arriving at any adequate knowledge of the proportion of the population swept away by the plague. Possibly the mortality may have been greater among ecclesiastics than among lay persons; but only from the number of the clergy carried off by the epidemic can an estimate be formed as to the number of lay people who died. Accordingly, in the course of this work, the mortality of the clergy is systematically investigated.

To understand the nature and value of the evidence thus afforded as to the extent of the mortality, a few words of explanation are necessary. In each diocese there was kept by the Bishop's Registrar a list of all the institutions made to vacant benefices by the Bishop. As a rule, not only was the name of the place and of the out-going and the in-coming incumbent, together with the date expressed, but the reason of the vacancy was stated, whether arising from death, exchange, or resignation. These lists, then, for the fatal period, or the autumn of 1348 and the year 1349, afford some means of gauging the extent of the mortality among the clergy. It must, however, be borne in mind that these registers record only the institutions of the actual incumbents, and take no account of the larger body of curates and chaplains, to say nothing of the monks, canons, and friars of a diocese. It has been calculated by a recent writer that non-beneficed clergy more than equal in numbers the holders of benefices, and that the total number of institutions of a diocese may fairly be doubled in estimating the deaths of the clergy during this epidemic.[1] These Books of Institutions, moreover, by furnishing the dates of the appointments made to various livings, afford a means of determining, at least approximately, the time when the plague was rife in a district, and even, making allowances for any delay in filling up the benefice, in any given place.

Besides the special register of each diocese a series of official State documents, called the *Patent Rolls*, contains much evidence of the destructive powers of the disease. On these rolls, amongst every variety of public document, are entered royal grants, licences, and presentations made by the Sovereign to such vacant ecclesiastical livings as were at the time in the royal gift. These were ordinarily—

(1) Benefices of which the King was by right the patron.

(2) Those to which he presented, as guardian of the sons of tenants *in capite* during their minority, and

(3) Livings to which bishops and abbots of Sees and monasteries, then vacant, ordinarily presented. At this period, 1348-9, moreover, the royal presentations were largely augmented by the patronage attached to the alien religious houses existing in England, the possession of which, "by reason of his war with France," as the official phrase runs, "the King had seized into his own hands."

---

[1] As will be seen subsequently, this estimate of Dr. Jessopp is certainly too low, and it is probably more correct to suppose that the non-beneficed clergy, including under that head the religious, were four times as numerous as those holding benefices.

The evidence of the mortality among the beneficed clergy during the great pestilence, as witnessed by the entries on the patent rolls, may be here briefly summarised. In 1348, in the period from January to May, the King presented to 42 livings, and to 36 during the following four months; so that in the eight months, immediately before the arrival of the plague in England, the average number of presentations monthly was below ten, the previous *yearly* average being hardly more than a hundred. The roll, upon which are entered the grants and presentations from September to the close of the year, affords conclusive proof that in the last four months of the year 1348 death had been busy among those holding royal preferments. Eighty-one more livings had to be filled up by the Sovereign during that period.

The patents for 1349, in the same way, occupy three parts, or rolls. On the first part are enrolled the presentations from January 25th to the end of May. This large roll is a curiosity, since a very great part of the parchment record is devoted to the entry of Royal presentations to the vacant livings, no fewer than 249 being recorded, as against 42 during the same period of the previous year. The second part registers the livings filled by King Edward from June to the middle of September, 1349, when the number reaches the extraordinary figure of 440, as against 36 in the corresponding period of 1348.

The third period, ending on January 24th, 1350, shows a decline in the number, although it still stands at the considerable total of 205. Altogether, therefore, from January 25th, 1349, to the same date in 1350, the King alone presented to 894 livings, which had become vacant. Comparing the figures thus obtained with the normal period of 1348 it may be said roughly that out of the 1,053 presentations, made by King Edward in the two years, at least 800 must have been due to the mortality caused by the great plague. This will be seen to be sufficiently terrible when it is remembered that, even allowing for the large number of presentations then in the hands of the King, they would form but a very small portion of the total number of institutions to vacant livings at this period.

The whole question of statistics in their details, as also any special indications of the effects which followed upon the ravages of the plague, will be dealt with in subsequent chapters in order to interfere as little as possible with the consecutive story of the visitation itself. Among the presentations made by the King, in the autumn of this year, frequent mention is made of vacancies in the diocese of Sarum, in which the county of Dorset is situated. From October 8th, 1348, to January 10th, 1349—that is, in the space of three months—the Crown presented to no fewer than 30 livings in the diocese. Most of these were in the county of Dorset, and Abbotsbury Abbey, apparently the first monastery attacked, and Bincombe rectory, to which Edward III presented on October 8th, 1348, were both close to Melcombe Regis, where the plague commenced its ravages.

Judged merely by the few royal presentations it is curious to observe how closely the epidemic in this country clung to the rivers and water-courses. The neighbourhood of Blandford, for instance, must have suffered severely enough during the November and December of 1348, the two Winterbournes and Spettisbury, together with Blandford—all four close on the river Stour—losing their incumbents. To Spettisbury, indeed, the King presented thrice in a very short space of time. Even before John le Spencer, of Grimsby, to whom the living was granted on December 7th, could have been installed in his cure—in fact, probably even before the grant was made—he was dead, for on December 10th, only three days later, another letter patent is issued, upon the death of Spencer, to Adam de Carleton. Adam in his turn did not hold the benefice long, and on January 4th, 1349, Robert de Hoveden was appointed in his place. Nor are these the only instances, even among the few presentations recorded on the patent rolls, of Dorset incumbents following one another in rapid succession during the last months of 1348.

Looking at the number of institutions in each month of this period, and making due allowance for the fact that the vacancy had probably occurred some little time before it was filled up, it is evident that the epidemic was prevalent in the county of Dorset from October, 1348, to February, 1349, and the mortality was highest in December and January.[1] The existence of the epidemic begins to be manifest in the institutions for

[1] The following table will show the actual number of institutions in Dorsetshire for some months:—

1348.			1349.			
Oct.	Nov.	Dec.	Jan.	Feb.	March.	April.
5	15	17	16	14	10	4

October, 1348. Previously only twelve institutions are recorded during that year. West Chickerell, a place close to Weymouth, received a new incumbent on October 14th, whilst to Bincombe, close by, which was then vacant, as is proved by the King's presentation on the 8th of the month, no new incumbent was inducted till November 4th. Warmwell and Combe Kaynes, a little to the eastward, received new parish priests on October the 9th and 19th, and Dorchester, the capital, was attacked apparently about the same time.

Following the indications afforded by the Bishop's registers the ravages of the pestilence are apparent on the coast early in November, when many vacancies begin to be noted in the coast towns. Bridport, East Lulworth, Tynham, Langton, and Wareham had all been visited by this time, whilst before the end of the month the epidemic had crossed the county and appeared at Shaftesbury. On December 3rd two vicarages in the south, quite close together, Abbotsbury and Portesham, received new incumbents.

At Shaftesbury appointments were made to St. Laurence's on the 29th of November, to St. Martin's on the 10th of December, to St. John's on the 6th of January, 1349, and to St. Laurence's again on the 12th of May. At Wareham, the small alien priory became vacant before November 4th, for on that day the King appointed a successor to Michael de Molis, lately dead,[1] and appointments were made to St. Martin's, Wareham, on the 8th of December, to St. Peter's on the 22nd of December, to St. John's on the 29th of May, and to St. Michael's on the 17th of June. Three changes were registered as having taken place at Winterbourne St.

[1] Originalia Roll, 22 Ed. III, m. 4.

Nicholas, between December 27th and May 3rd. As far as can be judged by the dates of these institutions it would appear as if a fresh outbreak of peculiar violence occurred towards the end of April.

The Bridport Corporation records show that four bailiffs held office in 1349, in place of the usual two, on account of the pestilence.[1] In common with most places in the land, Poole, which was then of sufficient importance to be called upon to furnish four ships and 94 men for the siege of Calais, suffered greatly from the pestilence, and received a considerable check to its prosperity. "At Poole," writes Hutchins, "a spot on the projecting slip of land, known as the *Baiter*, is still pointed out as the burial-place of its victims."[2] And the same writer adds that the country did not entirely recover for the next 150 years; since, in the reign of Henry VIII, "Poole and other towns in Dorsetshire" were included in that numerous list of places whose desolated buildings were ordered to be restored.

Before the close of the year 1348 the pestilence had spread itself far and wide in the western counties of England. The diocese of Bath and Wells, and that of Exeter, the former conterminous with the county of Somerset, and the latter comprising those of Devon and Cornwall, were infected in the late autumn of that year, and all over the west, as the old chronicle relates, the sickness "most pitifully destroyed people innumerable."

Indeed, so terrible had been the effect of the scourge among the clergy of Somerset that, as early as January 17th, 1349, the Bishop of Bath and Wells felt himself

[1] *Hist. MSS. Comm., Sixth Report*, p. 475.
[2] *History of Dorset*, i, p. 5.

constrained to address a letter of advice to his flock.
The document is of such interest, both as evidence of the
straits to which at that early date the diocese had been
reduced by the excessive mortality, and for the advice
that it contains, that it is here quoted at considerable
length, since it proves the depth of degradation to which
the whole religious life was reduced by the terror inspired
by the disease. Every bond was loosed, and every ordinary ecclesiastical regulation and provision set aside, because none could now be enforced, or, indeed, observed.
" The contagious nature of the present pestilence, which
is ever spreading itself far and wide," writes the Bishop,
" has left many parish churches and other cures, and
consequently the people of our diocese, destitute of
curates[1] and priests. And inasmuch as priests cannot be
found who are willing out of zeal, devotion, or for a
stipend to undertake the care of the foresaid places, and
to visit the sick and administer to them the Sacraments
of the Church (perchance for dread of the infection and
contagion), many, as we understand, are dying without
the Sacrament of Penance. These, too, are ignorant of
what ought to be done in such necessity, and believe that
no confession of their sins, even in a case of such need,
is useful or meritorious, unless made to a priest having
the keys of the Church. Therefore, desiring, as we are
bound to do, the salvation of souls, and ever watch-
ing to bring back the wandering from the crooked paths
of error, we, on the obedience you have sworn to us,
urgently enjoin upon you and command you—rectors,
vicars, and parish priests—in all your churches, and you
deans, in such places of your deaneries as are destitute

---

[1] *Curates* here and elsewhere is used for Rectors or Vicars, who
had the actual cure of souls.

of the consolation of priests, that you at once and
publicly instruct and induce, yourselves or by some
other, all who are sick of the present malady, or who
shall happen to be taken ill, that *in articulo mortis*, if
they are not able to obtain any priest, they should make
confession of their sins (according to the teaching of the
apostle) even to a layman, and, if a man is not at hand,
then to a woman. We exhort you, by the present letters,
in the bowels of Jesus Christ, to do this, and to proclaim
publicly in the aforesaid places that such confession
made to a layman in the presumed case can be most
salutary and profitable to them for the remission of their
sins, according to the teaching and the sacred canons
of the Church. And for fear any, imagining that these
lay confessors may make known confessions so made to
them, shall hesitate thus to confess in case of necessity,
we make known to all in general, and to those in particular who have already heard these confessions, or who
may in future hear them, that they are bound by the
precepts of the Church to conceal and keep them secret;
and that, by a decree of the sacred canons, they are for-
bidden to betray such confession by word, sign, and by
any other means whatever, unless those confessing so
desire. And (further) should they do otherwise, let such
betrayers know that they sin most gravely, and incur the
indignation of Almighty God and of the whole Church."
And further to stir up the zeal of both clergy and laity
to this work the Bishop grants ample indulgences to such
as follow the advice here given them.

" And since late repentance," he says "(when, for example, sickness compels and the fear of punishment
terrifies) often deceives many, we grant to all our subjects, who in the time of the pestilence shall come to

confession to priests having the keys of the Church and power to bind and to loose, before they are taken sick, and who do not delay till the day of necessity, forty days of indulgence. To every priest also who shall induce people to do this, and hear the confessions of those thus brought to confess whilst in health, we grant the same by the mercy of God Almighty, and trusting to the merits and prayers of His glorious Mother, of the Blessed Peter, Paul, and Andrew the Apostles, our patrons, and of all the Saints."

"You shall further declare," he adds, "to all thus confessing to lay people in case of necessity, that if they recover they are bound to confess the same sins again to their own parish priest. The Sacrament of the Eucharist, when no priest can be obtained, may be administered by a deacon. If, however, there be no priest to administer the Sacrament of Extreme Unction, faith must, as in other matters, suffice for the Sacrament."[1]

These large derogations from the usual ecclesiastical practice, though consonant alike with Christian charity and the teaching of the Church, are resorted to only in cases of the direst need, and the circular letter of the Bishop of Bath and Wells witnesses to the extreme gravity of the situation throughout the diocese, as early as the month of January, 1349. Already, as is certain from the Bishop's words, the dearth of clergy had made itself felt, and people were dying in the county of Somerset without the possibility of obtaining spiritual aid in their last hours, and no priests could be found to take the places of those who had already fallen victims to the disease. The list of institutions given in the register of Bishop Ralph of Shrewsbury shows that the mortality in

[1] Wilkins, *Concilia*, ii, pp. 735-6.

that county was considerable as early as the November of the previous year, 1348.

Taking the institutions of the diocese as a guide to the time when the plague was most violent, and bearing in mind that the death would have occurred some little time before the institution, and that according to the Bishop's letter some delay had been inevitable in the filling up of benefices, the months when the pestilence was at its height in the county of Somerset would appear to be December, 1348, and January and February, 1349, although the number of institutions each month remains high until June. The mortality was apparently highest about Christmastide, 1348.[1]

The Bishop of Bath and Wells remained at his manor of Wiveliscombe till the worst was past in May of 1349. Thither came the long procession of priests to receive their letters of institution to vacant benefices. Day after day for nearly six months the work went on with hardly any cessation. Singly, or in twos and threes, often four and five, once, at least, ten together, the clergy came to be instituted to cures which the disease had left without a priest.

How the epidemic entered into the county, and the

[1] The following is a table of the institutions in Somersetshire for some months:

1348.		1349.					
Nov.	Dec.	Jan.	Feb.	March.	April.	May.	June.
9	32	47	43	36	40	21	7

course it pursued, it would be now impossible, even if it were profitable, to discover. In December it would seem to have gained a foothold in most parts of the county. It was at Evercreech about November 19th, and about a fortnight later at Castlecary and Almsford, in the same neighbourhood. The fact that Bridgwater, Clevedon, Weston-super-mare, Portishead, and Bristol were amongst the earliest places in the county to be attacked would almost make it appear that the contagion was carried to these coast towns by a boat passing up the Bristol Channel. This supposition, moreover, is somewhat confirmed, as will be seen subsequently, by the fact that the towns of North Devon were attacked by the disease almost simultaneously with those on the south coast, and very much about the same time as those of North Somerset.

Bath suffered under the scourge in the early part of January, 1349, on the 9th and 10th of that month several institutions to livings, either in the city or the neighbourhood, being recorded. In the same month it had spread to the abbey of Keynsham, on the road between Bath and Bristol, and its path can almost be traced along the line of communication between Bath and Wells. Thus the villages of Freshford, Twerton, Hardington, Holcombe, Cloford, Kilmersdon, Babington, Compton, and Doulting, as well as several benefices in Wells itself, all fell vacant at this time.

It may be said with considerable certainty that fully half the number of beneficed clergy fell victims to the disease in this diocese. Many livings were rendered vacant two and three times during its course; whilst a not inconsiderable number had four changes of incumbents within these few months. Bathampton, for example,

H

had four parsons appointed in this period. At Hardington, not far from Frome, from January, 1349, to the
middle of March, there were certainly three and perhaps
four changes due to the disease; and at Yeovil, from the
15th December, 1348, to the 4th February, 1349, three
priests held the living, one after the other.

Little or no information is forthcoming as to the religious houses of the county at this time. Both Athelney
and Muchelney lost their abbots, and probably also many
of their members. The fact that the great abbey of
Glastonbury, which previously contained within its walls
a community of some 80 monks, is found in A.D. 1377 to
have 44, seems to indicate that it must have suffered
very severe losses through the epidemic.

At Bath, in 1344, only five years before the outbreak
of the disease, the community at the Priory consisted of
thirty professed monks under Prior John de Ford.[1] A
list on the roll of the Somerset clergy, on whom a clerical subsidy was levied at the close of Edward the Third's
reign, in 1377, shows that the number had been reduced
to sixteen,[2] and at this number it apparently remained
to the time of the final dissolution of the house in the
sixteenth century.[3]

It is not difficult to understand that the plague must
have raged with great virulence in the larger cities, where
in those days the most elementary notions of sanitation
were almost unknown. In the west, Bristol, of course,
suffered severely. "There," says the sub-contemporary

[1] Bath Chartulary (Lincoln's Inn MS.), p. 119. This has now been
edited for the *Somerset Record Society*, and the list is given at p. 73
of Mr. Hunt's edition.

R. O. Clerical Subsidy (Somerset), $\frac{4}{5}$.

See list given in *Deputy Keeper's Report*, vii, p. 280.

writer, Knighton, " died, suddenly overwhelmed by death,
almost the whole strength of the town, for few were sick
more than three days, or two days, or even half a day."
Nor need this be a subject of wonder when, according to
the description of a modern writer, speaking of the city
at this very period, the streets were very narrow; in the
busier parts the ground was honeycombed with cellars
for storing wine, salt, and other merchandise, whilst refuse streamed down the centre ditch. So small was the
distance between the houses that no vehicle was allowed
to be used in the streets, and all goods were carried on
pack-horses or porters, a custom which even in the seventeenth century excited the wonder of Samuel Pepys.[1]

"Here in Bristol," says the local historian Seyer,
quoting an old calendar of the town, " in 1348 the plague
raged to such a degree that the living were scarce able
to bury the dead. The Gloucestershire men would not
suffer the Bristol men to have access to them. At last
it reached Gloucester, Oxford, and London; scarce the
tenth person was left alive, male or female. At this period
the grass grew several inches high in High Street and
Broad Street; it raged at first chiefly in the centre of
the city. This pestilence came from abroad, and the
people near the sea-coast in Dorsetshire and Devon-
shire were first affected."[2] By the wholesale destruction
of the population of this western port the same authority
accounts for the reduction of the King's taxation of the
city from £245 to £158.

Lastly, in Bristol, as indeed without doubt in most
places, the cemeteries did not long suffice for the multitude of the dead. Of this there is an example upon the

[1] W. Hunt, *Historic Towns, Bristol*, p. 77.
[2] S. Seyer, *Memoirs of Bristol* (Bristol, 1823), ii, p. 143.

Patent Rolls. The parson of Holy Cross de la Temple soon found the necessity of enlarging his graveyard. For this purpose he obtained half an acre adjoining the old cemetery, and so great and pressing was the need of this fresh accommodation that it was done without the required royal license, for which subsequently a pardon had to be sued from the King.[1]

The diocese of Exeter, comprising the two counties of Devon and Cornwall, was stricken by the disease apparently about the same time as the county of Somerset.[2] For eight years before 1348 the average number of livings annually rendered vacant in the diocese was thirty-six, whilst in the single month of January, 1349, the Bishop instituted to some thirty livings, which shows that death had already been busy among the clergy.

The number of institutions in each month of the year points to the conclusion that the disease lingered somewhat longer in these counties than elsewhere. It is not till the close of September that any great decrease in the number of vacancies is seen, and although probably beginning in December, the height of the plague was not reached till March, April, and May.[3]

[1] Rot. Pat., 23 Ed. III, pars 3, m. 4.

[2] For information about the institutions of this diocese and other matters concerning Devon and Cornwall, I am indebted to the kindness of the Rev. Prebendary Hingeston-Randolph.

[3] The following table will give the number of institutions in Devon and Cornwall in each month:

1348.		1349.								
Nov.	Dec.	Jan.	Feb.	Mar.	April.	May.	June.	July.	Aug.	Sept.
10	6	30	34	60	53	47	45	37	16	23

Prebendary Hingeston-Randolph thus describes the state of the Exeter episcopal registers at this period:—
" There is very little direct information about the Black Death in Bishop Grandisson's register; but there is a great deal of indirect information. The *Registrum Commune*, which is wonderfully full before and after the fatal year, records scarcely anything during the year itself. The ordinary work of the diocese seems to have been all suspended, with a single exception. The register of institutions—a separate volume—is a record of incessant and most distressing work. Its very outward aspect for this period tells a tale of woe. The entries are made hurriedly and roughly, in striking contrast with the neatness and regularity of the rest of the Register. They are no longer grouped, as before, in years, but in months, and the changes in each month exceed the changes of a whole ordinary year, when there was no pestilence. The scribe leaves off the customary ' vacant *per mortem*,' as if he dreaded to write the fatal word. The clergy must have fallen by wholesale; evidently they were faithful, and, for their flock's sake, faced the foe without flinching. And, as each of them fell, another was ready at his Bishop's call fearlessly to fill the vacant place. Some incumbencies lasted but a few weeks. And, when all was over, the survivors were, comparatively, so few that there was no small difficulty in filling many a subsequent vacant benefice; this result of the sickness is to be traced for some time after the mortality had ceased.

" The Bishop never left his diocese, and the continuous presence of so strong, so earnest, and devoted a prelate must have been an unspeakable consolation and help to his grievously afflicted flock."

An examination of the institutions of the diocese, in relation to the time when the plague visited the various parts of it, appears to show that it commenced almost simultaneously in both north and south. In North Devon it is found at both Northam and Alverdiscott on the 7th of November, at Fremington in the same district on the 8th, and at Barnstaple on December the 23rd. It is found in November at villages on the Exe, and had possibly also reached Exeter before the close of the month. In the South, the fact of the close proximity of the part first infected to Dorsetshire explains the course of the epidemic; but the early outbreak in the coast villages at the mouth of the estuary leading to Barnstaple points to the conclusion that the infection was brought by a ship passing up the Bristol Channel, which subsequently infected other towns further up on the Somerset shore of the passage.

It is of interest also to note how greatly the coast towns generally appear to have suffered, as the contagion was very probably carried from one place to another by the fishing boats. Up some of the estuaries it would seem as if the passage of the disease could be traced by the dates of the institutions. Thus, to take one example, in March, 1349, there is an institution to a living at the mouth of the Fowey, in Cornwall; a week later there is another at St. Winnow's Vicarage higher up, and on March 22nd the sickness had reached Bodmin, at no great distance from the river, and a place with which, in all probability, the passage up the estuary of the Fowey would be an ordinary and usual means of communication.

As to the result of the sickness in the religious houses of the diocese some few details are known. At St.

Nicholas', Exeter, the Prior died in March, 1349; his
successor, John de Wye, was admitted on the 26th of
that month, but died almost immediately. The next
Prior was not installed until June 7th, and the house was
found to be in a deplorable state.[1] So also at Pilton
Priory two superiors died within a few weeks one of the
other. At the alien priory of Minster, Cornwall, William
de Huma, the Prior, was carried off by the sickness on
26th of April, 1349, and the house was so impoverished
by the death of tenants and labourers that it could not
support both its members and the chaplain they were
bound to find to do the parish work, as neither the prior
nor his brethren spoke English, "or rather Cornish."[2]

At the Cistercian Abbey of Newenham the register
records that "in the time of this mortality or pestilence
there died in this house twenty monks and three lay-
brothers, whose names are entered in other books. And
Walter, the abbot, and two monks were left alive there
after the sickness."[3]

At the Augustinian abbey of Hartland, Roger de
Raleghe, the abbot, died, and the proclamation of the
election of his successor is dated 18th March, 1349. At
Benedictine Tavistock also the abbot died, and his suc-

---

[1] The Prior of St. James', Exeter, also died: "postea tempore
pestilencie subito mortuus est" (Reg. Grand., i, fol. 27b).

[2] Rot. Pat., 29 Ed. III, pars 2, m. 19.

[3] B. Mus., Arund. MS. 17, fol. 55b. Oliver (*Monasticon Dioecesis
Exoniensis*, p. 359) adds: "And no fewer than 88 persons living
within the Abbey gates." In Noakes' *History of the Monastery and
Cathedral of Worcester*, p. 94, it is said that the virulence of the
plague of 1349 may be judged "from the fact that in the Abbey of
Newenham, in the West of England, out of a hundred and eleven
inmates, only the Abbot and two monks survived." No authority is
cited by these writers."

cessor, Richard de Esse, was taken ill after his confirmation, and, "detained by so grave a sickness," could not go to the King, who, on October 17th, commissioned Bishop Grandisson to receive his fealty.[1]

At Bodmin, according to a note taken by William of Worcester from a register in the Church of the Friars Minor there, it was estimated that 1,500 persons died of this sickness.[2] Amongst these was the Vicar, whose successor was appointed on April 8th, 1349. The Augustinian priory in the town was almost depopulated. The prior, John de Kilkhampton, and all his brethren but two were carried off by the sickness. The two survivors, on March 17th, wrote to the Bishop saying that they "were left like orphans," and begging that he would provide a superior for their house at once. The next day, March the 18th, 1349, an inquisition was held under a writ of the Prince of Wales. The jury found that the priory was free, and that the last prior had died "on Friday, next after the feast of St. Peter in Cathedra then last past" (February 27th).[3]

On March 19th Bishop Grandisson wrote to the prior of Launceston setting forth the facts, and appointing a member of that house to the office. Three days later the mandate for his induction was issued, in the hopes that "by his careful watchfulness the said priory may recover from the calamity."[4]

The plight to which the Augustinians of Bodmin were reduced by the disease is, after all, typical of that of many religious houses throughout the country. Mean-

[1] Reg. Grandisson, i, 26b.
[2] *Itinerarium*, ed. J. Nasmith, p. 112.
[3] Sir J. Maclean, *Deanery of Trigg Minor*, i, p. 128.
[4] Reg. Grandisson, i, 26b.

time, however, the epidemic had not confined its ravages
to the western counties, but continued to spread the
same desolation in every direction, as the wave of
pestilence rolled onward over the length and breadth of
the land.

CHAPTER VI

PROGRESS OF THE DISEASE IN LONDON AND THE SOUTH

FOR a time the people of Gloucester strove, but in vain, to protect their city by prohibiting all intercourse with plague-stricken Bristol. The contagion passed from one district to another, from town to town, and village to village, soon involving the entire land in one common misfortune. " There was no city, nor town, nor hamlet, nor even, save in rare instances, any house," writes an English contemporary, " in which this plague did not carry off the whole, or the greater portion, of the inhabitants." And so great was the destruction of life " that the living scarcely sufficed to tend the sick and bury the dead." . . . In some places, on account of the deficiency of cemeteries, the Bishop consecrated new burial grounds.

" In that time there was sold a quarter of wheat for 12*d.*, a quarter of barley for 9*d.*, a quarter of beans for 8*d.*, a quarter of oats for 6*d.*, a large ox for 40*d.*, a good horse for six shillings, which formerly was worth 40 shillings, a good cow for two shillings, and even for eighteenpence. And even at this price buyers were only rarely to be found. And this pestilence lasted for two years and more before England was freed from it."

" When, by God's mercy it ceased, there was such a scarcity of labourers that none could be had for agricultural purposes. On account of this scarcity, women, and even small children, were to be seen with the plough and leading the waggons."[1]

The rapidity with which the contagion spread from place to place makes it now impossible to follow its course with any certainty; the more so because it seems likely that many towns on the southern and western coasts became fresh starting points for the disease. London, in constant communication with other ports, is said by one contemporary to have been attacked as early as September 29th, 1348,[2] whilst other authorities fix, at latest, All Saints' day—November 1st—as the date when the epidemic declared itself in London. It lasted in the city and its neighbourhood till about the feast of Pentecost next following, and, according to the contemporary Robert of Avesbury, it was most severe in the two months from February 2nd to Easter. During the time, he says, "almost every day there were buried in the new cemetery, then made at Smithfield, more than 200 bodies of the dead, over and above those buried in other cemeteries of the city."[3]

Parliament, which was to have assembled at Westminster in January, 1349, was at the beginning of the month prorogued, because, as the King says, "the plague of deadly pestilence had suddenly broken out in the said place and the neighbourhood, and daily increased in severity so that grave fears were entertained for the safety of those coming there at the time."[4] The church-

[1] *Eulogium Historiarum* (Rolls series), iii, p. 213.

[2] *Annales de Bermundeseia* in *Annales Monastici* (Rolls series), iii, p. 475.

[3] *De gestis Edwardi III.* (Rolls series), p. 406.

[4] Rymer, *Fœdera*, v, p. 655.

yards of the city were quickly found to be insufficient, and two, if not three, cemeteries were opened. Of the one in Smithfield referred to in the quotation already given from Robert of Avesbury, the historian Stowe gives the following account·—" In the year 1348 (23 Edward III) the first great pestilence in his time began, and increased so sore that from want of room in church-yards to bury the dead of the city and of the suburbs, one John Corey, clerk, procured of Nicholas, prior of the Holy Trinity within Aldgate, one toft of ground near unto East Smithfield for the burial of them that died, with condition that it might be called 'the churchyard of the Holy Trinity;' which ground he caused, by the aid of divers devout citizens, to be enclosed with a wall of stone. Robert Elsing, son of William Elsing, gave five pounds thereunto; and the same was dedicated by Ralph Stratford, Bishop of London, where innumerable bodies of the dead were afterwards buried, and a chapel built in the same place, to the honour of God." Subsequently Edward III founded there a monastery of Cistercian monks dedicated to our Lady of Graces.[1]

The same author also relates the establishment of the better-known new cemetery, where subsequently the Charterhouse was founded. " The churchyards," he writes of this time, " were not sufficient to receive the dead, but men were forced to choose out certain fields for burials. Whereupon Ralph Stratford, Bishop of London, in the year 1348, bought a piece of ground, called 'No man's land,' which he enclosed with a wall of brick and dedi-cated for the burial of the dead, building thereupon a proper chapel, which is now (*i.e.*, 1598) enlarged and made a dwelling-house; and this burying plot is become

[1] *Survey of London* (ed. Strype), ii, p. 13.

a fair garden, retaining the old name of ' Pardon Churchyard.'

"After this, in the year 1349, the said Sir Walter
Manny, in respect of the danger that might befall in this
time of so great a plague and infection, purchased thirteen acres and a rood of ground, adjoining to the said
' No man's land,' and lying in a place called 'Spittle
Croft,' because it belonged to St. Bartholomew's Hospital (since that called ' New Church Haw '), and caused it
to be consecrated by the said Bishop of London to the
use of burials.

" In this plot of ground there were (in that year) more
than 50,000 persons buried, as I have read in the Charters
of Edward the Third.

" Also I have seen and read an inscription, fixed on a
stone cross sometime standing in the same churchyard,
and having these words: *Anno Domini* 1349. *Regnante*,
&c. That is in English, ' A great plague raging in the
year of our Lord 1349, this churchyard was consecrated;
wherein, and within the bounds of the present monastery, were buried more than 50,000 bodies of the dead,
besides many others from thence to the present time,
whose souls God have mercy upon. Amen."[1]

Whilst it is perfectly possible, and even probable, that
the number 50,000, named by Stowe as buried in one
churchyard, is an exaggerated estimate, it is on the
other hand more than likely that the pestilence found

---

[1] Dr. Creighton, *History of Epidemics in Britain*, p. 128, quotes
Rickman, *Abstract of the Population Returns of* 1831, as estimating
the total deaths in London at 100,000, and considers even the
50,000 as altogether impossible. In fact, he is inclined to think that
in 1349 the population of London "was probably not far from "
44,770 only.

the sanitary condition of the London of that period very favourable for its rapid development. The narrow and ill-cleansed streets, the low, unventilated and undrained houses, and the general condition of living at the time would all favour the growth of so contagious a disease as that which visited the city in the middle of the fourteenth century. One slight glimpse of the state of the streets about this time is afforded in a document issued by the King to the Mayor and Sheriffs, when in 1361 a second visitation threatened to become as destructive to human life as that of 1349. "Because," says the royal letter, "by the killing of great beasts, from whose putrid blood running down the streets and the bowels cast into the Thames, the air in the city is very much corrupted and infected, whence abominable and most filthy stench proceeds, sickness and many other evils have happened to such as have abode in the said city, or have resorted to it; and great dangers are feared to fall out for the time to come, unless remedy be presently made against it; we, willing to prevent such dangers, ordain, by consent of the present Parliament, that all 'bulls, oxen, hogs, and other gross creatures' be killed at either Stratford or Knightsbridge."[1]

There are indeed many indications that the number of those who died in the city was very great.[2] The extra-

---

[1] Brooke Lambert, *London*, i, p. 241.

[2] Dr. Creighton (*ut. sup.*, p. 129) mentions that "in the charter of incorporation of the Company of Cutlers, granted in 1344, eight persons are named as wardens, and these are stated in a note to have been all dead five years after, that is to say, in the year of the Black Death, 1349, although their deaths are not set down to the plague. Again, in the articles of the Hatters' Company, which were drawn up only a year before the plague began (December 13, 1347) six persons are named as wardens, and these according to a note

ordinary increase in the number of wills proved in the "Court of Hustings" affords some indication of this. During the three previous years the average number in that Court was twenty-two. In 1349 they reached the number of 222; and the wills themselves afford further evidence of the rapidity with which members of the same family followed each other to the grave. In one instance a son, who was appointed executor to his father's will, died before probate could be obtained, and his own will was passed through the Court together with that of his father.[1] The number of probates granted in each month is some indication of the time when the mortality was highest. May, with a total of 121, and July, with 51, are the largest numbers, whilst it is curious to observe that the large number in May is accounted for by the fact that none were proved in April.[2] It may be surmised that this was brought about by the complete paralysis of all business about the month of April in consequence of the sickness; this view being strengthened by the fact that no Easter sittings of the Courts of Justices were held.

of the time were all dead before the 7th of July, 1350, the cause of the mortality being again unmentioned, probably because it was familiar knowledge to those then living. It is known also that four wardens of the Goldsmiths' Company died in the year of the Black Death."

[1] *Calendar of Wills in the Court of Hustings, London*, ed. R. R. Sharpe, i, p. xxvii.

[2] The following is a table of the numbers:

Jan.	Feb.	March.	April.	May.	June.	July.
18	42	41	0	121	31	51

Westminster was grievously visited by the sickness. On March 10th, 1349, in proroguing the Parliament for the second time, the King declared that the plague had increased in Westminster and London more seriously than ever.[1] Some weeks later the great monastery was attacked; early in May abbot Bircheston died, and at the same time twenty-seven of his monks were committed to a common grave in the southern walk of the cloister. To relieve the urgent necessities of the house and those about it, jewels and other ornaments to the value of £315 13s. 8d.—a large sum in those days— were sold during the visitation out of the monastic treasury.[2]

At Westminster, too, the Hospital of St. James was left without inmates. "The then guardian and all the other brethren and sisters, except one," had died; and in May, 1349, William de Weston, the survivor, was appointed guardian. Charged with dilapidation, he was deposed in 1351, but in 1353 the house still remained without inmates.[3]

What happened at St. Albans has been recorded by Walsingham in the *Gesta Abbatum*. Speaking of abbot Michael Mentmore, he writes: "The pestilence, which carried off well-nigh half of all mankind, coming to St. Albans, he was struck by a premature death, being touched by the common misery amongst the first of his monks, who were carried off by the deadly disease. And although on Maundy Thursday (*i.e.*, Thursday in Holy Week) he felt the beginning of the ailment, still out of devotion to the feast, and in memory of our Lord's humi-

---

[1] Rymer, *Fœdera*, v, p. 658.
[2] B. Mus. Cotton MS. Vitell. E. xiv, f. 129b.
[3] R. O., L. T. R. Memoranda Roll, 25 Ed. III, m. 26.

lity, he celebrated solemnly the High Mass, and after that, before dinner, humbly and reverently washed the feet of the poor. Then, after partaking of food, he washed and kissed the feet of all the brethren. And all the offices of that day he performed alone and without assistance.

"On the morrow, the sickness increasing, he betook himself to bed, and like a true Catholic, having made, with contrite heart, a sincere confession, he received the Sacrament of Extreme Unction. And so in sorrow and sadness he lasted till noon of Easter-Day.

" And because the plague was then raging, and the air was corrupt, and the monks were dying day by day," he was buried as quickly as possible   " And there died at that time, forty-seven monks over and above those who were carried off in great numbers, in (the monasteries which are) the cells (of St. Albans)."[1]

In another place the same writer adds: "" By God's permission came the pestilence which swept away such numbers. Amongst the abbots was Dom Michael of pious memory, abbot of St. Albans. At that same time the prior of the monastery, Nicholas, and the sub-prior of the place also died. By the advice, therefore, of those learned in the law the convent chose Dom Thomas de Risburgh, professor of Holy Scripture, as prior of the Monastery."[2]

From the date of the death of the abbot of St. Albans, on April the 12th, 1349, it would appear that the epidemic was then at its height in that part of Hertfordshire. The institutions for the portion of the county in the diocese of Lincoln, however, show that it must have

[1] *Gesta Abbatum S. Albani* (Rolls series), ii, p. 369.
[2] *Ibid.*, p. 381.

lingered on, at any rate in the northern part, till the late summer.[1]

" In Hertfordshire Manors," writes Mr. Thorold Rogers, " where it (*i.e.*, the great plague of 1349) was specially destructive, it was the practice, for thirty years, to head the schedule of expenditure with an enumeration of the lives which were lost and the tenancies which were vacated after 1348."[2]

The neighbouring counties of Bedfordshire, Buckinghamshire, and Berkshire suffered in the same way. Although the chronicles make no special mention of the ravages of the epidemic in them, it would, indeed, from other sources of information, appear that during the first half of 1349 the mortality in this district was as great as in most other parts of the country. Thus, the general state of the country after the plague had passed may be illustrated from a class of documents known as *Inquisitiones post mortem*. Theoretically, at least, the whole country belonged to the Sovereign; the actual possessors holding as tenants of the Crown, just as the smaller farmers and peasants held from the tenant *in capite*. On the death of landowners, therefore, the Crown exercised certain rights and claimed certain dues, which it levied on the estates, the King's officers holding them until the

---

[1] The following is a table of the Institutions given in Clutterbuck's *Hertfordshire*:

June.	July.	Aug.	Sept.	Oct.	Nov.	Dec.
6	8	4	4	0	2	1

[2] *Six Centuries of Work and Wages*, i, p. 225.

rights of the Sovereign over the in-coming heir were satisfied. To secure these in each county. an official was appointed known as the Escheator, whose duty it was, on the death of any landowner, in response to the King's writ, to summon a jury bound by oath to inquire into, and testify to, the extent and value of the land held by the deceased person. The record of their sworn verdict is known as the *Inquisitio post mortem.*

These returns made into the King's Court of Chancery even as they now exist—many of them having been lost, or having otherwise disappeared—show a great increase in number in the year 1349. The average number of these inquisitions for the two years, 1346 and 1347, is less than 120; in 1348 there are 130, whilst in 1349 there still exist 311 such records. That the number was very considerably more than this appears from the entry of the writs to the various Escheators upon the " Originalia Roll " for 1349. From this source it may be gathered that the number of writs issued by the King upon information of the death of landed proprietors was 619. Sometimes several such writs are addressed at one time to the Escheator to inquire into many deaths in the same place.[1]

These records afford evidence of the numbers of land-owners swept off by the scourge, but their special value lies in the testimony they afford to the state of various manors and holdings examined in regard to their value after the plague had abated. The smaller tenants paying rent or performing land services were, of course, the chief element in the value of an estate, and especially

[1] Thus, some eight standing on the roll together direct inquiries into deaths of various landed proprietors at Hornseaburton, in Holderness, R. O., Originalia Roll, 23 Ed. III, m. 17.

where the land was in common, as was generally the case, empty farmsteads and cottages meant a proportional decrease in the yearly value.

Thus, to take some examples of the evidence of the epidemic in this district. Of the manor of Sladen in Buckinghamshire, not far from Berkhampstead, a jury, about the beginning of August, 1349, declared upon oath that the mill was of no value, since the miller was dead, and there were no tenants left to want any corn ground, "because of the mortality." The rents derived hitherto from the free tenants, natives of the soil and cottagers, had been £12 a year, now it is declared that there are no tenants at all and that the land is lying untilled and useless. On the whole manor one little cottage, with a strip of land, held by one John Robyns on a service rent worth seven shillings a year, was apparently all that was considered to be worth anything. At another place on the same estate all the tenants and cottars except one were dead, and at a third not one had survived.[1]

In Bedfordshire, by the end of May, 1349, the same tale is told. A cloth mill on the manor of Storington is said to be idle and worthless, and the reason assigned is that "it stands empty through the mortality of the plague, and there is no one who wishes to use it or rent it for the same reason." Land, too, is described as lying uncultivated, and woods cannot be sold because there is no one to buy.[2]

In Berkshire, in July, 1349, on a manor belonging to the Husee family the rents and services of the natives of the soil, "now dead," which were formerly worth thirty-

[1] R. O., Chancery Inq. post mortem, 23 Ed. III, No. 85.
[2] *Ibid.*, No. 75.

two shillings a year, are declared to be without any value at all, because, as the Inquisition says, " there is no one willing to buy or to hire the land of the said dead tenants," and since the land lay all in common it could not be cultivated, and was thus useless.[1] In the same way, on the manor of Crokham, which had belonged to Catherine, wife of the Earl of Salisbury, even as early as April 23rd of this year the free tenant and other holders, who had paid yearly £13, were all dead, and no tenants could be got to take up their lands.[2] In other places there are no Court fees, no services performed, and no mills used, because all on the land are dead; houses and tenements also are in hand, and rents everywhere are either reduced or are nothing at all, because some or all of those who held the lands and cottages have been swept away.[3]

The institutions for the county of Buckinghamshire show that in the year 1349[4] there were eighty-three appointments made to vacant livings. This is slightly less than half the total number of benefices in the county, which appears to have been 180. From the appointments that are dated it appears probable that the sickness was at its worst in the county in the months from May to September, 1349.[5]

[1] R. O., Chancery Inq. post mortem, 23 Ed. III, No. 77.
[2] *Ibid.* (second numbers), No. 58.
[3] *Cf.* four inquisitions in this county: Escheator's Inq. post mortem, file 103.
[4] See Lipscombe's *History of Buckinghamshire.*
[5] The following is a table of the dated institutions:

May.	June.	July.	Aug.	Sept.	Oct.	Nov.
3	10	23	11	13	3	3

On the other side of London, the dioceses of Canterbury and Rochester divided between them the county of
Kent. The Archbishop had jurisdiction over the south-
eastern portion with its long line of coast stretching
from the Medway to the boundaries of Sussex. The
diocese of Rochester included the western portion of
Kent, which lies on the southern bank of the Thames
from London to Sheerness. The diocese of Canterbury
was in many respects peculiarly exposed to the chances
of contagion. In it were situated both Dover and
Sandwich, the two chief points of communication with
the ports of France, and through the city of Canterbury
passed the main line of road between the coast and
London.

Thrice, within a few months, the Archiepiscopal See
was deprived by death of its ruler; and one, at least, of
these, and very probably two, died of the prevailing
sickness. The register of the prior and convent of
Christchurch, Canterbury, during the vacancy, shows
that institutions to livings in the diocese followed one
another in rapid succession, and that deaths must have
occurred in a large proportion of the benefices of this
part of England.[1] " In the year of our Lord, 1348, immediately after the close of the Nativity," writes Stephen
Birchington, in his history of the Archbishops of Canterbury, " arrived the common death of all people; and it
lasted continuously till the end of the month of May, in
the year 1349. By this pestilence barely a third part of
mankind were left alive. Then, also, there was such a
scarcity and dearth of priests that the parish churches
remained almost unserved, and beneficed persons, through

---

[1] *Hist. MSS. Comm., Eighth Report*, p. 336.

fear of death, left the care of the benefices, not knowing where to go." [1]

At Canterbury itself there is some evidence of the epidemic. The abbot of St. Augustine's had died of the disease at Avignon; but no information has been preserved of what took place at the monastery itself, although the fact that abbot Thomas asked for and obtained from Pope Clement VI dispensations, "on account of defect of birth," for six monks, whom he desired to have ordained at this time, makes it more than probable that the pestilence had carried off many members of the community, whose places it was necessary to fill.

At Christchurch only four of the community died at the time, and this comparative immunity has been ascribed to the excellent water supply obtained a century before for the monastery from the hills.[2] Later on in the summer, however, when the new abbot of St. Albans rested at Canterbury, on his way to the Pope at Avignon, one of the two companions whom he had with him died of the sickness there.[3] In the city, also, two masters were appointed to the Hospital of Eastbridge, one quickly after the other. The prioress of St. Sepulchre's and the prior of St. Gregory's both died; but we can only suspect what happened in the communities at this anxious time, and among the people at large. At Sandwich, in the June of 1349, the plague was still raging. The old cemetery was full to overflowing, and the suffragan bishop was commissioned to proceed thither and

[1] Wharton, *Anglia Sacra*, i, p. 42.
[2] J. E. Thorold Rogers, *Six Centuries of Work and Wages*, i, p. 221.
[3] *Gesta Abbatum* (Rolls series).

consecrate a new piece of ground, given for the purpose by the Earl of Huntingdon.[1]

One example may be given here of the rapidity with which during the great sickness members of a family followed one another to the grave. Sir Thomas Dene, of Ospring, about three miles from Faversham, in the northern part of the diocese of Rochester, died on May the 18th, 1349. At the time of his death he had four daughters —Benedicta, five years old, Margaret, four years, and Martha and Joan, younger still. By July the 8th Martha, the wife of Sir Thomas, had also died, and from the inquisition, taken on Monday, the 3rd of August, 1349, it appears that of the children the two youngest were now also dead. Thus, out of a family of six, the father, mother, and two children had been carried off by the disease.[2]

In this second half of the county of Kent, which forms the diocese of Rochester, the sickness was felt as severely as in the Canterbury diocese. What happened here is told in the account of William Dene, a monk of Rochester, and a contemporary of the events he describes. "A plague such as never before had been heard of," he writes, "ravaged England in this year. The Bishop of Rochester, out of his small household lost four priests, five gentlemen, ten serving men, seven young clerks, and six pages, so that not a soul remained who might serve him in any office. At Malling (a Benedictine nunnery) he blessed two abbesses, and both quickly died, and there were left there only four professed nuns and four novices. To one of these the Bishop committed the charge of the temporals, to another that of the spirituals, because no proper person for abbess could be found."

[1] *Hist. MSS. Comm., Eighth Report*, p. 336. Batteley's copy of this commission is in B. Mus. Add. MS., 22665, fol. 183.

[2] Escheator's Inq. p.m., 23 Edw. III, Kent.

"The whole of this time," says the writer in another place, "the Bishop of Rochester remained at Halling[1] and Trotterscliff,[2] and he conferred orders in both places at certain intervals. Alas, for our sorrow! this mortality swept away so vast a multitude of both sexes that none could be found to carry the corpses to the grave. Men and women bore their own offspring on their shoulders to the church and cast them into a common pit. From these there proceeded so great a stench that hardly anyone dared to cross the cemeteries."

The chronicler calls attention, in the most distinct terms, to a fact mentioned by Birchington of Canterbury, and touched on by the Bishop of Bath and Wells (p. 93), namely, that dread of the contagion interfered even with the exercise of priestly functions. These are, perhaps, the only cases in England which recall the terrible and uncontrollable fear which in Italy issued in an abandonment of all principle.

Again, he says: "In this pestilence many chaplains and paid clerics refused to serve, except at excessive salaries. The Bishop of Rochester, by a mandate addressed to the archdeacon of Rochester, on the 27th of June, 1349, orders all these, on pain of suspension, to serve such cures;"[3] "and some priests and clerics refuse livings, now vacant in law and fact," writes the Bishop, "because they are slenderly provided for; and some, having poor livings, which they had long ago obtained, are now unwilling to keep them, because their stipend, on account of the death of their parishioners, is so

---

[1] Some six miles from Rochester.
   Nine miles from Maidstone.
[3] Wharton, *Anglia Sacra*, i, pp. 375-6. This is an abstract of Dene's account in the Rochester cartulary, B. Mus., Cotton MS., Faust. B. v, ff. 96 *et seqq. Cf.* also Vitell. E. xiv, ff. 375 *et seqq.*

notoriously diminished that they cannot get a living and bear the burden of their cure. It has accordingly happened that parishes have remained unserved for a long time, and the cure attached to them has been abandoned, to the great danger of souls. We, desiring to remedy this as soon as possible, by the present letters permit and grant special leave to all rectors and, vicars of our city and diocese instituted, or hereafter to be instituted, to such slender benefices as do not produce a true revenue of ten marks sterling a year, to receive during their poverty an anniversary mass, or such a number of masses as may bring their stipends to this annual sum."[1]

Then after noting that the Archbishop of Canterbury, Thomas Bradwardine, had died in the Bishop of Rochester's palace in London, William Dene continues: "So great was the deficiency of labourers and workmen of every kind in those days that more than a third of the land over the whole kingdom remained uncultivated. The labourers and skilled workmen were imbued with such a spirit of rebellion that neither king, law, nor justice could curb them. The whole people for the greater part ever became more depraved, more prone to every vice, and more inclined than before to evil and wickedness, not thinking of death, nor of the past plague, nor of their own salvation. ... And priests, little weighing the sacrifice of a contrite spirit, betook themselves to places where they could get larger stipends than in their own benefices. On which account many benefices remained unserved, whose holders would not be stayed by the rule of their Ordinary. Thus, day by day, the dangers to soul both in clergy and in people multiplied."

[1] B. Mus. Faust. B., v, f. 98.

"Throughout the whole of that winter and spring the Bishop of Rochester, an old and decrepit man, remained at Trotterscliff, saddened and grieving over the sudden change of the age. And in every manor of the Bishopric buildings and walls fell to ruins, and that year there was hardly a manor which returned a hundred pounds. In the monastery of Rochester, also, there was such a scarcity of provisions that the community were troubled with great want of food; so much so that the monks were obliged to grind their own bread." The prior, however, adds the writer, always lived well. William Dene also relates much that will come under consideration when the results of the great pestilence are dealt with. Here, however, it may be noted that he speaks of "the Bishop visiting the abbey of Malling and the monastery of Lesnes," when he found them so poor "that, as is thought, from the present age to the Day of Judgment they can never recover." Moreover, he notes that Simon Islip, on the day of his enthronisation as Archbishop of Canterbury, did not keep the feast, as was usual, with great display, but to avoid all expense kept it simply with the monks in their refectory at Christchurch.[1]

To this account of the state of the diocese of Rochester, written at the time, it is only necessary to add that the number of benefices in this portion of Kent was some 230, which will serve as some indication of the number of clergy carried off by the prevailing sickness.

The diocese of Winchester includes the two counties of Surrey and Hampshire and the Isle of Wight. On the 24th of October, 1348, Bishop Edyndon, the occupant of the See, addressed a letter to his clergy ordering prayers.[2]

[1] B. Mus. Faust. B., v, fol. 99.
[2] For the use of his transcripts of the Bishop's Register, as well

It bears upon it the stamp of the horror which had seized upon the minds of all by reason of the reports now coming to hand of what had taken place in other countries. "William, by Divine providence, Bishop," he writes, "to the prior and chapter of our Church of Winchester, health, grace, and benediction. A voice in Rama has been heard; much weeping and crying has sounded throughout the various countries of the globe. Nations, deprived of their children in the abyss of an unheard-of plague, refuse to be consoled because, as is terrible to hear of, cities, towns, castles, and villages, adorned with noble and handsome buildings, and wont up to the present to rejoice in an illustrious people, in their wisdom and counsel, in their strength, and in the beauty of their matrons and virgins; wherein, too, every joy abounded, and whither multitudes of people flocked from afar for relief; all these have already been stripped of their population by the calamity of the said pestilence, more cruel than any two-edged sword. And into these said places now none dare enter, but fly far from them as from the dens of wild beasts. Every joy has ceased in them; pleasant sounds are hushed, and every note of gladness is banished. They have become abodes of horror and a very wilderness; fruitful country places, without the tillers, thus carried off, are deserts and abandoned to barrenness. And, news most grave which we report with the deepest anxiety, this cruel plague, as we have heard, has already begun singularly to afflict the various coasts of the realm of England. We are struck with the greatest fear lest, which God forbid, the fell disease ravage any part of our city and diocese. And

as for assistance in all that relates to the Winchester diocese, I am indebted to the kindness of F. J. Baigent, Esq., of Winchester.

although God, to prove our patience, and justly to punish our sins, often afflicts us, it is not in man's power to judge the Divine counsels. Still, it is much to be feared that man's sensuality, which, propagated by the tendency of the old sin of Adam, from youth inclines all to evil, has now fallen into deeper malice and justly provoked the Divine wrath by a multitude of sins to this chastisement.

"But because God is loving and merciful, patient, and above all hatred, we earnestly beg that by your devotion He may ward off from us the scourge we have so justly deserved, if we now turn to Him humbly with our whole heart. We exhort you in the Lord, and in virtue of obedience we strictly enjoin you to come before the face of God, with contrition and confession of all your sins, together with the consequent due satisfaction through the efficacious works of salutary penance. We order further that every Sunday and Wednesday all of you, assembled together in the choir of your monastery, say the seven penitential psalms, and the fifteen gradual psalms, on your knees, humbly and devoutly. Also on every Friday, together with these psalms, we direct that you chant the long litany, instituted against pestilences of this kind by the holy Fathers, through the market-place of our city of Winchester, walking in procession, together with the clergy and people of the said city. We desire that all should be summoned to these solemn processions and urged to make use of other devout exercises, and directed to follow these processions in such a way that during their course they walk with heads bent down, with feet bare, and fasting; whilst with pious hearts they repeat their prayers and, putting away vain conversation, say, as often as possible, the Lord's Prayer and Hail Mary. Also that they should remain in earnest prayer to the close of the Mass, which at the end of the procession we desire you to celebrate in your church." The Bishop then concludes by granting indulgences to those who approach the Sacrament of Confession, and shall in these public devotions pray that God "may cause the severity of the plague to be stayed." [1]

On the same day, October 24th, 1348, Bishop Edyndon issued other mandates to his clergy generally, and to the archdeacon of Surrey in particular. He charges them to see that, in view of the terrible plague which was approaching, all are exhorted to frequent the Sacrament of Penance and to join in the public prayers and processions to be made with bare feet in towns through the market-places, and in villages in the cemeteries round about the churches.

On November 17th, on the nearer approach of the epidemic, the Bishop granted faculties to absolve from all reserved cases, reminding his people of "the approved teaching of the holy Fathers, that sickness and premature death often come from sin; and that by the healing of souls this kind of sickness is known to cease." To guard against any possible danger of cloistered nuns being left by the death of their chaplains without confessors, he at the same time sent to every abbess and superior of religious women in his diocese permission to appoint two or three fit priests, to whom he gave faculties to hear the confessions of the nuns. [2]

Before Christmas time the sickness was already in the diocese, although it was only beginning. On the 19th of January, 1349, Bishop Edyndon wrote to his official that he had good tidings to announce—tidings which he had

[1] Reg. Edyndon, ii, fol. 17.   [2] *Ibid.*, ff. 17b-18.

received with joy—that "the most holy father in Christ, our lord the Supreme Pontiff, had in response to the petition of himself and his subjects, on account of the imminent great mortality, granted to all the people of the diocese, religious and secular, ecclesiastic and lay, who should confess their sins with sincere repentance to any priest they might choose—a plenary indulgence at the hour of death if they departed in the true faith, in unity with the holy Roman Church, and obedience and devotion to our lord the Supreme Pontiff and his successors the Roman Bishops." The Bishop consequently ordered that this privilege should be made known to all as quickly as possible.[1]

At Winchester, as at this time in other places, difficulties about the burial of the dead who were carried off by the pestilence soon arose. By January many benefices in the city had been rendered vacant, and without doubt the daily death-roll was becoming alarming. The clergy for many reasons were desirous of restricting burials to the consecrated cemeteries, but a party of the citizens had clearly made up their minds that in such an emergency as the present the ordinary rules and laws should be, and must be, set aside. In order, apparently, the better to enforce their views they set upon and seriously wounded a monk of St. Swithun's, who was conducting a funeral in the usual burial place. The Bishop took a serious view of the offence. On January

---

[1] Reg. Edyndon, ii, fol. 19. The Indulgence was to last until Easter, but the time was subsequently extended to the feast of St. Michael. This extension was notified from Avignon by letter dated 28th April, 1349; the Pope here granted the extension verbally. On 25th May, Bishop Edyndon sent out the announcement of the extension, and ordered it to be made known at once.

the 21st, 1349, he addressed an order to the prior of
Winchester and the abbot of Hyde ordering sermons to
be preached on the Catholic doctrine of the resurrection
of the flesh, and excommunication to be denounced
against those who had laid violent hands upon brother
Ralph de Staunton, monk of Winchester. " The Catholic
Church spread over the world," he says, " believes in the
resurrection of the bodies of the dead. These have been
sanctified by the reception of the Sacraments, and are
hence buried, not in profane places, but in specially
enclosed and consecrated cemeteries, or churches, where
with due reverence they are kept, like the relics of the
Saints, till the day of the resurrection." Winchester, he
continues,should set an example to the whole diocese, and
above other places ought to reflect the brightness of the
Catholic Faith. Some people there, however, not, he
thanks God, citizens, or even those born in the city (who
are wont to be conspicuous in their upright lives and in
their devotion to the Faith), but low class strangers and
degenerate sons of the Church, lately attacked brother
Ralph de Staunton whilst burying in the appointed
place, and when by his habit and tonsure they knew him
to be a monk, beat him and prevented him from con-
tinuing to bury the dead amongst those there waiting
for the resurrection. Thinking, therefore, that mischief
was likely to ensue in regard to the true Catholic belief
in the resurrection of the dead, he orders the doctrine to
be preached in the churches of Winchester. From all
this it is quite evident that the crisis had brought to the
surface, as it had previously done in Italy, a denial of
the first principles of the Catholic Faith.

Bishop Edyndon further adds that seeing that " at
this time" the multitude of the faithful who are dying

is greater than ever before, provision should be made
" that the people of the various parishes may have
prompt opportunity for speedy burial," and that the
old cemeteries should be enlarged and new ones dedicated.[1]

This, however, did not end the difficulties. On the
13th of February, 1349, letters were directed by the King
to the abbot of Hyde, John de Hampton, Robert de
Popham, and William de Fyfhide,[2] ordering them to
hear and determine a complaint made by the Venerable
Father, William de Edyndon, Bishop of Winchester,
concerning the breaking down of walls and other boundaries of the enclosure, whereon the abbey of Hyde
formerly stood, adjoining the cemetery of the Cathedral
church of St. Swithun's, Winchester, which had been
granted to the priory by the King, Henry I, on the
removal of the abbey. It appears from the document
that " the Mayor, bailiffs, and citizens had entered upon
the usurped portions of the said land, and employed the
site thereof to hold a market twice in the week and a
fair twice in the year." By this " the bodies of the dead
had been iniquitously disturbed, because, owing to the
great mortality and pestilence of late, and the smallness
of the parochial burial grounds, the Bishop, in the exercise of his office, had consecrated the said ground, and
many interments had taken place in it." The Commissioners, or two or three of them, are directed to view
the said area, cemeteries, and closes, " to empanel a

[1] Reg. Edyndon, i, fol. 19b.

[2] Any doubt about the pestilence to which this letter refers is
removed by the dates of the deaths of these last two named. John
de Hampton died 4th August, 1356, and William Fyfhide on 18th
May, 1361.

K

jury, and to examine evidence and generally to try the case." [1]

Taking the dates of the institutions to livings in the county of Hampshire [2] as some indication of the period when the deaths were most frequent, it would appear that the height of the plague was reached in the months of February, March, and April, 1349. In one month, May, indeed, the number of benefices filled was more than double the average of the whole twelve months of any of the three previous years.

In the county of Surrey, March, April, and May were apparently the worst months; and in the last named the number of clergy instituted to vacant livings was double that of the previous yearly average. [3]

[1] Winchester Cathedral Archives, Book ii, No. 80. In Book i, No. 120, is an "Exemplification of the record and proceedings by the Bishop of Winchester against the Mayor and others concerning the limits and boundaries of the churchyard, where the Abbey of Hyde once stood, called the cemetery of St. Peter," Anno 23 Ed. III (1349).

The following table will give the Institutions for Hants:

1348.	1349.								
Dec.	Jan.	Feb.	Mar.	April.	May.	June.	July.	Aug.	Sept.
7	12	19	33	46	29	24	18	11	12

[3] Table of Institutions for Surrey:

1349.								
Jan.	Feb.	Mar.	April.	May.	June.	July.	Aug.	Sept.
5	8	12	12	23	6	7	2	5

Some districts were affected more than others. Thus in the deanery of Basingstoke, in the north of Hampshire, at one time or other, and chiefly in the month of March, by far the greater proportion of benefices fell vacant. On the western side of the county several institutions are made in February, and a considerable number in March. Ivychurch priory, in Wiltshire, where the prior died on February 2nd, and all the rest of the community but one quickly followed him to the grave, is situated close to the boundaries of Hampshire, and an institution was made to a living not far distant on February the 7th. One of the earliest vacancies was Fordingbridge vicarage, also not far from Wiltshire, which appointment was made on the 21st of December, 1348. Only two days later there was apparently the first beginning of the plague at Southampton. The southern coast of the county generally round about Portsmouth and Hayling island suffered chiefly in April and March, and in the later month are recorded numerous institutions to livings in the Isle of Wight and in the country between the southdowns and the sea. On January the 14th, 1349, a new vicar was appointed to Wandsworth by Bishop Edyndon, "because to our pastoral office it belongs," he says, "to have charge of the churches, and to provide for the needs and wants, especially whilst the present mortality among men continues to rage." [1]

The ordinations held by Bishop Edyndon are further indications of the havoc wrought in the diocese of Winchester by the pestilence. In each of the two years 1349, 1350, disregarding the usual Ember week, he held six public ordinations as well as many private ones. On March 5th, 1349, a candidate was ordained *per saltum* to

[1] Reg. Edyndon, i, fol. 38.

the priesthood, and there are instances of two orders being conferred on the same candidate on the same day. The numbers at the usual ordinations leapt up from 57 in March, 1347, to 158 in March, 1349.[1]

The friars who mostly lived amid the denser popula-tions of our cities suffered naturally from the scourge even more than others. The Hampshire friaries appar-ently received a staggering blow, which is manifested in the presentations of subjects for ordination. The Austin Friars of Winchester, who had sent four of their number to be ordained priests between September, 1346, and June, 1348, next presented two, and that only in 1358. The Franciscans had two houses at Winchester and Southampton. For these, three were ordained in 1347 and 1348, but until Bishop Edyndon's death in 1359, only two more were presented. The Dominicans of Winchester in the same way could only manage to pre-sent one friar for the priesthood in the ten years which followed the great plague.

Mr. F. J. Baigent, who for many years has made the episcopal registers and other muniments of the diocese of Winchester his special study, writing of the effects of

[1] Dr. Cox in the "Ecclesiastical History" contributed to the *Victorian County History* for Hampshire, i, p. 34, has given the following table of ordinations:

Year.	Acolytes.	Subdeacons.	Deacons.	Priests.	Total.
March, 1347	8	17	14	18	57
March, 1348	9	22	22	22	75
March, 1349	48	62	25	23	158

this great epidemic, says: " We have no means of ascertaining the actual havoc occasioned among the religious houses of this diocese . . . but in the hospital of Sandown, in Surrey, there existed not a single survivor, and of other religious houses in the diocese (which comprises only two counties) there perished no fewer than 28 superiors, abbots, abbesses, and priors."

Of Sussex, the adjoining county to Hampshire, which is conterminous with the diocese of Chichester, the loss of the episcopal registers makes it difficult to speak with certainty as to the number of clergy swept off by the pestilence or as to its effect upon the religious houses. It is certain, however, that the disease was not less virulent here than in other places about which definite information is obtainable.

At Winchelsea the King, in the year of the plague, 1349, granted to John de Scarle, the parson, a messuage to the east of the cemetery of the church, which formerly belonged to Matilda Lycotin, who had died without leaving any heirs. " Out of devotion to St. Thomas," the King gives this house to the church for a rectory house for ever.[1] That the town suffered considerably seems clear from the fact that in this year, 1349, "ninety-four places in the said town lie together deserted and uninhabited."[2] And both here and at Rye the bailiffs claim that in 1354 they have not received £8 1s. out of £11 17s. 5d., supposed to be due from them, for taxes on these towns, "because so many houses are destroyed and lie desolate there."[3]

Incidentally it is known that John de Waring, abbot

[1] R. O., Originalia Roll, 23 Ed. III, m. 37.
[2] Pipe Roll, 23 Ed. III, m. 23.
[3] R. O., L. T. R. Memoranda Roll, 28 Ed. III.

of Boxgrove, died some time before May 20th, on which
day the monks had leave to elect another superior. Also
from a chance entry in the Ely registers it appears that
on July the 25th, 1349, a new vicar was instituted to
Whaddon, in Cambridgeshire, on the presentation of the
fourth prior of the Monastery of Lewes, to which the
living was appropriated. It is explained that the reason
why the fourth superior in the house had presented was
because "the prior, sub-prior, and third prior were all
dead."[1] Lastly, a year or two after the epidemic had
passed, even Battle abbey is said to be in great straits,
and "in many ways dilapidated" (*multipliciter dilapid-
atur*), about which the King orders an inquiry.[2]

[1] B. Mus. Cole MS., 5824, p. 78 (from Reg. Lisle, fol. 24).
[2] Rot. Pat., 27 Ed. III., pars 1, m. 4.

CHAPTER VII

THE EPIDEMIC IN GLOUCESTER, WORCESTER, WARWICK, AND OXFORD

IN the last two chapters an account has been given of the great plague of 1349 in the southern portion of England. In somewhat less detail the story of its ravages in Gloucester, Oxfordshire, and the Midlands must be here told. First, however, the general account given in the chronicle of Galfrid le Baker, who appears to have been a native of this district, may here find a place.

In all these narratives there is, of course, much repetition. But it is just this absolute coincidence, even to the use of the same terms, in writers of different countries, or even of the same country, who could not have had any communication with one another, that brings home to the mind the literal reality of statements which, when read each one by itself, inevitably appear as gross and incredible exaggeration. It so raged at Bristol, writes Le Baker, that the people of Gloucester refused those of Bristol access to their town, all considering that the breath of those so dying was infectious to the living. But in the end, Gloucester, and Oxford, and London, and finally all England, were so violently attacked that hardly a tenth part of both sexes survived. The cemeteries not being sufficient, fields were chosen as burial-places for the dead. The Bishop of London bought a croft, called "No man's Land," in London, and Sir Walter de Manny one called "The new church-hawe" (where he has founded a house of religious) to bury the dead. Cases in the King's Bench and in the Common Pleas necessarily ceased. A few nobles died, amongst whom was Sir John Montgomery, Captain of Calais and the Lord of Clistel (?) in Calais,[1] and they were buried at the Friars of the Blessed Mary of Carmel, in London. An innumerable number of the common people and a multitude of religious and other clerics passed away. The mortality attacked the young and strong especially, and commonly spared the old and weak. Scarce anyone dared to have contact with a sick person; the healthy fled, leaving the goods of the dead as if infected. Swellings suddenly breaking out in various parts of the body, racked the sick. So hard and dry were they that, when cut, scarcely any fluid matter came from them. From this form of the plague many, through the cutting, after much suffering, recovered. Others had small black pustules distributed over the whole skin of the body, from which very few, and indeed hardly anyone, regained life and strength.

"This terrible pestilence, which began at Bristol on the Feast of the Assumption of the Glorious Virgin, and in London about the Feast of St. Michael, raged in England for a whole year and more so severely that it completely emptied many country villages of every individual of the human species. . . . The following year

[1] At p. 92 of the printed edition of this chronicle the author describes the breaking out of the plague in France, just after the taking of Calais by the English. He attributes the truce between the French and the English to the epidemic.

it devastated Wales as well as England, and then passing over to Ireland it killed the English inhabitants there in great numbers, but the pure-blooded Irish, living in the mountains and high lands, it hardly touched till A.D. 1357, when unexpectedly it destroyed them everywhere."[1]

The mention by Le Baker of Wales and Ireland suggests a brief statement of what is recorded as to the ravages of the pestilence in these two countries. Of Wales hardly anything is known for certain, although the few items of information that we possess make it tolerably certain that Le Baker's statement that it " devastated " the country is not exaggerated. In April, 1350, Thomas de Clopton, to whom the lands of the late Earl of Pembroke, Laurence de Hastings, had been leased during the minority of the heir, petitioned the King for a reduction of £140 out of the £340 he had engaged to pay. The property was chiefly situated in the county of Pembroke, and the petitioner urges that, " by reason of the mortal pestilence lately so rife in those parts, the ordinary value " of the land could not be maintained. Upon inquiry the statement was found to be true, and £60 arrears were remitted, as well as £40 a year taken off the rent.[2] No institutions for any of the four Welsh dioceses are forthcoming; but on the supposition that half the number of beneficed clergy in the Principality were carried off by the sickness, the number of benefices in Wales being about 788, the total mortality among the beneficed clergy would be nearly 400.

With regard to the religious houses in Wales also,

---

[1] *Chronicon Galfridi Le Baker de Swynebroke*, ed. Sir E. M. Thompson, pp. 98-9.

[2] R. O., Originalia Roll, 24 Ed. III, m. 8.

little is known as to the effect of the pestilence. The priory of Abergavenny, an alien priory then in the King's hands, was forgiven the rent due to the King's exchequer, as the prior found it impossible to obtain payment at this time for his lands.[1] And seven-and-twenty years later, the small number in some fairly large religious houses raises the suspicion that they, like so many English monasteries at this time, had not regained their normal strength after their losses. Thus the Cistercian abbey of Whitland, in Carmarthen, in 1377 had only a community of the abbot and six monks; the Augustinian priory at Carmarthen had but five besides the prior; the Premonstratensian abbey of Talley only an abbot and five canons, whilst the prior of Kidwelly, a cell of Sherborne abbey in Dorset, had not even a socius with him.[2]

Some account of what happened in Ireland may be gathered from the relation of friar John Clyn, a Minorite of Kilkenny, who himself apparently perished in the epidemic. "Also this year (*i.e.*, 1349),"[3] he writes, "and particularly in the months of September and October, bishops, prelates, ecclesiastics, religious, nobles and others, and all of both sexes generally, came from all parts of Ireland in bands and in great numbers to the pilgrimage and the passage of the water of That-Molyngis. So much so, that on many days you could see thousands of people flocking there, some through devotion, others (and indeed

---

[1] R. O., Rot. Claus., 25 Ed. III, m. 9.
[2] R. O., Clerical Subsidy, $\frac{1}{7}$ (51 Ed. III.).
[3] The author seems to imply that the plague reached Ireland in 1348. It is, however, probable that 1349 was in reality the date, for in that year, on July 14, Alexander de Biknor, the Archbishop of Dublin, died, and also the Bishop of Meath in the same month (*cf.* Gams, *Series Episcoporum*, p. 219).

most) through fear of the pestilence, which then was very prevalent. It first commenced near Dublin, at Howth[1] and at Drogheda. These cities—Dublin and Drogheda—it almost destroyed and emptied of inhabitants, so that, from the beginning of August to the Nativity of our Lord, in Dublin alone, 14,000 people died."

Then after speaking of the commencement of the plague and its ravages at Avignon, the author continues: " From the beginning of all time it has not been heard that so many have died, in an equal time, from pestilence, famine, or any sickness in the world; for earthquakes, which were felt for long distances, cast down and swallowed up cities, towns, and castles. The plague too almost carried off every inhabitant from towns, cities and castles, so that there was hardly a soul left to dwell there. This pestilence was so contagious that those touching the dead, or those sick of it, were at once infected and died, and both the penitent and the confessor were together borne to the grave. Through fear and horror men hardly dared to perform works of piety and mercy; that is, visiting the sick and burying the dead. For many died from abscesses and from impostumes and pustules, which appeared on the thighs and under the arm-pits; others died from affection of the head, and, as if in frenzy; others through vomiting of blood.

" This year was wonderful and full of prodigies in many ways; still it was fertile and abundant, although sickly and productive of great mortality. In the convent of the Minorites of Drogheda 25, and in that of Dublin 23, friars died before Christmas.

" The pestilence raged in Kilkenny during Lent, for by the 6th of March eight friars Preachers had died since

[1] Dalkey *in the margin.*

Christmas. Hardly ever did only one die in any house, but commonly husband and wife together, with their children, passed along the same way, namely the way of death.

" And I, Brother John Clyn, of the order of Minorites, and the convent of Kilkenny, have written these note-worthy things, which have happened in my time and which I have learned as worthy of belief. And lest notable acts should perish with time, and pass out of the memory of future generations, seeing these many ills, and that the world is placed in the midst of evils, I, as if amongst the dead, waiting till death do come, have put into writing truthfully what I have heard and verified. And that the writing may not perish with the scribe, and the work fail with the labourer, I add parchment to con-tinue it, if by chance anyone may be left in the future and any child of Adam may escape this pestilence and continue the work thus commenced."[1]

This account of Friar Clyn is borne out by one or two documents on the Patent Rolls. Thus in July, 1350, the Mayor and Bailiffs of Cork stated in a petition for relief " that, both because of the late pestilence in those parts, and the destruction and wasting of lands, houses, and possessions, by our Irish enemies round about the said city," they were unable to pay the tax of 80 marks upon the place.[2] Also the citizens of Dublin, in begging to be allowed to have 1,000 quarters of corn sent for their relief, state in the petition of their Mayor " that the merchants and other inhabitants of the city are gravely impoverished by the pestilence lately existing in the

[1] Friar John Clyn's *Annals of Ireland* (ed. *Irish Archæological Society*, 1849).

[2] Rot. Pat., 25 Ed. III, pars 2, m. 19.

said country, and other many misfortunes which had happened there."[1] Lastly, the tenants of the royal manors in Ireland asked the King for special protection. They urged that "both by reason of the pestilence lately existing in the said country, and because of the excessive price of provisions and other goods charged by some of the officers of the land to the tenants, they are absolutely reduced to a state of poverty."[2]

After this brief digression upon the plague in Wales and Ireland, a return may be made to England. The county of Worcester suffered from the disease chiefly in the summer months of the year 1349. The institutions to livings in the county, show that in 67 parishes out of 138 the incumbent changed at this time. In several instances there are recorded more than one change, so that fully half of the total number of benefices in the county were at one time or other vacant during the progress of the disease. The highest number of appointments to livings in the county in any one month was in July, whilst each month from May to November gives indication of some special cause at work producing the vacancies. In the first four months of the year and in December only six institutions are recorded.[3] As examples

[1] Rot. Pat., 26 Ed. III, pars 1, m. 11.
[2] R. O., L. T. R. Memoranda Roll, 27 Ed. III, Hilary term, m. 7.
[3] The following is a table showing the Institutions in some months:

1349.						
May.	June.	July.	Aug.	Sept.	Oct.	Nov.
5	9	23	11	3	5	8

of benefices which fell vacant more than once during the
period there may be adduced Great Malvern, to which
priests were presented on the 10th of July and the 21st
of August; and Powick, near Worcester, to which institutions are registered on the 15th of May and the 10th
of July.

In the city of Worcester, as early as the middle of
April, difficulties as to the disposal of the bodies of the
dead were foreseen and provided against by the Bishop,
Wulstan de Braunsford, who himself, an old and infirm
man, died on the 6th of August, 1349. On the 18th of
April, this year, the Bishop wrote from Hartlebury to
his officials at Worcester, to the following effect: "Carefully considering and not without anxiety of heart often
remembering how dangerously and excessively, alas, the
burials have in these days, to our sorrow, increased, in
the cemetery of our cathedral church at Worcester (for
the great number of the dead in our days has never
been equalled); and on this account, both for our brethren in the said church ministering devoutly to God and
His most glorious Mother, for the citizens of the said
city and others dwelling therein, and for all others
coming to the place, because of the various dangers
which may probably await them from the corruption
of the bodies, we desire, as far as God shall grant us,
to provide the best remedy. Having deliberated over
this, we have ordained, and do ordain, that a place fit
and proper for the purpose, namely, the cemetery of
the hospital of St. Oswald, Worcester, be made to
supply the deficiency in the said cemetery of our cathedral church arising from the said cause." He consequently orders that it be made known to the sacrist
that all burials may at his discretion, "in the time

of this mortality, be made in the said cemetery of St. Oswald."[1]

Leland mentions this cemetery in his Itinerary, where, speaking of the "long and fayre suburbe by north without the foregate," he says there was a chapel to St. Oswald, afterwards a hospital; "but of later times it was turned to a free chapel, and beareth the name of Oswald, and here were wont corses to be buried in time of pestilence as in a publicke cemitory for Worcester."[2]

The general state of the country parts in the county may be gauged by the account given by the King's Escheator for Worcester at this time. This officer, named Leo de Perton, was called upon, amongst other duties, to account for the receipts of the Bishop of Worcester's estates, from his death in August to the appointment of a successor at the end of November, 1349. The picture of the county generally which is presented in his reply is most distressing; tenants, he says, could not be got at any price, mills were vacant, forges were standing idle, pigeon houses were in ruins and the birds all gone, the remnant of the people were everywhere giving up their holdings; the harvest could not be gathered, nor, had this been possible, were there any inhabitants left in the district to purchase the produce.

[1] Nash, *Worcestershire*, i, p. 226.

[2] Green (*Worcester*, p. 144) speaks of the measures taken by the Bishop for the public safety as relieving the city "from an alarming evil," and by it the parishes of St. Alban, St. Helen, St. Swithun, St. Martin, St. Nicholas, and All Saints, "whose churchyards were very confined and not equal to the reception of the parochial deceased, were permitted to partake of the same advantages of sepulture. . . . Hence St. Oswald's burial ground has accumulated that prodigious assemblage of tumulation which, at this time, cannot be viewed with indifference by the most cursory beholder."

Coming to the particular case of the Bishop's temporalities, he claims that of £140 supposed to be due, on the calculation of normal years, so much as £84 was never received. For in that year, 1349, the autumn works of all kinds were not performed. "On the divers manors of the said bishopric they did not, and could not, obtain more than they allowed, on account of the dearth of tenants, who were wont to pay rent, and of customary tenants, who used to perform the said works, but who had all died in the deadly pestilence, which raged in the lands of the said bishopric, during and before the date of the said account."

In the inquiry, the Escheator produced a letter from the King,[1] saying that he had no wish that his official should be charged more than he received. As a consequence of this, two commissions were sent into the country to try, with a jury, the matter at issue. The Escheator put in lists of tenants from whom alone he had received anything, and in the end the jury came to the conclusion that his statement was correct. The particulars disclose some matters of considerable interest in the present inquiry. For example, on the manor of Hartlebury there had been thirty-eight tenants called *virgates*, because each had farmed a virgate of land; thirteen called nokelonds, twenty-one called arkmen and four cottars, who rendered certain services, valued at 106 shillings and $11\frac{1}{2}d$. a year, including a custom called "yardsilver." Nothing could be got of these services, "because all the tenants had died in the mortal sickness, before the date of this account," and in the return of the jury there are said to be only four tenants on the land paying 2s. 10d.[2]

[1] Dated October 26th, 1352.
[2] R. O., L. T. R. Memoranda Roll, 26 Ed. III.

That this was not a mere passing difficulty appears certain when, some years later, in 1354, the same Escheator asks for relief of £57 15s. 5¼d., which he could not then obtain on the same estates, once again in his hands, by the translation of the Bishop to another See. Speaking of the work of the customary tenants, he says: " That he has not obtained, and could not obtain any of these, because the remnant of the said tenants had changed them into other services, and after the plague, they were no longer bound to perform services of this kind." [1]

The results in the neighbouring county of Warwick are naturally similar. With the counties of Gloucester and Worcester it formed the ancient see of Worcester. The institutions of clergy in the county, given in Dugdale's *History of Warwickshire*, show that before April and after October only seven of such institutions were made, so that the pestilence was rife in the county in the summer months of 1349, the institutions in the two months of June and July being the highest. [2]

In some instances the changes were very rapid; thus at Ditchford Friary an incumbent came on July the 19th, and by August the 22nd his successor was appointed. Kenilworth, too, was thrice vacant between May and

---

[1] R. O., L. T. R. Memoranda Roll, 28 Ed. III, Mich. term, m. 19.

[2] The following table gives the number of Institutions in some months:

April.	May.	June.	July.	Aug.	Sept.	Oct.
4	13	17	20	15	7	10

August. At Coventry, on May 10th, Jordan Shepey, the Mayor, "who built the well called Jordan well," died.[1] In July the archdeacon of Coventry and a chantry priest at Holy Trinity were carried off. In August the Cathedral prior, John de Dunstable, was elected to fill the vacancy at the priory, and shortly after Trinity church had a new incumbent. At Pollesworth the abbess, Leticia de Hexstall, died, and a successor was appointed on October 13th, 1349.

In Oxfordshire, which at the time of the great visitation of the plague, formed part of the large diocese of Lincoln, the number of benefices, exclusive of the Oxford colleges, was some 220. Half this number consequently may be estimated as that of the deaths of the beneficed clergy. The disease was probably prevalent in the county about the same time as in the adjacent places —that is, in the spring and summer months of 1349. The prioress of Godstowe, for example, died some time before May the 20th, on which day the royal permission was given to elect a successor, and the prior of St. Frideswide, Oxford, very much about the same time; since on June 1st Nicholas de Hungerford received the temporalities upon his election.

The city of Oxford, with its large population of students, appears to have suffered terribly. "Such a pestilence," writes Wood, "that the like was never known before in Oxon. Those that had places and houses in the country retired (though overtaken there also), and those that were left behind were almost totally swept away. The school doors were shut, colleges and halls relinquished, and none scarce left to keep possession, or make up a competent number to bury the dead. 'Tis

[1] Dugdale, *Warwickshire* (ed. Thomas), p. 147.

reported that no less than 16 bodies in one day were carried to one churchyard to be buried, so vehemently did it rage."[1] The celebrated FitzRalph, Archbishop of Armagh, who had been Chancellor of the University before the event, declares that in his time of office there were 30,000 students at Oxford.[2] In this statement he is borne out by Gascoigne, who, writing his *Theological Dictionary*, in the reign of Henry VI, says: " Before the great plague in England there were few quarrels between the people and law cases, and so there were also few lawyers in the kingdom of England and few in Oxford, when there were 30,000 scholars at Oxford, as I have seen on the rolls of the ancient Chancellors, when I was Chancellor there."[3] This concourse was diverted by the pestilence, since in 1357 FitzRalph declares that there were not a third of the old number at the schools.

In the year of the visitation Oxford had no fewer than three Mayors. Richard de Selwood died on the 21st April of this year, and the burgesses then made choice of Richard de Cary. Before he could reach London to

---

[1] Wood, *History and Antiquities of the University of Oxford* (ed. Gutch), p. 449.

[2] Harl. MS., 1900, fol. 11[b]. Trevisa's translation of FitzRalph's *Propositio coram Papa:* " So yt yet in my tyme, in ye University of Oxenford were thritty thousand scolers at ones, and now beth unnethe six thousand."

[3] Gascoigne, *Loci ex Libro Veritatum*, ed. J. E. Thorold Rogers, p. 202. The editor on the passage says: " They (*i.e.* the students) come from all parts of Europe. The number seems incredible, but Oxfordshire was, to judge from its rating for exceptional taxation, after Norfolk, then at the best of its industries, the wealthiest county in England by a considerable proportion. . This concourse of students was diverted by the great plague. . I see no reason to doubt the statement about the exceeding populousness of Oxford in the first half of the 14th century."

take the oath to the King he was taken sick, and the abbot of Osney was named as Commissioner to attend at Oxford and administer the oath of office to him. On May 19th the abbot certified that he had done this, but on the 16th of June, letters dated from Oxford two days previously were received in London announcing the Mayor's death and the election of John Dereford in his place.[1]

Without doubt Oxford had its plague pit like other cities. The late Professor Thorold Rogers, writing about this pestilence, says: " I have no doubt that the principal place of burial for Oxford victims was at some part of New College garden, for when Wykeham bought the site it appears to have been one which had been previously populous, but was deserted some thirty years before during the plague and apparently made a burial ground by the survivors of the calamity."[2]

[1] R. O., L. T. R. Memoranda Roll, 23 Ed. III, Mich.
[2] *Six Centuries of Work and Wages*, i, p. 223.

CHAPTER VIII

STORY OF THE DISEASE IN THE REST OF ENGLAND

THE history of the great pestilence in the diocese of Norwich which includes the two eastern counties of Norfolk and Suffolk, has been graphically described by Dr. Jessopp.[1] The results at which he has arrived by a careful study of the episcopal registers of the diocese and the court rolls of sundry manors may be very briefly summarised here. The epidemic was at its height in the East of England in the summer months of 1349,[2] and the deaths in the ranks of the clergy were very alarming. The average number of institutions in the diocese yearly for five years before the sickness was seventy-seven. In this single year 800 parishes lost their incumbents, 83 of them twice, and ten three times, in a few months; and by the close of the year two-thirds of the benefices in the diocese had become vacant.

Of the seven convents of women in this district, five

---

[1] *The Coming of the Friars,* pp. 166-261.
[2] The following is a table of the Institutions during four months:

1349.			
April.	May.	June.	July.
23	74	139	209

149

lost their superiors, and in at least twelve of the religious houses of men, including the abbey of St. Benet's Hulme, the head died. How many of the subjects in these 19 monastic establishments were carried off by the sickness can never be known; but bearing in mind what was remarked at the time, that the disease hardly ever entered a house without claiming many victims, and what we know of other places of which there is definite information, the suspicion may be allowed that the roll of the dead in the religious houses of East Anglia was very large. At Heveringland the prior and canons died to a man, and at Hickling only one survived; neither house ever recovered. In the college of St. Mary-in-the-Fields, at Norwich, five out of the seven prebendaries were carried off, whilst the Friars of our Lady, in the same city, are said all to have died. Altogether, Dr. Jessopp calculates that some 2,000 clergy in the diocese must have been carried off by the disease in a few months.

From the court rolls the same evidence is adduced for the terrible mortality among the people. Dr. Jessopp had collected many striking proofs of this, from which one or two examples may be quoted. On a manor called Cornard Parva there were about 50 tenants. On 31st March three men and six women are registered as having died in two months. During the next month 15 men and women, seven without heirs, were carried off, and by 3rd November there are 36 more deaths recorded, and of these 13 had left no relations. Thus during the incidence of the plague some 21 families on this one manor had disappeared. The priest of the place had died in September.[1]

To take another example. At Hunstanton on the

[1] *The Coming of the Friars*, p. 200.

16th of October, 1349, it was found that in two months 63 men and 15 women had been carried off. In 31 instances only women and children had been left to succeed, and in nine there were no known heirs. In this small parish, and in only eight months, 172 persons who were tenants of the manor had died. Of these, 74 had left no heirs male, and 19 no blood relations at all.[1]

To these examples may be added one taken from the court roll of the manor of Snetterton, about the centre of the county of Norfolk. A court of the manor was held on Saturday in the feast of St. James the Apostle, that is July 25th, 1349, and it is called ominously the *Curia pestilencie*, the Court of the Plague. At this meeting 39 tenants of the manor are named as having died, and in many cases no heir is forthcoming. One tenant is specially named as holding his house and ten acres on condition of keeping three lamps ever burning before the Blessed Sacrament in the parish church. He is dead, and has left no other relation but a son 16 years of age.

The larger cities of East Anglia, such as Norwich and Yarmouth, suffered no less than the country districts from the all-pervading plague. The historian of Norfolk has estimated the population of Norwich before this catastrophe at 70,000.[2] It was unquestionably one of the most flourishing cities of England, and possessed some 60 parish churches, seven conventual establishments, as well as other churches in the suburbs; and on the authority of an ancient record in the Guildhall, Blomefield put down the number of those carried off by the

---

[1] *The Coming of the Friars*, p. 203.
[2] Blomefield, *History of Norfolk* (folio ed.), ii, p. 681.

epidemic at 57,374. Such a number has been considered
by many as altogether impossible, but that the city was
reduced considerably does not appear open to doubt in
view of the fact that by 1368 ten parishes had disappeared and fourteen more were subsequently found to
be useless. "The ruins of twenty of these," says a
modern writer, "may still be seen." [1]

Yarmouth in the middle of the fourteenth century was
a most flourishing port. When, to assist the attack of
Edward on Calais, but two years before the plague,
London furnished 25 ships and 662 mariners, Yarmouth
is said to have sent 43 ships and 1,950 sailors. [2] William
of Worcester, in his Itinerary, after speaking in praise of
the town, says: "In the great pestilence there died
7,000 people." [3] This statement is probably based upon
the number of persons buried in one churchyard. For in
a petition of burgesses of Yarmouth in the beginning of
the sixteenth century to Henry VII it is asserted that
the prosperous condition of the town was destroyed by
the great plagues during the reign of Edward III. In
the thirty-first year of this reign, they say—probably
mistaking the year—7,052 people were buried in their
churchyard, "by reason whereof the most part of the
dwelling-places and inhabitations of the said town stood
desolate and fell into utter ruin and decay, which at this
day are gardens and void grounds, as it evidently appeared."

It is, moreover, certain that Yarmouth Church, large
as it appears in these days, was, before the plague of

---

[1] F. Seebohm, *The Black Death and its place in English History*
(in *Fortnightly Review*, Sept. 1st, 1865).

[2] Fuller, *Worthies*, ed. Nicholas, ii, p. 132.

[3] Ed. Nasmith, p. 344.

1349, not ample enough for the population,[1] and preparations had already been made for considerably enlarging its nave. Owing to the pestilence the work was not carried out. Nor is this the only instance in the county where the enlargement of churches already vast was rendered unnecessary by the diminution of inhabitants through the sickness. It is impossible to examine the great churches which abound in the counties of Norfolk and Suffolk without coming to the conclusion that they were built to serve the purposes of a large population.

To take one example, the tax on the town of Dunwich had been granted by the King to the monastery of Ely; but in 1351 the inhabitants petitioned for relief as they were quite unable to find the money for the royal collectors. The King gave way to what he calls "the relation of the men of the town of Dunwich," which recited that "the said town, which before this time was completely inhabited by fisher-folk had been rendered desolate by the deadly plague late raging in those parts, and by our enemies the French seizing and killing the fishermen at sea, and still remained so."[2]

From Norfolk and Suffolk we pass to the adjoining county of Cambridge, which is conterminous with the diocese of Ely. The Bishop of the diocese, Thomas de Lisle, was abroad at the time when the plague broke out in the county. On the 19th of May he wrote to the clergy of his diocese, forwarding the letter of Stephen,

---

[1] Professor Seebohm thinks that Yarmouth had probably a population of 10,000 before 1349. This seems much too low. It had 220 ships.

[2] R. O., Rot. Claus., 26 Ed. III, m. 5d. This is repeated on two occasions in the next year.

Archbishop of Arles, and Chamberlain of the Pope, already referred to elsewhere. By this anyone was empowered to choose his own confessor, " since in all places now is, or will be, the epidemic or mortality of people which at present rages in most parts of the world."[1] The Bishop had made arrangements for the government of his See during his absence abroad, but on April 9th, 1349, he wrote from Rome, making other dispositions in view of the plague. " By reason of the epidemic, as it is called, wonderfully increasing in the diocese," as he has lately understood by people from thence, he " for fear his former Vicars General should die," augments their number. And, further, "considering how difficult it is for two people to agree about the same sentence, he appoints John, prior of Barnwell, singly and solely to dispose of all vacant benefices, and in case of his death, or refusal to act, then Master Walter de Peckham, LL.D., to be sole disposer of them," and then six others in order; a provision which itself shows how slight he considered the chance of life for any individual. In other matters any of his Vicars General could act; and " in case of any death putting a stop to business, as was likely in such a mortality," whichever Vicar General was present should act until the arrival of the three specially appointed.[2]

The foresight of the Bishop was not unnecessary. From the month of April vacancies followed quickly one upon another. For three years previous to 1349 the average number of institutions recorded in the episcopal registers was nine, and in 1348 it was only seven. In this year of the great sickness 97 appointments to liv-

[1] B. Mus. Cole MS., 5824, fol. 73. Extracts from Reg. Lisle.
[2] Ibid., fol. 76.

ings in the diocese were made by the Bishop's Vicars, and in July alone there were 25.[1] The prior of Barnwell died early in the course of the sickness, probably even before he could have received the Bishop's commission to act for him in the matter of vacant benefices.

In June there are evidences of the mortality in the Cathedral priory of Ely. On the 23rd of the month John de Co, Chancellor of the diocese, acting as the Bishop's representative, according to the commission, appointed a new sub-prior to the monastery, and again on July 2nd a cellarer and camerarius. A week later, on the 9th of July, 1349, "Brother Philip Dallying, late sacrist of Ely, being dead, and the said Brother Paulinus (the camerarius) being likewise dead and both of them buried, he appointed to both offices, namely, Brother Adam de Lynsted as sacrist, and Brother John of St. Ives as camerarius."[2] At the same time also two chantries in the Cathedral became vacant; one, called "the green chantry," twice in two months.

[1] The following table will give the number for some months:

1349.						
April.	May.	June.	July.	Aug.	Sept.	Oct.
6	8	19	25	13	6	7

The total number of benefices in the diocese at this time was 142.

[2] Cole MS., *ut supra*. Apparently another sacrist of Ely, called John of Wisbeach, died on 16th June, 1349, "during the building of the Lady Chapel" (see D. J. Stewart, *Hist. of Ely*, p. 138; and *Angl. Sacra*, i, p. 652).

The number of clergy carried away by the sickness in this diocese may be estimated from the number of vacant benefices. Deducting the average number of yearly institutions, it is fair to consider that 89 priests holding benefices died at this time.[1] The proportion of non-beneficed clergy to those beneficed was then probably about the same as it was in the second year of King Richard II. The clerical subsidy for that time shows 140 beneficed clergy against 508 non-beneficed, including the various religious.[2] On this basis at least 350 of the clerical order must have perished in the diocese of Ely.

The University town of Cambridge did not escape. On May 24th, 1349, the church of St. Sepulchre's fell vacant, and already in July several of the churches were without incumbents. Towards the end of April the Master of the hospital of St. John died, and one Robert de Sprouston was appointed to succeed. Then he died a short time after, and one Roger de Broom was instituted on May 24th; but in his turn Roger died, and another took his place.

Cambridge, too, had probably its common plague pit. "Some years ago," writes the late Professor Thorold Rogers, "being at Cambridge while the foundations of the new Divinity School were being laid, I saw that the ground was full of skeletons, thrown in without any at-

[1] Bentham, *History of the Cathedral Church of Ely*, i, p. 161, has the following note: Register L'Isle, fol. 17-21. Hinc obiter notandum duxi, numerum clericorum parochialium in tota Diocesi Elien. hoc tempore fuisse 145, aut circiter; ex hoc autem numero, constat ex Registro 92 Institutiones fuisse infra annum 1349 (anno incipiente 25 die Martii).

[2] Clerical Subsidy, $\frac{2}{1}$.

tempt at order, and I divined that this must have been a Cambridge plague pit." [1]

A curious document preserved in the Bishop's archives shows how severely some parishes must have suffered. It is a consent given by the prior and convent of Ely to a proposal of the Bishop to unite two parishes in Cambridge. It mentions the churches of All Saints' and St. Giles', of Cambridge, near the castle, and states that the parishioners of the former are, for the most part, dead in the pestilence, and those that had been left alive had gone to the parishes of other churches. It also says that the people of St. Giles' have died, and, further, that the nave of All Saints' is in a ruinous state, " and the bones of the dead exposed to beasts." The Bishop consequently proposes to unite these two ancient parishes of Cambridge, and in this consent to the proposal a glimpse is almost accidentally afforded of the desolation wrought in the University town by the terrible scourge. [2]

An example of what was probably very general throughout the county is afforded by a roll of accounts for a Cambridgeshire manor in this year. Considerable decay of rents is noted, and no wonder, for it would seem that 50 tenements and 22 cottages were in hand, and that the services which the holders would otherwise have rendered had to be paid for. At Easter 13 copyholders' tenements are vacant, and by Pentecost another 30 are added to the long list. [3]

---

[1] *Six Centuries of Work and Wages*, i, p. 223.

[2] *Hist. MSS. Comm., Sixth Report*, p. 299. This document is dated 27th May, 1366, and consequently may refer also to the effects of the plague of 1361.

[3] R. O., Duchy of Lancaster, Mins. Accts., Bundle 288, No. 471.

The clergy were reduced to the greatest straits in consequence of the deaths among their parishioners, leading to a proportional diminution of their incomes. On September 20th, 1349, the Bishop's Vicar addressed a letter to John Lynot, vicar of All Saints', Jury, Cambridge.[1] "We are informed," he says, "by your frequent complaint that the portion coming to you in the said church is known to consist only of offerings of the parishioners, and that the same parishioners have been so swept away by the plague notoriously raging in this year that the offerings of the said church do not suffice for the necessities of life, and that you cannot elsewhere obtain help to bear the burden laid upon you. On this account you have humbly petitioned us to be allowed to have for two years an anniversary (Mass) for your necessary support. Since your position in God's Church does not make it fitting that you should seek alms, particularly for necessities in food and clothing, we grant you the permission asked on the condition that as soon as the fruit and revenue of the said portion be sufficient to furnish you properly with necessaries you altogether give up the income of this anniversary (Mass)."[2] At the same time a similar permission was granted to John Atte Welle, vicar of St. John, "in Meln-street," Cambridge.

The adjoining county of Huntingdon forms a portion of the great diocese of Lincoln. In it there were some 95 benefices, which may give some indication of the probable number of deaths in the ranks of the clergy of the county.

The abbot of Ramsey died on the 10th of June, 1349,

---

[1] It was this church which some years later was declared to be in a ruinous state.

[2] Cole MS., 5824, fol. 81.

and the King did not, as usual, claim the temporalities during the vacancy, but allowed the monks to pay a smaller sum than was usual; "and, be it remembered," says the document allowing this, "that because of the depression of the said abbey by the present mortal pestilence raging in the country, the said custody is granted to the prior and convent for a lesser sum to pay to the King than at the time of the last vacancy." [1]

Among the *Inquisitiones post mortem* is one relating to the manor of Caldecot, in Huntingdonshire. It formed part of the estates of Margaret, Countess of Kent, who died on St. Michael's day, 1349. Many houses of the manor are represented as ruinous, and of no value. Rents of assize, formerly worth £8 a year, this time produced but fifty shillings; an old mill, which hitherto had been let with land for two pounds a year, is now only worth 6s. 8d., "because of the pestilence it could be let at no higher rate." And, lastly, the fees of the manor court had sunk from 13s. 4d. to 3s. 4d. "through dearth of tenants there." [2]

Proceeding westward from Huntingdonshire, the county of Northampton next claims attention. Judged by the lists of institutions given in Bridges' history of the county, there were changes at this period in 131 instances out of 281. In fifteen cases two or more changes occurred in the same place in 1349, and the number of institutions was greatest in August, when 36 appoint-

---

[1] R. O., Originalia Roll, 23 Ed. III, m. 6. Among the Ministers' Accounts (Q. R., Mins. Accts., General Series, 874, No. 9) is a set belonging to a Ramsey manor at this time. "Many holdings of natives" are said to be in hand "on account of the pestilence," and in one place "22 virgates of land" for the same reason.

[2] R. O., Chancery Inq. p. m., 23 Ed. III, No. 88.

ments were made.[1] From the institutions it appears
likely that the town of Northampton was attacked most
severely about the October of the year 1349; at least, on
November 1st two appointments were made to livings
there.

As to the religious houses, at Luffield all are said to
have died of the plague. William de Skelton, the prior,
was carried off by the sickness, and the rental of the
house was subsequently declared to be inadequate for
its support. At Delaprey Convent, Catherine Knyvet,
the abbess, fell a victim to the disease. At Worthop, the
superior, Emma de Pinchbeck, died, and probably many
of the Augustinian nuns there. The Bishop appointed
Agnes Bowes to succeed, but the convent never recovered, and in 1354 was, at the petition of its patron
Sir Thomas Holland, united to the convent of St. Michael
near Stamford. In the royal licence it is stated "that
the convent, being poorly endowed, was, by the pestilence which lately prevailed, reduced to such poverty that
all the nuns but one, on account of their penury, had
dispersed."[2]

[1] The following table will show the number of Institutions in
Northamptonshire for some months; before May and after October,
1349, some 34 institutions are recorded:

1349.					
May.	June.	July.	Aug.	Sept.	Oct.
8	15	25	36	10	7

[2] R. O., Rot. Pat., 28 Ed. III, pars 1, m. 16.

The inquiry just referred to, as to the estates of the Countess of Kent upon her death in 1349, reports as to the state of a manor in Northamptonshire. It is the same tale of depression and desolation as appears everywhere else throughout England. Pasture formerly worth forty shillings now yields only ten, and some even brought in only five shillings in place of eighteen; and the sole reason assigned is "the mortality." A watermill and a wind-mill "for the same cause" were let for 6s. 8d., instead of the old 56 shillings.

The priory of Stamford itself moreover was in sad distress. The rents from five free tenants and eighteen customary tenants, were just one-third of their former value "for the same cause." And the same nuns, in place of 19s. 8d. which they used to get for thirteen tenements, now received only four shillings, whilst their yearly tenants, who should pay 13 lbs. of pepper, at 12d. the pound, have paid nothing; moreover the fines of the manor, estimated to produce twenty shillings a year, have brought in but two.

A third example is given in the case of a manor near Blisworth, in which two mills are let for twenty, in place of the old rent of sixty-five shillings; and two carucates of land produced only some fifteen shillings the carucate, "and not more, on account of the mortality in those parts."[1]

Of the small county of Rutland, lying at the north of Northamptonshire, little can be said. It likewise formed part of the diocese of Lincoln, and contained some 57 benefices. From an inquisition we learn that on one manor for nine virgates of land there could be estimated nothing in the way of rent, "because all the tenants died

[1] R. O., Chancery Inq. p. m., 23 Ed. III, No. 88.

M

before the feast of Easter (1349). They (*i.e.*, the jury) also say that the natives and cottars did not work this year." In another place, a house and garden formerly let for forty shillings, now produces only twenty shillings; 240 acres of arable land are let for half their former value, and 180 acres of meadow are worth 10*d.* per acre, in place of eighteenpence.[1]

Eastward, the county adjoining Northampton is Leicester. For this county there exists the local account of Knighton, a canon of Leicester abbey. As far as concerns England his relation may fitly find a place here. " The sorrow-bearing pestilence," he writes, " entered the sea coast at Southampton, and came to Bristol, and almost the whole strength of the town died as if struck with sudden death, for there were few who kept their beds beyond three or two days or even half a day. Then the terrible death rolled on into all parts according to the course of the sun, and at Leicester, in the little parish of St. Leonard, there died more than 380; in the parish of Holy Cross more than 400; in that of St. Margaret, Leicester, more than 700; and so in every parish great numbers.

" The Bishop of Lincoln sent through his diocese a general power to all and every priest, both regular and secular, to hear confessions and to absolve with full and entire episcopal power, except only in the case of debt. In that case, if able (the penitent) himself was to make satisfaction whilst he lived, or at least others should do so with his property, after his death. In the same way the Pope granted a full remission from all sins, to be obtained once only by every one in danger of death, and he allowed this faculty to last till the next

[1] Escheator's Inq. p. m., Series i, file 201.

Easter following, and each to choose at will his own confessor.

"In the same year, there was a great mortality of sheep everywhere in the kingdom; so much so, that in one place there died in one pasture more than 5,000 sheep, and they were so putrid that neither beast nor bird would touch them. The price for everything was low; through fear of death, very few cared for riches and the like. And then a man could purchase a horse for half a mark, which before had been worth forty shillings; a large fat ox for 4s.; a cow for 12d.; a bullock for 6d.; a fat wether for 4d.; a sheep for 3d.; a lamb for 2d.; a large pig for 5d.; and a stone of wool for nine pence; and sheep and cattle roamed about, wandering in fields and through the growing harvest, and there was no one to drive them off or collect them; but in ditches and thickets they died in innumerable quantities in every part, for lack of guardians; for so great a dearth of servants and labourers existed that no one knew what to do. Memory could not recall so universal and terrible a mortality since the time of Vortigern, king of the Britons, in whose reign, as Bede in his *De gestis Anglorum* testifies, the living did not suffice to bury the dead.

"In the following autumn no one could get a harvester at a lower price than eight pence with food. For this reason many crops perished in the fields for lack of those to gather them; but in the year of the pestilence, as said above of other things, there was such an abundance of crops of all kinds that no one, as it were, cared for them." [1]

In the absence of any definite information as to the institutions made at this time in the county of Leicester

[1] Twysden, *Historiae Anglicanae Scriptores Decem*, col. 2699.

it is only necessary to note that the number of benefices was about 250 at this period. There were also some twelve religious houses and several hospitals. In 1351, as we learn from the records, Croxton abbey still "remained quite deserted." The church and many of the buildings had been burnt, and "by the pestilence the abbey was entirely deprived of those by whose ability the monastery was then administered" (the abbot and prior alone excepted). The abbot was sick, "and the said prior (in November, 1351) was fully occupied in the conduct of the Divine Office and the instruction of the novices received there into the community, after the pestilence."[1]

A slight confirmation of Knighton's account of the distress in the country parts after the plague had passed, if any were needed, is found in an inquisition made upon the death of Isabella, wife of William de Botereaux, who died upon St. James' Day, 1349. The manor held by her was at a place called Sadington, in Leicestershire, and two carucates of land are represented as lying uncultivated and waste "through the want of tenants."[2]

The adjoining county of Staffordshire formed part of the diocese of Coventry and Lichfield. It comprised 165 benefices, which may form some basis on which to calculate in estimating the number of clergy who were carried off by the pestilence. Some lands in this county, near Tamworth, belonged to the Earl of Pembroke. Upon his death, whilst the heir was a minor, they were farmed out at a rent of £38 per annum, to be paid to the King. In 1351 the man who had agreed to pay that sum petitioned to have it reduced, because "the tenements with the said land so let are so deteriorated by the

---

[1] Rymer, *Foedera*, v, p. 729.
[2] R. O., Escheator's Inq. p. m., 23 Ed. III, Series i, file 240.

pestilential mortality lately raging in those parts that they do not reach their wonted value." After inquiry, his rent is reduced by £8 the year.[1]

Of the two counties bordering upon Wales, Hereford and Shropshire, not much is known at this time. There can be little doubt, however, that they suffered quite as severely from the epidemic as the other counties of England.

In the diocese of Hereford, including that county and a portion of Shropshire, the average number of institutions to benefices, during three years before and after the epidemic, was some 13. In 1349 there are recorded in Bishop Trileck's register no fewer than 175 institutions, and in the following year the number of 45 vacant benefices filled up, points to the fact that many livings had probably remained for some months without incumbents. This suspicion is further strengthened by the frequent appearance of the words "by lapse" in the record of institutions at this period, which shows that for six months the living had not been filled by the patron. It is probable, therefore, that in the diocese of Hereford about 200 beneficed clergy fell victims to the disease. Taking the dates of the institutions as some indication of the period when the epidemic was most severe in the diocese, it would appear that the worst time was from May to September, 1349.[2]

[1] Originalia Roll, 25 Ed. III, m. 11.
[2] The following table will give the number of Institutions in the diocese of Hereford for some months:

1349.					
May.	June.	July.	Aug.	Sept.	Oct.
13	14	37	29	27	13

One fact bearing upon the subject of the great mortality in the pestilence of 1349 in the county of Hereford is recorded in the episcopal register. In 1352 the Bishop united into one parish the two churches of Great Colington and Little Colington, about four miles from Bromyard. The patrons of the two livings agreed to support a petition of the parishes to this effect, and in it they say "that the sore calamity of pestilence of men lately passed, which ravaged the whole world in every part, has so reduced the number of the people of the said churches, and for that said reason there followed, and still exists, such a paucity of labourers and other inhabitants, such manifest sterility of the lands, and such notorious poverty in the said parishes, that the parishioners and receipts of both churches scarcely suffice to support one priest."[1] The single church of Colington remains to this day as a memorial of the great mortality in that district. Even among the inhabitants the memory of the two Colingtons has apparently been lost.

In Salop the historians of the county town record that "through all these appalling scenes (consequent upon the great mortality of 1349) the zeal of the clergy, both secular and monastic, was honourably distinguished. The episcopal registers of the diocese, within which Shrewsbury is situated, bear a like honourable testimony to the assiduity of the secular clergy of the district."[2] From the same source it appears that the average number of institutions to benefices vacant by death during ten years before 1349 and ten years after are only 1½ per annum, or 15 for the whole period. In that year the number of institutions to vacancies known to

[1] Reg. Trileck, fol. 103.
[2] Owen and Blakeway, *Shrewsbury*, i, p. 165.

have been caused by *death* was 29. If this number be taken as a guide for the general mortality, Shropshire would appear to have suffered in an exceptional manner. Besides these, however, there are a number of other institutions registered at this time, the cause of which is not specified, and many of them most probably were also caused by the great epidemic.

As an example of the general destitution caused by the great sickness, Owen and Blakeway quote an *Inquisitio post mortem*, taken in the year of the plague, upon the estate of a Shropshire gentleman, John le Strange of Blakmere. By that record he is found by the jury to have died, seized with various lands, etc., amongst others, the three water-mills, "which used to be worth by the year 20 marks, but now they are worth only half that sum, by reason of the want of those grinding, on account of the pestilence." The same cause is assigned for the diminution of other parts of his revenue, as tolls on markets, rent of assize, etc.

In the manor of Dodington, proceeds the record of the inquiry, "there are two carucates of land which used to be worth yearly sixty shillings, and now the said jurors know not how to value the said land, because the domestic and labouring servants (*famuli et servientes*) are dead, and no one is willing to hire the land." The water-mill has sunk in value from thirty shillings to six-and-eightpence, because the tenants are dead; the pond was valueless since the fish had been taken out, and it had not been stocked again.[1]

This John le Strange, of Whitchurch, died on August

[1] Owen and Blakeway, *Shrewsbury*, i, p. 165. The Inquisition is to be found in the Record Office; Chancery Inq. p. m., 23 Ed. III, No. 78.

20th, 1349, and the inquisition held upon his estates names three sons—Fulk, the eldest, who was married; Humphrey, the second; and John, who was 17 years of age; and it notes that if Fulk were to die then Humphrey his brother was the heir. The inquiry was held upon August 30th, ten days after the death of John, and at this very time when Fulk was thus declared to be the heir he had himself been dead two days. Apparently also Humphrey was carried off by the sickness as well; because in the inquisition subsequently held upon the estate of Fulk, John, the third brother, is named as the heir. In this inquiry the jury bear out the declarations of that which had testified to the condition of the estates upon the death of the father. On one manor it is stated that the rent of assize, which used to be £20, is now only forty shillings, and the court fees have fallen from forty to five shillings, "because the tenants there are dead." And in another Shropshire hamlet the rent of assize, formerly £4, was now "from the said cause" only eight shillings.[1]

North of a line drawn from the Wash to the Dee, the four counties of Chester, Derby, Nottingham, and Lincoln stretch across England from west and east. A brief record of the pestilence in each of these counties is all that need be here given. In its main lines, and, indeed, almost in its every detail, the story of one county is that of every other, and it is only by chance that the account of definite incidents has been preserved.

The benefices in the county of Chester numbered some 70. In the four months June, July, August, and September, thirty institutions are entered in the registers of Coventry and Lichfield for the archdeaconry of Chester

---

[1] Chancery Inq. p. m., 23 Ed. III, No. 79.

alone. The most numerous are in the month of September.[1] The non-beneficed clergy are, of course, not included in this number; and in the city alone, at the end of Edward the Third's reign, there were at least fifty or sixty of this class. In one parish, for example, that of St. John by the Riverside, there were nine non-beneficed vicars and six chaplains.[2] In August a new prioress was installed at St. Mary's, Chester, and a new prior at Norton.

From the ministers' accounts for the County Palatine of Chester, at this period, some facts can be gleaned as to the general state of desolation to which the great sickness reduced it. Thus, in the manor of Frodsham, the bailiff returns the receipt of only twenty shillings rent for the lands of the manor farm, "received for 66 animals feeding on them." He adds, "and not more this year, because he could get no tenants by reason of the pestilence." Further, he notes the general prices as being low, and names a mill and a bakehouse that cannot be let. As an instance of the decay of rent it is noted that in the town of Netherton, more than a year after the plague had ceased, eleven houses and a great quantity of land, which fell into the hands of the lord in the last year through the pestilence, "remain yet in his hands;" the same also is remarked of other townships, and in one place the miller had been allowed a reduction in his rent on account of the way his business had fallen off since the disease.[3]

In the same way on another manor, that of Bucklow, at Michaelmas 1350, it is stated that 215 acres of arable

---

[1] B. Mus. Harl. MS. 2071, ff. 159-160.
[2] R. O., Clerical Subsidy, 51 Ed. III, $\frac{14}{5}$.
[3] R. O., Q. R. Mins. Accts., Bundle 801, No. 14.

land are lying waste, " for which no tenants can be found
through the pestilence," which had visited the place the
previous year. Further, those who had held a portion of
the manor land during the last year had given their
holdings up at the feast of St. Michael at the beginning
of the account (*i.e.*, 1349). On the same estate the rent
of a garden was put down at only 12*d.*, because there
was no one to buy the produce. One of the largest
receipts was 3*s.* 6*d.*, paid by one Margery del Holes,
" for the turf of divers tenants of the manor who had
died in the time of the pestilence." On the whole of the
estate there is represented to be a decrease of £20 9*s.* 2¾*d.*
in the rent of this year, and a good part of the deficit is
accounted for by the fact that 34 tenants owe various
sums, but cannot pay as they have nothing but their
crops, and that 46 of the tenants had been carried off by
the epidemic.

On the estate, moreover, it is not uninteresting to note
that a portion—no less, indeed, than a third part—of the
rent was remitted at this time. The remission, however,
hardly appears to have been made willingly, but in consequence of a threat on the part of the holders of the
manor lands that unless it was granted they would leave.
This is noted upon the roll: " In money remitted to the
tenants of Rudheath (some four miles from Northwich)
by the Justices of Chester and others, by the advice of
the lord, for the third part of their rent by reason of the
plague which had been raging, because the tenants there
wished to depart and leave the holdings on the lord's
hands, unless they obtained this remission until the
world do come better again, and the holdings possess a
greater value . . . £10 13*s.* 11¾*d.*[1]

[1] R. O., Q. R., Mins. Accts., Bundle 801, No. 4.

Eastward, the adjoining county is Derbyshire. An examination of the institutions for this county has been made by the Rev. Dr. Cox for his work on the *Churches of Derbyshire*. The result of his studies may here be given almost in his words. In May, 1349, there is evidence that the plague had reached Derbyshire. At that period the total number of benefices in the county was 108, and the average number of institutions registered yearly during the century was only seven. In 1346 the actual number had been but four, in 1347 only two, and in 1348 it was eight. In the year of the plague, 1349, no fewer than sixty-three institutions to vacant benefices are registered, and "in the following year (many of the vacant benefices not being filled up till then) they numbered forty-one." In this period seventy-seven of the beneficed clergy died; that is considerably more than half the total number, and twenty-two more resigned their livings.

" Of the three vicars of Derby churches two died, whilst the third resigned. The chantry priest of our Lady at St. Peter's Church also died. The two rectors of Eckington both died, and of the three rectors who then shared the rectory of Derley two died and one resigned. The rectories of Langwith and Mugginton, and the vicarages of Barlborough, Bolsover, Horsley, Longford, Sutton-on-the-Hill, and Willington were twice emptied by the plague, and three successive vicars of Pentrich all fell in the same fatal year. Nor were the regular clergy more fortunate, for the abbots of Beauchief, Dale, and Derley, the prior of Gresley, the prior of the Dominicans at Derby, and the prioress of King's Mead, were all taken."[1]

[1] *Notes on the Churches of Derbyshire.* Introduction, p. viii.

The same author has called attention to some obituary notes in the calendar prefixed to the Chartulary of Derley abbey.

"A glance at this obituary," he says, "is sufficient to draw the attention of the reader to the remarkable number of deaths in the year 1349. . . . Of the character of the plague we can form some idea when we consider the extent of its ravages in a single household—a household the most wealthy of the neighbourhood, and situated in as healthy and uncrowded a spot as any that could be found on all the fair hillsides of Derbyshire. Within three months Sir William de Wakebridge lost his father, his wife, three brothers, two sisters, and a sister-in-law. Sir William, on succeeding to the Wakebridge estate, through this sad list of fatalities, appears to have abandoned the profession of arms and to have devoted a very large share of his wealth to the service of God in his own neighbourhood. The great plague had the effect of thoroughly unstringing the consciences of many of the survivors, and a lamentable outbreak of profligacy was the result."

The accounts for the Lordship of Drakelow, some four miles from Burton-on-Trent, may be taken as a sample of what must have been the case elsewhere. There is noted a loss, to begin with, "upon turf sold from the waste of the manor to tenants who had died in the time of the pestilence." The decrease of rent is very considerable. From "the customs of the manor there is nothing, because all these tenants died in the time of the plague." Then follow the names of seventy-four tenants, from all of whom only 13s. 9¾d. had been received in the period covered by the account, and practically from the entire manor there had been no receipt except for grass. Then, instead of the harvest being gathered in, as before it had been, by means of the services of the tenants, this year paid-labour had to be employed at a cost of £22 18s. 10d. On the receipt side of the account appear the values of the cows, oxen, and horses of tenants who had died, and whose goods and animals passed into the possession of the lord of the manor.[1]

In Nottinghamshire the proportion of deaths among the beneficed clergy is found, as in other cases, to be fully one-half the total number. Out of 126 benefices in the county the incumbent died in sixty-five.[2]

Eastwards, again, the county of Lincoln lies between Nottinghamshire and the sea. At an early period Pope Clement VI granted to the priests and people of the city and diocese of Lincoln great indulgences at the hour of death, " since on their behalf a petition had been made to him which declared that the deadly pestilence had commenced in the said city and diocese."[3] The extent of the county is large, and its endowed livings numerous. In all, not including its forty-nine monasteries, the beneficed clergy of the county numbered some 700, and from this some estimate may be formed of the probable number of clerics who died in Lincolnshire in the year 1349.

The chronicle of Louth Park, a Cistercian abbey in the county, contains a brief note upon the epidemic. " This plague," it says, " laid low equally Jew, Christian, and Saracen; together it carried off confessor and peni-

---

[1] R. O., Q. R. Mins. Accts., Bundle 801, file 3.
[2] Seebohm, *Black Death*, in *Fortnightly Review*, Sept. 1, 1865, p. 150.
[3] Vatican Archives, Reg. Pontif., Rubrice Litterarum Clem. VI.

tent. In many places it did not leave even a fifth part of the people alive. It struck the whole world with terror. Such a plague has not been seen, or heard of, or recorded before this time, for it is thought so great a multitude of people were not overwhelmed by the waters of the deluge, which happened in the day of Noah. In this year many monks of Louth Park died; amongst them was Dom Walter de Luda, the Abbot, on July 12th, who was much persecuted because of the manor of Cockrington, and he was buried before the high altar by the side of Sir Henry Vavasour, Knight. To him Dom Richard de Lincoln succeeded the same day, canonically elected according to the institutes of our Lord and the Order." [1]

From a document relating to the Chapter of Lincoln it would appear that the Courts of Law did not sit every term, during the universal visitation. The dean and chapter complain that, whereas " from time beyond all memory" they had received 6s. 8½d. for some 66 acres of arable and four acres of meadow at Navenby, this year they had not done so. Still they were called upon to pay the King's dues. They appealed; but there was no cause tried at Trinity anno 23° (1349) " because of the absence of our judges assigned to hold the common pleas, by reason of the plague then raging." [2]

The audit of the Escheator's accounts for the county of Lincoln proves that the distress was very real. Saier de Rocheford, who held the office for Rutland and Lincoln in 1351, sought to be relieved of £20 18s. 1d., which he was charged to pay for money he should have received, on the ground that he had got nothing, " because

---

[1] *Chronicon de Parco Lude* (Lincoln Record Society), pp. 38-39.
[2] R. O., Rot. Claus., 24 Ed. III, m. 7.

of the mortality."[1] Three years later, moreover, he again pleads that he is unable to raise more, "because of the deadly pestilence of men and of tenants of the land, who died in the year 1349, and on account of the dearth of tenants" since.

The people, he adds, were so impoverished that they could pay nothing for "Wapentakes."[2]

Archbishop Zouche of York was apparently one of the first of the English prelates to recognise the gravity of the epidemic, which in 1348 was devastating Southern Europe, and ever creeping northwards towards England. Before the end of July, 1348, he wrote to his official at York, ordering prayers. "Since man's life on earth is a warfare," he writes, "those fighting amidst the miseries of this world are troubled by the uncertainty of a future, now propitious, now adverse. For the Lord Almighty sometimes permits those whom he loves to be chastised, since strength, by the infusion of spiritual grace, is made perfect in infirmity. It is known to all what a mortal pestilence and infection of the atmosphere is hanging over various parts of the world, and especially England, in these days. This, indeed, is caused by the sins of men who, made callous by prosperity, neglect to remember the benefits of the Supreme Giver." He goes on to say that it is only by prayer that the scourge can be turned away, and he, therefore, orders that in all parish churches, on every Wednesday and Friday, there shall be processions and litanies, "and in all masses there be said the special prayer for the stay of pestilence and infection of this kind."[3]

---

[1] R. O., L. T. R. Memoranda Roll, 25 Ed. III.

[2] *Ibid.*, 28 Ed. III, Trinity term.

[3] Raine, *Historical Papers from Northern Registers* (Rolls series), p. 395.

Judging from a reply of the Pope to a petition of the Archbishop, it would be necessary to conclude that the plague had reached York as early as February, 1349. It is, however, more probable that the petition was sent in the expectation that the scourge would certainly come sooner or later, and it was best to be prepared. From the dates of the institutions to vacant benefices, more-over, it would seem that the province of York suffered chiefly in the summer and autumn of the year 1349. Pope Clement VI, by letters to Archbishop Zouche, dated from Avignon as early as March 23rd, 1349, be-stowed the faculties and indulgences already mentioned as having been granted to other Bishops. This he did, as the letter says, "in response to a petition declaring that the deadly pestilence has commenced to afflict the city, diocese, and province of York." [1]

The county of York contained at this date some 470 benefices; or, counting monastic houses and hospitals, some 550. It has been pointed out that out of 141 livings in the West Riding, in which the incumbent changed in 1349, ninety-six vacancies are registered as being caused by death, and in the East Riding 65 incumbents died against 61 who apparently survived. [2] In the deanery of Doncaster, [3] out of fifty-six lists of incumbents, printed

[1] Raine, *Historical Papers from Northern Registers* (Rolls series), p. 399.

[2] Seebohm, *Fortnightly Review*, Sept. 1st, 1865.

[3] Joseph Hunter, *Deanery of Doncaster.* The following table will give the institutions in this deanery for some months of 1349:

1349.					
July.	Aug.	Sept.	Oct.	Nov.	Dec.
2	3	7	7	3	4

in the local history, a change is recorded in thirty. It may be concluded with certainty, from an examination of the printed lists of institutions for Yorkshire, that one-half at least of the clergy, generally, were carried off by the sickness. So serious did the mortality among the cathedral officials become that steps were taken to prevent the total cessation of business. In July, 1349, for instance, " it was ordained on account of the existing mortality of the pestilence that one canon, with the auditor and chapter clerk, might, in the absence of his fellows, grant vicarages and transact other matters of business as if the other canons were present, notwithstanding the statutes." [1]

The Archbishop, too, sought and obtained from Pope Clement VI faculties to dispense with the usual ecclesiastical laws as to ordinations taking place only in the Ember weeks. "For fear the Divine worship may be diminished through want of ministers, or the cure and ruling of souls be neglected," writes the Pope, we grant leave to hold four extra ordinations during the year, since you say "that on account of the mortal pestilence, which at present rages in your Province," you fear that "priests may not be sufficient for the care and guidance of souls." [2] With this the Archbishop gives a specimen of the testimonial letters to be granted to such as were ordained under this faculty, reciting that it was given " because of the want of ecclesiastical ministers carried off by the pestilence lately existing in our Province."

There is little doubt that the religious houses of the diocese suffered in a similar way. The abbots of Jervaulx

[1] B. Mus. Harl. MS., 6971, fol. 110b.
[2] Raine, *Historical Papers from Northern Registers*, p. 491.

and Rievaulx, Welbeck and Roche, the priors of Thurgarton, and Shelford, of Monkbretton, of Marton, of Haltemprice and Ferriby, are only some few of the superiors of religious houses who died at this time.

For one of the monasteries of the county, Meaux, there exists a special account in the chronicles of the house. Abbot Hugh, it says, "besides himself had in the convent 42 monks and seven lay brethren; and the said abbot Hugh, after having ruled the monastery nine years, eleven months and eleven days, died in the great plague which was in the year 1349, and 32 monks and lay brethren also died.

"This pestilence so prevailed in our said monastery, as in other places, that in the month of August the abbot himself, 22 monks and six lay brethren died; of these, the abbot and five monks were lying unburied in one day, and the others died, so that when the plague ceased, out of the said 50 monks and lay brethren, only ten monks with no lay brethren were left.

"And from this the rents and possessions of the monastery began to diminish, particularly as a greater part of our tenants in various places died, and the abbot, prior, cellarer, bursar, and other men of years, and officials dying left those, who remained alive after them, unacquainted with the property, possessions, and common goods of the monastery. The abbot died on 12th August, A.D. 1349."[1]

In the Deanery of Holderness, in which Meaux Abbey was situated, there is evidence of great mortality. It is striking to observe how frequently the bailiffs and collectors of royal rents and taxes are changed. It is by no means uncommon to find an account rendered by the

[1] *Chronicon Monasterii de Melsa* (Rolls series), iii, 37.

executors of executors to the original official.[1] This
evidence as to the great extent of the mortality here as
in other places of England, and as to the consequent
distress, is borne out by the *Inquisitiones post mortem*
for the period. In one case, where the owner of the property had died on 28th July, 1349, it is said that 114
acres of pasture were let at 12*d.* a year, "and not more
this year because of the mortality and dearth of men."
At Cliffe, on the same estate, the rents of customary
tenants and tenants at will are stated to have been
usually worth £10 5*s.* a year; but in this special year
they had produced only two shillings.[2]

The chronicler of Meaux has described the disastrous
consequences of the sickness in his own monastery.
That this condition was not soon mended appears certain from the fact that in 1354 it was found necessary to
hand over the abbey, "on account of its miserable condition," to a royal commission.[3]

The account of the King's Escheator in Yorkshire for
the year, from October, 1349, to October, 1350, states
that he could in no way obtain the sum of £4 12*s.* 2*d.*,
"due on certain lands and tenements from which he had
levied and could levy nothing during the said time
because of the mortality amongst men in those parts,
and owing to the dearth of tenants willing to take up
the said land and tenements." Then follows a list of
houses standing vacant.[4]

---

[1] *Cf.* for example Mins. Accts. Yorks., Holderness, 23-25 Ed. III,
Bundle 355.

[2] R. O., Chancery Inq. p. m., 23 Ed. III, 1st series, No. 72. *Cf.*
also No. 88.

[3] Rot. Pat., 28 Ed. III, pars 1, m. 3.

[4] R. O., L. T. R. Memoranda Roll, 25 Ed. III.

As another instance may be quoted a case related in the history of the deanery of Doncaster. "John FitzWilliam, the heir of Sir William, had a short enjoyment of the family estates. He died in the great plague of 1349. I transcribe, to show public feeling at the time, from a chronicle: 'And in these daies was burying withoute sorrowe and wedding without frendschippe and fleying without refute of socoure; for many fled from place to place because of the pestilence; but yet they were effecte and myghte not skape the dethe.'

"In another part of the deanery we find a person willing that his goods shall be divided among such of his children as shall remain alive. In the FitzWilliams MS. is a contemporary memorandum that John FitzWilliam, the father, gave in the time of the pestilence before his death all his goods and chattels, movable and immovable, to Dame Joan, his wife, John, his son, and Alleyn, late parson of Crosby, amounting to the sum of £288 3s. 8½d." [1]

An incident recorded by the same writer will serve to show how uncertain people, at this time, regarded the tenure of life, a feeling hardly to be wondered at when so many were dying all round them. Thomas Allott, of Wombwell, in the deanery of Doncaster, in his will, proved 14th September, 1349, after desiring to be buried at Darfield, says: "Item I leave, etc., to my sons and daughters living after this present mortal pestilence." [2]

These notes upon the evidence for the plague in Yorkshire may be concluded by a brief account of the state of Hull in consequence of the mortality and other causes.

---

[1] Hunter, *Deanery of Doncaster*, i, p. 1. The *Inquisitio post mortem* of John Fitz William is in 1350.

[2] *Ibid.*, ii, p. 125.

In 1353 the King, "considering the waste and destruction which our town of Kingston-on-Hull has suffered, both through the overflow of the waters of the Humber and other causes, and that a great part of the people of the said town have died in the last deadly pestilence which raged in these parts, and that the remnant left in the town are so desolate and poverty-stricken in money," grants them permission to apply the fines ordered to be imposed on labourers and servants demanding higher wages than before, to the payment of the fifteenth they owe the royal exchequer.[1]

Westward of Yorkshire the extensive but then sparsely populated county of Lancashire stretches between it and the Irish sea. Of this county there is practically little to be recorded. The number of benefices which existed in the county was about 65, whilst the number of chaplains and non-beneficed clergy generally must have greatly exceeded that number. In the deanery of Blackburn alone there were at the close of the reign of Edward III at least 55 capellani without benefices.[2] One document, of its kind unique, relating to Lancashire and to this great plague, is preserved in the Record Office. It was long ago referred to by the late Professor Thorold Rogers, and is now printed in the *English Historical Review*. It is a statement of the supposed number of deaths during the incidence of the great pestilence in the deanery of Amounderness. Unfortunately, as perhaps might be expected in such a mortality, when death came so suddenly and men followed one another so rapidly to the grave that vast numbers had to be cast as quickly as possible into the

---

[1] Rot. Pat., 27 Ed. III, pars 1, m. 18.
[2] R. O., Clerical Subsidy, ¼.

same plague pit, the figures are clearly only approximate, being in every instance round numbers. Still, as they were adduced at a legal investigation and before a jury, when the facts of the visitation of Providence must have been fresh in the minds of those who heard the evidence, it is difficult to suppose that they are mere gross exaggerations, and may at least be taken as proof that the mortality in this district of Lancashire was very considerable.

The paper in question is the record of a claim for the profits received, or supposed to have been received, by the dean of Amounderness, acting as procurator for the Archdeacon of Richmond, for proof of wills, administration of intestate estates, and other matters, during the course of the plague of 1349. Ten parishes are named in the claim, including Preston, Lancaster, and Garstang. In those ten parishes it supposes that some 13,180 souls had died between September 8th, 1349, and January 11th, 1350. In both Preston and Lancaster 3,000 are said to have been carried off, and in Garstang, 2,000. Nine benefices are declared to have been vacant, three of them twice, whilst the chapel of St. Mary Magdalene, at Preston, is stated to have been unserved for seven weeks. The Priory of Lytham is also noted as having been rendered vacant by the sickness, whilst 80 people of the village were said to have died at the same time.[1]

From the Patent rolls it would appear that Cartmel Priory, also, about this time lost its superior, as upon September 20th, 1349, the King's licence was granted to the community to proceed to a new election.[2]

---

[1] R. O., Exchequer, Treasury of Receipt $\frac{2}{3}\frac{1}{3}$, in *English Historical Review*, v, p. 525 (July, 1890).

[2] Rot. Pat., 23 Ed. III, pars 3, m. 25.

The counties of Westmoreland, to the north of Lancashire, with Cumberland, still further to the north again, carry the western part of England to the borders of Scotland. In the former there were some 57 beneficed clergy, and in the latter about 85. From these figures the approximate number of beneficed priests who died in the pestilence in the two counties may be guessed at about 72.

The state of this borderland county of Cumberland was, even before the arrival of the plague in the district, deplorable. The Memoranda rolls of the period contain ample evidence that the Scottish invasions had rendered the land desolate and almost uninhabitable. Still the mortality added to the misery of the people. The few *Inquisitiones post mortem* afford little knowledge, beyond the fact that here also the dearth of tenants was severely felt.[1] The audit of the accounts of Richard de Denton, late Vice-Sheriff of the County, is more precise in its information. He declares, in excuse for the smallness of his returns, that "the great part of the manor lands, attached to the King's Castle at Carlisle," has remained until the year of his account, 1354, waste and uncultivated, "by reason of the mortal pestilence lately raging in those parts." Moreover, for one and a half years after the plague had passed, the entire lands remained "uncultivated for lack of labourers and divers tenants. Mills, fishing, pastures, and meadow lands could not be let during that time for want of tenants willing to take the farms of those who died in the said plague."

Richard de Denton then produced a schedule of particulars, which may now be seen stitched on to the roll. This gives the items of decrease in rents; for instance,

[1] *E.g.*, Escheator's Inq. p. m., series i, 430.

there are houses, cottages, and lands to let, which used to bring in £5, and now but £1; " the farm of a garden belonging to the King, called King's Mead, is rented now at 13 shillings and fourpence less than it used to be," and so on. The jury, who were called to consider these statements, concluded that Richard de Denton had proved them, and they enter a verdict to that effect, giving a list of the tenants, and adding " the said Richard says that all the last-mentioned tenants died in the said plague, and all the tenements have stood since empty through a dearth of tenants."[1]

An indication of the same difficulties which beset the people of Cumberland at this time is found in the case of the prior of Hagham, an alien house, to farm which, during the time it was in the King's hands on account of his French war, the prior had been appointed, on condition of his paying the sum of threepence a day in rent to be paid to the Bishop of Carlisle. At this time he could not get even this out of the land, and could not live, by reason of the great dearness of provisions.[2]

The city of Carlisle also in 1352 was relieved of taxation to a great extent, because " it is rendered void, and more than usual is depressed, by the mortal pestilence lately raging in those parts."

The two remaining counties of England, Durham and Northumberland, were no exceptions to the general mortality. In the former there were some 93 beneficed clergy, and in the latter about 72, figures from which, on the usual calculation, may be deduced the numbers of the beneficed clergy who died at this time.

In the Durham Cursitor records of this time a glimpse

---

[1] R. O., L. T. R. Memoranda Roll, 28 Ed. III, m. 9.
[2] R. O., Rot. Claus., 25 Ed. III, m. 16.

is afforded of the state of these northern counties. The Halmote courts were similar to the manor courts, and were held by commissioners appointed under the great seal of the Palatinate of Durham, by the Bishop's certificate, to receive surrender of copyhold lands, to settle fines, contentions, and generally to transact the business of the estates. At one of these Halmote courts, held at Houghton on the 14th of July, 1349, it is recorded: "that there is no one who will pay the fine for any land, which is in the lord's hands through fear of the plague. And so all are in the same way of being proclaimed as defaulters until God shall bring some remedy." At another court "all refused their fines on account of the pestilence." In another, after stating the receipts, the record adds: "And not more on account of the poverty and pestilence;" and one tenant "was unwilling to take the land in any other way, since even if he survived the plague, he absolutely refused to pay a fine." There are many similar instances in the records at this period, and in one case it is noted that "a man and his whole family had fled before the dreaded disease."[1]

In Northumberland the case of the people was so desperate that in 1353 more than £600, which was owing to the King for taxes for five and twenty parishes named, was allowed to stand over for some months since it was hopeless to press for payment.[2]

Of Newcastle the same story is told. "It has been shown us," writes the King, "in a serious complaint by the men of Newcastle-on-Tyne, that, since very many merchants and other rich people who were wont to pay the greater part of the tenth, fifteenth, and other burdens

[1] R. O., Durham Cursitor Records, Bk. ii, ff. 2b, *seqq.*
[2] Rot. Claus., 27 Ed. III, m. 10d.

of the town, have died in the deadly pestilence lately
raging in the town, and since the population remaining
alive, who were wont to live by their trading, are by the
said pestilence and other adverse causes in this time of
war, so impoverished that they hardly possess sufficient
to live upon," [1] they cannot now pay what is due.

At Alnwick, still further north, the plague may be
traced into the spring of the following year, 1350; at
least, the chronicle of the abbey there states that " in the
year 1350 (which for them began March 25th) John,
abbot of Alnwick, died in the common mortality." [2]
Lastly, it is related by two contemporary authors that
the Scotch carried the disease over the borders into
their own country. " The Scots," writes Knighton,
" hearing of the cruel pestilence among the English,
thought this had happened to them as a judgment at
the hand of God. They laughed at their enemies, and
took as an oath the expression, ' Be the foul deth of
Engelond,' and so thinking that the terrible judgment of
God had overwhelmed the English, they assembled in
the forest of Selkirk with the intention of invading
England. The terrible mortality, however, came upon
them, and the Scotch were scattered by the sudden and
cruel death, and there died in a short time about five
thousand." [3]

An account of the visitation given in the continuation
of a chronicle, probably written at the time, and possibly

[1] Rot. Claus, 24 Ed. III, pars 2, m. 5.
[2] B. Mus. Cott. MS., Vitell., E. xiv, fol. 256.
[3] Dr. Creighton (*History of Epidemics in Britain*, p. 119), speaking of Scotland, says : " The winter cold must have held it in check
as regards the rest of Scotland; for it is clear from Fordoun that
its great season in that country generally was the year 1350."

by a monk at Tynemouth, may fitly conclude this review of the course of the epidemic in England; telling, though it does, ever the same story, and reading like an echo of the plaint first raised in Europe on the shores of the Bosphorus and in the islands of the Mediterranean. "In the year of our Lord 1348, and in the month of August," writes this chronicler, "there began the deadly pestilence in England which three years previously had commenced in India, and then had spread through all Asia and Africa, and coming into Europe had depopulated Greece, Italy, Provence, Burgundy, Spain, Aquitaine, Ireland, France, with its subject provinces, and at length England and Wales, so far, at least, as to the general mass of citizens and rustic folk and poor, but not princes and nobles.

"So much so, that very many country towns and quarters of innumerable cities are left altogether without inhabitants. The churches or cemeteries before consecrated did not suffice for the dead; but new places outside the cities and towns were at that time dedicated to that use by people and bishops. And the said mortality was so infectious in England that hardly one remained alive in any house it entered. Hence flight was regarded as the hope of safety by most, although such fugitives, for the most part, did not escape death in the mortality, although they obtained some delay in the sentence. Rectors and priests, and friars also, confessing the sick, by the hearing of the confessions, were so infected by that contagious disease that they died more quickly even than their penitents; and parents in many places refused intercourse with their children, and husband with wife." [1]

[1] B. Mus. Cott. MS., Vitell., A. xx, fol. 56.

CHAPTER IX

THE DESOLATION OF THE COUNTRY

SO far, the course of the epidemic in England has been followed from south to north. It is now necessary to consider some statistics and immediate results of the plague.

The diocese of Salisbury comprised the three counties of Dorset, Wilts, and Berkshire. The total number of appointments made by the Bishop, in his entire diocese, is said to have been 202 in the period from March 25th, 1348, to March 25th, 1349; and 243 during the same time in the year following.[1] Of this total number of 445 it is safe to say that two-thirds were institutions to vacancies due to the plague. Roughly speaking, therefore, in these three counties, comprised in the diocese of Sarum, some 300 beneficed clergy, at least, fell victims to the scourge.

The county of Dorset may first be taken. The list of institutions taken from the Salisbury episcopal registers, given in Hutchins' history of that county, numbers 211. During the incidence of the plague ninety of these record a change of incumbent, so that, roughly, about half the benefices were rendered vacant. In several cases, moreover, during the progress of the epidemic, changes are recorded twice or three times, so that the

[1] B. Mus. Harl. MS. 6979, f. 64.

total number of institutions made to Dorsetshire livings at this time was 110. As regards the non-beneficed clergy, secular and regular, their proportion to those holding benefices will be considered in the concluding chapter. Here it is sufficient to observe that the proportion commonly suggested is far too low.

It is almost by chance that any information is afforded as to the effect of the visitation in the religious houses. All contemporary authorities, both abroad and in England, agree in stating that the disease was always most virulent and spread most rapidly where numbers were gathered together, and that, when once it seized upon any house, it usually claimed many victims. Consequently when it appears that early in November, 1348, the abbot of Abbotsbury died, and that about Christmas Day of that year John de Henton, the abbot of the great monastery of Sherborne, also died, it is more than probable that many of the brethren of those monasteries were also carried off by the scourge.

In the county of Wilts the average number of episcopal institutions, for three years before and three years after the mortality, was only 26. In the year 1348 there are 73 institutions recorded in the registers, and in 1349 no less a number than 103,[1] so that of the 176 vacancies filled in the two years the deaths of only some 52 incumbents were probably due to normal causes, and the rest, or some 125 priests holding benefices in the county, may be said to have died from the plague.

A chance entry upon the Patent roll reveals the state of one monastery in this county. The prior of Ederos, or Ivychurch, a house of Augustinian canons, died on

---

[1] *Institutiones clericorum in Comitatu Wiltoniae*, ed. Sir J. Phillipps.

February 2nd, 1349.[1] On February 25th the King was informed that death had carried off the entire community with one single exception. " Know ye," runs the King's letter, dated March 16th, "that since the Venerable Father Robert, Bishop of Salisbury, cannot hold the usual election of prior in the Monastery of Ederos in his diocese, vacant by the death of the last prior of the same, since all the other canons of the same house, in which hitherto there has been a community of thirteen canons regular, have died, except only one canon, brother James de Grundwell, we appoint him custodian of the possessions, the Bishop testifying that he is a fit and proper person for the office.[2]

The general state of the county of Wilts after the epidemic had passed is well illustrated from some Wiltshire *Inquisitiones post mortem*. Sir Henry Husee, for instance, had died on the 21st of June, 1349. He owned a small property in the county. Some 300 acres of pasture were returned upon oath, by a jury of the neighbourhood, as "of no value because all the tenants are dead."[3] Again John Lestraunge, of Whitchurch, a Shropshire gentleman, had half the manor of Broughton, in the county of Wilts. He died on July the 20th, 1349, and the inquisition was held on August the 30th. At that time it is declared that only seven shillings had been received as rent from a single tenant, "and not more this year, because all the other tenants, as well as the natives, are dead, and their land is all in the hand of the lord."[4]

---

[1] Originalia Roll, 23 Ed. III, m. 37.
[2] Rot. Pat., 23 Ed. III, pars 1, m. 20.
[3] R. O., Chancery Inq. p. m., 23 Ed. III (1st numbers), No. 77.
[4] *Ibid.*, No. 78.

So, too, on the manor of Caleston, belonging to Henry de Wilington, who died on May the 23rd, 1349, it is said that water-mills are destroyed and worthless; of the six native tenants two have died, and their lands are in hand; and of the ten cottars, each of whom paid 12*d.* for his holding, four have been carried off with all their family.[1] In other places of the same county woods are declared to be valueless, " for want of buyers, on account of the pestilence amongst the population; "[2] from tenants who used to pay £4 a year there is now obtained only 6*s.*, because all but three free tenants have been swept away;[3] 140 acres of land and twelve cottages, formerly in the occupation of natives of a manor, are all now in hand, "as all are dead."[4] So, too, at East Grinstead, seven miles from Salisbury, on the death of Mary, wife of Stephen de Tumby, in the August of 1349, it is found that only three tenants are left on the estate, " and not more because John Wadebrok and Walter Wadebrok, Stephen and Thomas and John Kerde, Richard le Frer, Ralph Bodde, and Thomas the Tanner, tenants in bondage," who held certain tenements and lands, are all dead, and their holdings are left in the hands of the lord of the manor. Also, on the same estate, William le Hanaker, John Pompe, Edmund Saleman, John Whermeter, and John Gerde, jun., have also been swept away by the all-prevailing pestilence.

Such examples as these will enable the reader to understand the terrible mortality produced by this visitation, and in some measure to appreciate the social difficulties and changes produced by the sudden re-

---

[1] R. O., Chancery Inq. p. m., 23 Ed. III (1st numbers), No. 74.
[2] *Ibid.*, No. 87.
[3] Escheator's Inq. p. m., Series i, file 95.   [4] *Ibid.*

moval of so large a number of the population from every
part of the country.

To pass on to the neighbouring county of Somerset.
The institutions given in the episcopal registers of the
diocese of Bath and Wells show that the mortality had
already commenced in the county as early as November,
1348. The average number of inductions to livings in
the county in each month of 1348, previous to November,
was less than three; in November it was nine, and in the
following month thirty-two. During the next year,
1349, the total number of clergy instituted to the vacant
livings of the diocese by the Bishop was 232, against an
average in a normal year of 35. For the two years,
1348 and 1349, consequently, out of the 297 benefices
to which institutions were made, some 227 may be
said, with fair certainty, to have been rendered vacant
by the great mortality which then raged in this and
other counties of England.

It must be borne in mind that the death of every
priest implied the deaths of very many of his flock, so
that, if no other information were attainable, some idea
of the extent of the sickness among the laity may be
obtained. It cannot but be believed that the people
generally suffered as greatly as the clergy, and that,
proportionally, as many of them fell victims to the
scourge. If the proportion of priests to lay folk was
then (as some writers have suggested) about one to fifty
—an estimate, however, which would seem to be considerably above the actual relation of laymen to those
in sacred orders at that time—the reader can easily form
some notion of the terrible mortality among the people
of Somersetshire in the first half of 1349.

Some slight information, however, is afforded as to the

actual state of the county in one or two instances. In
each manor throughout the country there was held
periodically what was known as the Court of the manor.
At this assembly the business of the estate, so far as the
tenants were concerned, was transacted before a chosen
and sworn jury. Holders of land under the lord of the
manor came before the court to claim their tenements
and land as the rightful heirs of tenants deceased, to pay
their heriots or fines due to the lord on every entry of a
new holder. At this assembly, too, matters of police, the
infringement of local customs, and often disputes between the tenants themselves, were disposed of by the
officials of the manor. The record of the business of
such courts is known as the Court roll, and these documents give some information about the extent of the
mortality among the manorial tenants. Here, however,
just as in the case of the institutions of clergy, where the
actual incumbent only is registered and no account is
taken of the larger body of non-beneficed clergy, so on
the Court roll only the actual holder of the land is
entered, and no notice is taken of the members of his
family, or of others in the district, such as labourers and
servants, etc., who were not actual tenants of the manor.

Unfortunately the Court rolls for this period are
often, if not generally, found to be missing. They are
either lost, or the disorganised state of the country consequent upon the great mortality did not permit of the
court being held. There are, however, quite sufficient of
these records to afford a tolerably good idea of what
must have happened pretty generally throughout the
country. Dr. Jessopp has been able by the use of the
Norfolk Court rolls to present his readers with a vivid
picture of the havoc made by the plague in East Anglia.

O

As an illustration of the same, some notes from a few Court rolls of West of England manors may here be given.

The records of the royal manor of Gillingham, in the county of Dorset, show that at a court, held on " Wednesday next after the feast of St. Lucy (13 December), 1348," heriots were paid on the deaths of some twenty-eight tenants, and the total receipts on this account, which at ordinary courts amounted to but a few shillings, were £28 15s. 8d. Further, at the same sittings, the bailiff notes that he has in hand the lands and tenements of about thirty tenants, who had apparently left no heir to succeed to their holdings. In numbers of cases it is declared that no heriot has been paid, and this although the receipts on this score at the sitting of the court, and on many subsequent sittings, are unusually large. At another court, held early in the following year (1349) the names of two-and-twenty tenants of the manor are recorded as having died, and two large slips of parchment, belonging to the court held on May 6th, give the lists of dead tenants. Thus in the tything of Gillingham alone forty-five deaths are recorded, and in the neighbouring tything of Bourton seventeen.[1]

The next example may be taken from the rolls of a Wiltshire manor, and ought, perhaps, to have been given in the account of the plague in that county. On June the 11th, 1349, a court was held at Stockton, some seven miles from Warminster, consequently only a short distance from the boundaries of Somerset. The manor, be

[1] Records of the Manor of Gillingham, which I was permitted to examine by the kindness of the present Steward of the Manor, R. Freame, Esq., of Gillingham.

it remarked, was evidently only a very small one. On the parchment record it is stated that since the previous Martinmas (November 11th, 1348) no court had been held, and from the entries upon the roll it appears that out of a small body of tenants on this estate fourteen had died. How many had been carried off in each household does not, of course, appear, but in the majority of instances it looks very much as if the dead tenant had left no heir behind him.[1]

A third instance is taken from the Court roll of the manor of Chedzoy, near Bridgwater. The plague had made its appearance at Bridgwater, as before related, some time previous to November 21st, 1348. It was to be expected, therefore, that the rolls of a manor only three miles off would show some sign of the mortality among the tenants about the same period. As a matter of fact a glance through the parchment record of a court held on St. Katherine's day, November 25th, 1348, shows that it had made its appearance some time between September 29th and November 25th. On this latter day some few of the tenants of the manor are noted as dead, and three or four fairly large holdings have also fallen into the hands of the lord of the manor, no heirs being forthcoming. Amongst others, one William Hammond, who had rented and worked a water-mill, at a place called *le Slap*, had been carried off by the sickness. The house, it is noted, had since, up to the date of the court, stood vacant. The mill wheel no longer spun round at its work, for William Hammond, the miller, had left no one to succeed him in his occupation.

But this was only a beginning. The next court was held on Thursday after the Epiphany, January 8th, 1349.

[1] B. Mus. Add. Roll 24,335.

What a terrible Christmas time it must have been for those Somersetshire villagers on the low-lying ground about Bridgwater, flooded and sodden by the long months of incessant rain! At least twenty more tenants are marked off upon the roll as dead, and as in this case the actual days of their deaths are given, it is clear the plague claimed many victims in this neighbourhood about the close of December, 1348.

Between this and March 23rd, 1349, the sickness was at its worst in this manor of Chedzoy. The record of the proceedings at the court, held on " Monday after the feast of St. Benedict," 1349, occupies two long skins of parchment closely written on both sides. Some 50 or 60 fines are paid by new tenants on their taking possession of the lands and houses, which had belonged to others now dead and gone. Again, who can tell how many had perished in each house? One thing is absolutely clear. In this single Somerset village many homes had been left vacant without a solitary inhabitant; many were taken over by new tenants not connected with the old occupier; and in more than one instance people came forward to act as guardians to young children who had apparently been left alone in the world by the death of every near relative. Take an instance. At this court one John Cran, who, by the way, took up the house and lands formerly held by his father, who is said to have died, also agreed with the officer of the court to take charge of William, the son of Nicholas atte Slope, for the said Nicholas, and apparently every other near relative of the boy William had perished in the sickness.

In this same court of March 23rd also several law cases are disposed of, for they had been settled by the death of one or other or both of the parties. Thus, in

January, 1349, a claim had been laid, at the sitting of
the court, against one John Lager, for the return of some
cattle by three tenants, William, John, and Roger Riche-
man. At the March sitting of the court in due course
the case was called on. No plaintiffs, however, appeared,
and inquiry elicited the fact that all three had died in
the great pestilence.

The actual document which contains these particulars
has, moreover, a tale of its own to tell. The long entries
on these two skins of parchment are not all in the same
hand. Before the record of the heavy business done at
this court had been all transcribed, the clerk was changed.
The hand which had so long kept the rolls of these
Manor Courts ceases to write. What happened to him?
Did he too die? Of course nothing can be known for
certain, but it is not difficult to conjecture why another
at this very time takes up the writing of the Chedzoy
manor records.[1]

Another glimpse of the desolate state to which the
country was generally reduced by this disastrous sickness is afforded by the case of Hinton and Witham, the
two Somerset Carthusian houses. The King had endeavoured by every means in his power to restrain the
tenants, who survived the plague, from leaving their old
holdings and seeking for others where they could better
themselves. Not only were fines ordered to be inflicted
upon such labourers and tenants as endeavoured to take
advantage of the market rise in wages, but under similar penalties landowners were prohibited from giving
employment to them. That such a law must have

[1] B. Mus. Add. Rolls 15,961-6. Perhaps the Richard Hammond
capellanus who had a mill and six acres, and who is reported as
among the dead, may have been the scribe.

proved hard in the case of those owning manors, in which some or all of the tenants and labourers had died, is obvious. It was this hardship which some years after the epidemic, in 1354, made the Carthusians of Witham plead for some mitigation of the royal decree. " Our beloved in Christ, the prior and brethren of the Carthusian Order at Witham, in the county of Somerset," runs the King's reply, "have petitioned us that since their said house and all their lands and tenements thereto belonging are within a close in the forest of Selwood, placed far from every town, and they possess no domain beyond the said close, they have nothing to support the prior and his brethren," (and this) " both because almost all their servants and retainers died in the last pestilence, and because by reason of a command lately made by us and our Parliament, in which *inter alia* it is ordered that servants should not leave their villages and parishes in which they dwelt, as long as they could be hired there, they have been brought to great need on account of the want of servants and labourers. Further, that a large part of their lands (for this same reason) remain waste and untilled, and the corn in the rest of their estate, which had been sown at the time of harvest, had miserably rotted as it could not be gathered for lack of reapers. By this they have been brought into great and manifest poverty." Looking at the circumstances, therefore, the King permits them for the future to engage servants and workmen on reasonable wages above the legal sum, provided that their time of service elsewhere had expired.[1]

The second instance is recorded in the following year, 1355, and has reference to difficulties springing from the

---

[1] Rot. Pat., 28 Ed. III, pars 1, m. 20 (16th January, 1354).

same regulations as to the employment of labourers: "The prior and brethren of the Carthusians of Hinton, in the county of Somerset, have petitioned us," says the King, "that seeing that they have no support except by the tillage of their lands, and that the greatest part of their estates, for want of workmen and servants from the time of the last pestilence, have been unused and still remain uncultivated, and that they cannot get any labourer to work their lands," (and further) "that as many people and tenants were wont to weave the woollen cloth for the clothes of the brethren from their wool, and do other various services for them, now through fear of our orders as to servants that they may not receive greater salaries and stipends from the said brethren, do not dare to serve them as before, and so leave their dwelling, so that the brethren cannot get cloth to clothe themselves properly," they beg that these orders may be relaxed in their regard. To which petition the King assented, allowing the Carthusians of Hinton to pay the wages they had been used to do.[1]

The diocese of Exeter, comprising the two counties of Devon and Cornwall, was stricken by the disease apparently about the same time as the county of Somerset. The institutions made by the Bishop of the diocese, in January, 1349, number some 30, which shows that death had already been busy among the clergy. The average number of livings annually rendered vacant in the two counties during the eight years previous to 1348 was only 6. In the year 1349 the vacancies were 382, and the number of appointments to vacant livings, in each of the five months from March to July, was actually larger than the previous yearly average. It would appear,

[1] Rot. Pat., 29 Ed. III, pars 2, m. 4 (October 5th, 1355).

therefore, that in 1349 some 346 vacancies may reason-
ably be ascribed to the prevailing sickness.

In looking over the lists of institutions it is evident
that the effect of sickness was felt for some years. It is
not until 1353 that the normal average is again reached.
The year following the epidemic the number of vacancies
filled up was 80, and even in 1351 it still remained at the
high figure of 57. It is curious to note in these years
that numerous benefices lapsed to the Bishop. These
must have been vacant six months, at least, before the
dates when they were filled by Bishop Grandisson.
Sometimes, no doubt, patrons were dead, leaving no
heirs behind them. Sometimes, in all probability, the
patron could find no one to fill the cure. Further, the
number of resignations of benefices during this period
would appear to point to the fact that many livings were
now found to be too miserably poor to afford a bare
maintenance.

After the sickness was over here, as in other parts of
England, the desolation and distress is evidenced by
chance references in the inquisitions. Thus at Lylford,
a manor on Dartmoor, the King's escheator returns the
value of a mill at fifteen shillings, in place of the previous
value of double that amount, because " most of the tenants, who used to grind their corn at it, have died n the
plague." It is the same at other places in the county,
and in one case 30 holdings are named as having fallen
into the hands of the lord of the manor.[1]

A bundle of accounts for the Duchy of Lancaster
gives a good idea of the effect of the pestilence in Cornwall. The roll is for the year from Michaelmas 1350,
and includes the accounts of several manors i the

[1] R. O., Escheator's Accts., $\frac{838}{40}$.

Deanery of Trigg, such as Helston, Tintagel, and others, in the district about the river Camel. In one it is noted that "this year there are no buyers;" in another only two youths pay poll tax, two more have not paid, as they have been put in charge of some land, "and the rest have died in the pestilence." In the same place pasture, which usually let for 3*s.* 4*d.*, now, "because of the pestilence," fetched only 20*d.*; the holdings of five tenants are named as in hand, as well as nine other tenements and 214 acres of land. Again, in another place the rent has diminished by £7 14*s.*, because 14 holdings and 102 acres are in hand, together with two fulling mills; on the other hand credit is given for 8*s.* 11*d.*, the value of the goods and chattels of the natives of the manor who have died. And so the roll proceeds through the accounts of some twelve or fourteen manors, and everywhere the same story of desolation appears. Besides numerous holdings and hundreds of acres, represented as in hand and producing nothing, entire hamlets are named as having been depopulated. The decay in rent of one manor alone is set down at £30 6*s.* 1¾*d.*

Attached to the account of Helston, in Trigg, is a skin giving a list of goods and effects of different tenants named which the lord Prince "occupied." There are 57 items in this list, which includes goods of all sorts, from an article of female dress and a golden buckle to ploughs and copper dishes; and the total value of the goods which thus fell into the hands of the Black Prince, presumably by the death of his tenants without heirs, is £16 18*s.* 8*d.*

At Tintagel it is noted that the "fifty shillings previously paid each year as stipend to the chaplain who celebrated in the chapel, was not paid this year, because no one would stay to minister there for the said stipend."[1]

On the 29th May, 1350, the Black Prince, in view of the great distress throughout the district, authorised his officials to remit one-fourth part of the rents of the tenants who were left, "for fear they should through poverty depart from their holdings."[2] But John Tremayn, the receiver of the revenues of the Prince in Cornwall, states that even in the years 1352 and 1353, so far from the estates there showing any recovery, they were in a more deplorable state still. "For the said two years," he relates, "he has not been able to let (the lands), nor to raise or obtain anything from the said lands and tenements, because the said tenements for the most part have remained unoccupied, and the lands lain waste for want of tenants (in the place of those) who died in the mortal pestilence lately raging in the said county."[3]

The loss of the episcopal registers of London for this period makes it impossible to form any certain estimate of the deaths in the ranks of the clergy of the capital during the progress of the epidemic. London contained within its walls, at that time, some 140 parish churches, exclusive of the large number of religious houses grouped together in its precincts. It is not unreasonable to suppose that the mortality here was greater than elsewhere. The population was closely packed in narrow streets, the religious houses were exceptionally numerous, and many of them, from their very situation, could have had but very little space. It has already been seen how fatal was the entry of the plague into any house,

[1] R. O., Duchy of Lancaster Mins. Accts., No. 817.
[2] Ibid.
[3] R. O., L. T. R. Memoranda Roll, 28 Ed. III (Trinity Term).

and consequently the proportion of deaths among the regulars in London was doubtless greater than elsewhere, whilst other causes must have also contributed to raise the roll of death among the seculars.[1]

The diocese of London included, with Middlesex, the county of Essex and a portion of Hertfordshire. The benefices of the county of Essex were in number some 265, and, like the actual institutions of the Middlesex clergy for this period, those made in the county of Essex are unknown. By July, 1349, the consequences of the scourge clearly appear in the *Inquisitiones post mortem* for this county. In one manor ten acres of meadow, which had formerly been let for twenty shillings, this year produced only half that amount, "because of the common pestilence." For the same reason the arable land had fallen in value, and a water-mill was idle, as there was no miller. In another place a holding of 140 acres of arable land was lying waste. "It cannot be let at all," says the Inquisition, "but if it could be let, it would be worth but eleven shillings and sixpence" only, in place of twenty-three shillings. Here, too, pasture had fallen fifty per cent. in value, and the wood that had been cut could not be sold. So, too, at a manor near Maldon, in this county, prices had fallen to half the previous value, and here the additional information is given that, out of eleven native tenants of the manor eight have died, and their tenements and land were in hand. It is the same in every

---

[1] Judging by the ordination lists in the London Registers, the proportion of non-beneficed clergy was very large. In the twelve years, from 1362 to 1374, Bishop Sudbury ordained to the priesthood 456 regulars and 809 non-beneficed clergy, against 237 beneficed priests. According to this proportion, the non-beneficed would be six times as numerous as the beneficed.

instance; rents had dropped, owing to the catastrophe, to one-half. Arable, meadow, and pasture could be obtained this year in Essex anywhere at such a reduction. Other estate receipts had fallen equally. In one place court fees were three in place of the usual six shillings, and the manor dove-house brought in one instead of two shillings. Water-mills were at a greater discount even than this. One, at a place called Longford, was valued at twenty shillings in place of sixty shillings, and even at this reduction there is considerable doubt expressed whether it will let at all.

Lastly, to take one more example in the county of Essex. An inquiry was made as to the lands held by the abbot of Colchester, who died on August the 24th, 1349. In this it appears that, in the manors of East and West Denny, 320 acres of arable land had fallen in yearly value from four to two pence an acre; 14 acres of meadow from 18*d.* to 8*d.*; the woods are valueless, "because there are no buyers;" and out of six native tenants two are dead. In another place four out of six have been carried off; in another, only two are left out of seven. The rent of assize, it is declared, is only £4, "and no more, because most of the land is in hand." [1]

No account has been preserved of the ravages of the pestilence at the abbey of Colchester; but the death of the abbot at this time makes it not unlikely that the disease was as disastrous here as in other monasteries of which there is preserved some record. It is known that the town suffered considerably. "One of the most striking effects was," writes one author, "that wills to the

[1] R. O., Escheator's Inq. p. m., Series i, file 165. Also *ibid.*, file 166. Esch. Accts., $\frac{838}{23}$; $\frac{848}{31}$. *Cf.* also, Exch. Q. R. Mins. Accts., Bundle 869, No. 9.

unusual number of 111 were enrolled at Colchester, which at that time had the privilege of their probate and enrolment." [1]

Talkeley, an alien priory in Essex, was reduced to complete destitution. It was a cell of St. Valery's Abbey, in Picardy, and when seized into the King's hands on account of the war with France, the prior was allowed to hold the lands on condition of his paying £126 a year into the royal purse. Two years after the plague had visited the county this payment had fallen into arrears, "by reason of the pestilence lately raging, from which time the said land remained uncultivated, and the holdings, from which the revenues of the priory were derived, remained unoccupied after the death of the tenants. So terribly is it impoverished that it has nothing upon which to live, and on account of the arrears no one is willing to rent the lands and tenements of the priory." In the end the King was compelled to forgive the arrears of rent. [2]

In the county of Hertfordshire 34 benefices were in the diocese of London, whilst 22 more were under the jurisdiction of no Bishop, but formed a peculiar of the abbey of St. Alban's. In both of these consequently the actual institutions made in the year of the great plague are unknown. For the portion within the diocese of Lincoln 27 institutions were made in the summer of 1349; so that probably at least 50 Hertfordshire clergy died at this time.

The values of land and produce fell, as in other places. In one instance, given in an *Inquisitio post mortem* into the estate of Thomas Fitz-Eustace, the lands and tene-

---

[1] T. Cromwell, *History of Colchester*, i, p. 75.
[2] R. O., Originalia Roll, 25 Ed. III, m. 10.

ments, formerly valued at 67 shillings, were on the 3rd of August this year, 1349, estimated to produce only 13 shillings, and this only "if the pasture can be let."[1] In the same way the Benedictine convent of Cheshunt, in the county, is declared shortly afterwards "to be oppressed with such poverty in these days that the community have not wherewith to live."[2]

Again the destitution and poverty produced by the pestilence is evidenced in the case of some lands in the county, given by Sir Thomas Chedworth to Anglesey priory in Cambridgeshire. It had been agreed, shortly before the scourge had fallen upon England, that the monastery should for this benefaction endow a chantry of two secular priests. In 1351, however, the state of Anglesey priory, consequent on the fall in rents, made this impossible, and the obligation was, through the Bishop, readjusted, and the new document recites: "Carefully considering the great and ruinous miseries which have occurred on account of the vast mortality of men in these days, to wit, that lands lie uncultivated in innumerable places, not a few tenements daily decay and are pulled down, rents and services cannot be levied, nor the advantage thereof, generally had, can be received, but a much smaller profit is obliged to be taken than heretofore," the community shall now be bound to find one priest only, whose stipend shall be five marks yearly instead of six as appointed, the value of the property being thus estimated at less than half what it had been before.[3]

---

[1] Escheator's Inq. p. m., Series i, file 165.

[2] Rot. Pat., 25 Ed. III, pars 3, m. 4.

[3] B. Mus. Cole MS., 5824, fol. 86. *Cf.* Dr. Cunningham, *Growth of English Industry and Commerce*, p. 305.

In Buckinghamshire there were at the time between 180 and 200 benefices, in the county of Bedford some 120 and in Berkshire 162. From these a calculation of the probable number of incumbents carried off in 1349 by the sickness may be made.

As some indication of the state to which these counties were reduced by the scourge, a petition of the sheriff of Bedfordshire and Buckinghamshire, made to the King in 1353, may be here mentioned. He declared that it was impossible then to pay into the Exchequer the old sums for the farming of the hundreds, which had been usual "before the late pestilence." Coming before the King in February, 1353, he not only urged his petition, but claimed to have £66 returned to him, which he had paid over and above his receipts. For the years 1351 and 1352 he had paid £132 for these rents, as had been usual since 1342; but he claimed that "from the time of the pestilence the bailiffs of the hundreds had been unwilling to take them on such terms." An inquiry by a jury was held in both counties, and it was declared "that since 1351 the bailiffs of the hundreds had been able to obtain nothing for certain—except what they could get by extortion—from the county. Further, that the inhabitants of the said county were now so diminished and impoverished that the bailiffs were able to get nothing for the farms in that year, 1351." In the same way also John Chastiloun, the sheriff, had received nothing whatever for his office. In the end the sum claimed was allowed.[1]

In the Canterbury portion of the county of Kent there were some 280 benefices, which number may form the

[1] R. O., L. T. R. Memoranda Roll, 27 Ed. III (Hilary term), m. 7.

basis for a calculation of the death roll. The condition
to which this portion of England was reduced may be
estimated from one or two examples. In 1352 the
prioress and nuns of the house of St. James' outside
Canterbury were allowed to be free from the tax of a
fifteenth granted to the King, because they were reduced to such destitution that they had nothing beyond
what was necessary to support them.[1] Even the Cathedral priory of Christchurch itself had to plead poverty.
About 1350 the monks addressed petitions to the Bishop
of Rochester asking him to give them the church of
Westerham "to help them to maintain their traditional
hospitality." They say that "by the great pestilence
affecting man and beast," they are unable to do this, and
as arguments to induce the Bishop to allow this impro-
priation, they state that they have lost 257 oxen, 511
cows, and 4,585 sheep, worth together £792 12s. 6d.
Further they state that "1,212 acres of land, formerly
profitable, are inundated by the sea," apparently from
want of labourers to maintain the sea walls.[2]

The neighbouring county of Sussex, at the time of the
appearance of the disease, counted some 320 benefices.
From the Patent rolls it appears that in 1349 the King
presented to as many as 26 livings in the county;
amongst these no less than five were at Hastings, at All
Saints', St. Clement's, St. Leonards, and two at the Free
Chapel.[3]

In Hampshire, including the Isle of Wight, the aver-

---

[1] Rot. Claus., 26 Ed. III, m. 7.

[2] *Hist. MSS. Comm., Fifth Report*, p. 444. These lands were
apparently the Appledore Marshes, which subsequently cost the
monastery £350 to reclaim.

[3] *Sussex Archæological Society*, vol. xxi, pp. 44, *seqq.*

age annual number of appointments to benefices for three years previous to the pestilence was 21; in 1349 no fewer than 228 institutions are registered, so that it may fairly be said that over 200 beneficed clergy were carried off by the sickness.

In the county of Surrey the total number of institutions in 1349 was as high as 92, against a previous average of a little over nine yearly, so that here, as in Hants, the number of vacancies of livings was this year increased tenfold. It may fairly be argued that of the number 92, some 80, at least, of the vacancies were caused by the epidemic. Several examples have already been given of the havoc wrought by the epidemic in religious houses in which it had effected an entrance. Where the head of a community was carried off, it is practically certain many of the members also would have perished, and it can be doubted by no one who examines the facts that the pestilence was not only terrible at the time, but had a lasting and permanent effect upon the state of the monastic houses. This point may be illustrated by some of the monasteries of the diocese of Winchester.

In the city itself the prior of St. Swithun's and the abbess of St. Mary's Benedictine convent both died, and there is evidence that a large proportion of both these communities must have perished at the same time, as well as many at the abbey of Hyde. To take the cathedral priory of St. Swithun's first. In 1325, four and twenty years before the great mortality, the monks in the house were 64 in number.[1] Of these the 12 juniors on the list had not at that time received the subdiaconate. The 34th in order in the community had been ordained

[1] Reg. Pontissera, fol. 143.

P

deacon on December 19th, 1310, and all the thirty below him were his juniors. It is fair to consider that about 60 was the normal number previous to the year 1349.[1] After that date they were reduced to a number which varied between 35 and 40. In 1387 William of Wykeham exhorted the community to use every effort to get up their strength to the original 60 members;[2] but notwithstanding all their endeavours they were on Wykeham's death, in A.D. 1404, only 42. At Bishop Wayneflete's election, in 1447, there were only 39 monks; three years later only 35; and in A.D. 1487 their number had fallen to 30, at which figure it remained till the final dissolution of the house in the reign of Henry VIII.[3]

[1] This may be considered the number in the previous century from the *Annales de Wintonia.*

[2] Reg. Wykeham, ii, fol. 226.

[3] The following table gives the number of monks belonging to Winchester Cathedral Priory at the annexed dates:

Date.	Occasion.	Number.
A.D. 1260	Episcopal Election	62
A.D. 1325	Living in the Priory on October 9th	64
A.D. 1404	Episcopal Election	42
A.D. 1416-17	On Chamberlain's Rolls	39 and 2 juniors at schools
A.D. 1422-3	On Chamberlain's Rolls	29 to 32 and 8 juniors at schools.
A.D. 1427-8	On Chamberlain's Rolls . .	35 to 36
A.D. 1447	Episcopal Election on the death of Cardinal Beaufort	39
A.D. 1450	Election of Prior .	35
A.D. 1468	Episcopal Election .	30 and 2 or 3 at Oxford
A.D. 1498	Election of Prior	31
A.D. 1524	Election of Prior	30 (none below subdeacons named)

The neighbouring abbey of Hyde, a house of considerable importance, with a community of probably
between thirty and forty monks, a century later had
fallen to only twenty. In 1488 it had risen to twenty-
four, and eight of these had joined within the previous
three years. At the beginning of the sixteenth century,
in 1509, the community again consisted of twenty; but
on the eve of the final destruction of the abbey there are
some signs of a recovery, the house then consisting of
twenty-six members, four of whom were novices. So
impoverished was the house by the consequences of the
great mortality that in 1352 the community were forced
in order "to avoid," as they say, "the final destruction
of their house," and "on account of their pitiful poverty
and want, to relieve their absolute necessity," to surrender their possessions into the hands of Bishop
Edyndon.[1]

Financial difficulties also overwhelmed and nearly
brought to ruin the Benedictine Convent of St. Mary's,
which was reduced to about one half their former number. To the same generous benefactor, Bishop Edyndon,
they were indebted for their escape from extinction. In
fact, it would appear that at this time many, if not most,
of the religious houses of the diocese were protected and
supported by the liberality of the Bishop and his relatives, whom he interested in the work of preserving
from threatened destruction these monastic establishments. In the document by which the nuns of St.
Mary's acknowledge Bishop Edyndon as their second
founder, they say that "he counted it a pious and
pleasing thing mercifully to come to their assistance
when overwhelmed by poverty, and when, in these days,

[1] Harl. MS., 1761, f. 20.

evil doing was on the increase and the world was growing worse, they were brought to the necessity of secret begging. It was at such a time that the same father, with the eye of compassion, seeing that from the beginning our monastery was slenderly provided with lands and possessions, and that now we and our house, by the barrenness of our land, by the destruction of our woods, and by the diminution or taking away from the monastery of due and appointed rents, because of the dearth of tenants carried off by the unheard-of and unwonted pestilence," came to our assistance to avert our entire undoing.[1]

Six months later the nuns of Romsey, in almost the same words, acknowledged their indebtedness to the Bishop.[2] Here the results of the pestilence upon the convent, as regards numbers, are even more remarkable than in the instances already given. At the election of an abbess in A.D. 1333 there were present to record their votes 90 nuns. Early in May, 1349—that is only 16 years later—the abbess died, for the royal assent was given to the election of her successor, Joan Gerneys, on May 7th of that year.[3] What happened to the community can be gathered by the fact that in 1478 their number is found reduced to 18, and they never rose above 25 until their final suppression.

The various bodies of friars must have suffered quite as severely as the rest of the clergy. It is, however, very difficult to obtain any definite information about these mendicant orders; but some slight indication of the dearth of members they must have experienced at this

[1] Rot. Claus., 28 Ed. III, m. 3d (dated February 6th, 1353).

[2] Ibid., m. 6 (July 8th).

[3] Rot. Pat., 23 Ed. III, pars 1ª, m. 13.

period in common with all other bodies in England, ecclesiastical and lay, is to be found in the episcopal registers of the period. In the diocese of Winchester, for
example, the Augustinians had only one convent, at
Winchester. From September, 1346, to June, 1348, they
presented four subjects for ordination to the priesthood; from that time till Bishop Edyndon's death, in
October, 1366, only two more were ordained, both on
22nd December, 1358. The Friars Minor had two
houses, one at Winchester, the other at Southampton;
for these, in 1347 and 1348, three priests were ordained.
From that time till the 21st of December, 1359, no more
received orders. Then two were made priests; but no
further ordinations are recorded until after Bishop Edyndon's death. The same extraordinary want of subjects
appears in the case of the Carmelites. With them, between 1346 and 1348, eleven subjects received the priesthood. The next Carmelite ordained was in December,
1357, and only three in all were made priests between
the great plague and the close of the year 1366. The
Dominicans also had only one priest ordained in ten
years, that is in the period from March, 1349, to December, 1359.

Owing to the mortality having swept away so many
of their tenants, and other consequences traceable to the
mortality, the priory of St. Swithun's became heavily
involved in debt. On the 31st of December, 1352,
Bishop Edyndon determined to make a careful inquiry
into the state of his cathedral monastery, and wrote to
that effect to the prior and convent. He says in his letter that he has heard how the temporalities have suffered
severely "in these days, both by the deaths of tenants of
the church, from which there has come a grave diminu-

tion of rent and services, and from various other causes unknown, and that it is burdened with excessive debts." As he himself was occupied in the King's service, he proposes to send some officers to inquire into these matters, and begs the monks to assist them in every way. He further says that it is reported to him "that in this our church the former fervour of devotion in the divine service and regular observance has grown lukewarm;" that both the monastery and out-buildings are falling to ruins; that "guests are not received there so honourably as before; on which account we wonder not a little," he continues, "and are troubled the more because so far you have not informed us" of these things. He appoints January 21st, 1353, for the beginning of the inquiry, and in a second document names three priests, including a canon of the diocese of Sarum and the rector of Froyle, in Hampshire, to hold it.[1]

Shortly after this, on January 14th, 1353, Bishop Edyndon ordered a similar inquiry to be made as to the state of Christchurch priory, which was also heavily in debt.[2] That the house had been seriously diminished in members seems more than probable in view of the fact that from the date of the plague till the beginning of 1366 no subject of the house was ordained priest.

The hospital of Sandown, in Surrey, was left, as before said, without a single inmate. On June 1st, 1349, the Bishop, in giving it into the care of a priest named William de Coleton, says: "Since all and everyone of the brethren of the Hospital of the blessed Mary Magdalen of Sandown, in our diocese, to whom on a vacancy of the office of prior, or guardian, the election belonged, are dead in the mortality of men raging in the kingdom

---

[1] Reg. Edyndon, ii, ff. 27b, 28.   [2] *Ibid.*, fol. 28.

of England, none of the brethren being left, the said
hospital is destitute both of head and members."[1]

The same state of financial ruin is known to have
existed in the case of Shireborne priory. On 8th June,
1350, Bishop Edyndon wrote to the abbot and convent
of St. Vigor of Cérisy saying that Shireborne, which was
said to be a dependency of the abbey, was fallen into
great poverty. "The oblations of sacrifices had ceased,
and from very hunger the devotion of priests was grown
tepid; the buildings were falling to ruins, and its fruitful
fields, now that the labourers were carried off, were
barren." The priory could not hope, he considered, to
recover "in their days," and so, with the consent of the
patron, he requested the abbot to recall four of the monks
to the abbey, the priory then containing the superior and
seven religious. The same day a letter was sent to the
prior of Shireborne directing that this should be at once
carried out.[2]

One fact will be sufficient to show the state to which
the diocese was reduced after the plague had passed.
On the 9th of April, 1350, the Bishop issued a general
admonition to his clergy as to residence on their cures.
It had been reported to him, he says, that some priests,
to whom the cure of souls had been committed, "neglect-
ing, with danger to many souls," this charge, "have most
shamefully absented themselves from their churches," so
that "even the divine sacrifices," for which these churches
had been built and adorned, "had been left off." The
sacred buildings were, he says, "left to birds and beasts,"
and they neither kept the church in repair nor repaired
what was falling to ruins, "on which account the general
state of the churches is one of ruin." He consequently

<hr />

[1] Reg. Edyndon, i, fol. 49b.   [2] *Ibid.*, ii, fol. 23b.

orders all priests to return to their cures within a month,
or to get proper and fitting substitutes.[1]

In the June of the same year (1350) a special moni-
tion was issued to William Elyot, rector of a church near
Basingstoke, to return at once to his living, as the church
had been left without service. A month later, on the
10th of July, 1350, the Bishop published a joint letter of
the Archbishop and Bishops ordering priests to serve
the churches at the previous stipends, and he adds that
every parish church must be contented with one chaplain
only, "until those parish and prebendal churches and
chapels which are now, or may hereafter be, unserved, be
properly supplied with chaplains.[2]

There are many indications of the misery and suffering to which the people generally were reduced in these
parts. Thus, for example, the King, whose compassion
and tenderness, by the way, are very rarely manifested,
remits the tax of the fifteenth due to him in the case of
his tenants in the Isle of Wight. This he does, "taking
into account the divers burdens which" these tenants
have borne, "for the men and tenants of our manors now
dead and whose lands and tenements by their deaths
have come into our hands."[3] A glance at the institutions
to benefices in the island will show that at one time
or another during the prevalence of the plague nearly
every living became vacant, and some more than once.

The town of Portsmouth, also, was forced to plead
poverty, and ask the remission of a tax of £12 12s. 2d.,
because "by the attacks of our enemies the French,
fires, and other adverse chances the inhabitants were

[1] Reg. Edyndon, ii, fol. 22b.
[2] *Ibid.*, ii, fol. 23b.
[3] Rot. Claus., 27 Ed. III, m. 19.

very much depressed."[1] That the "other adverse
chances" refers to the desolation caused by the pestilence
appears from another grant, of relief for eight years,
made to the town the previous year, because it was so
impoverished "both by the pestilence and by the burning and destruction of the place by our enemies."[2]

The neighbouring island of Hayling was in even a
worse plight after the pestilence. "The inhabitants of
Stoke, Eaststoke, Northwood, Southwood, Mengham,
Weston, and Hayling, in the island of Hayling, have
shown to us," says the King, in 1352, "that they are
greatly impoverished by expenses and burdens for the
defence of the said island against the attacks of the
French, and by the great wasting of their lands by in-
road of the sea, as well as by the abandonment of the
island by some who were wont to bear the burdens of
the said island. Those consequently who are left would
have to pay more than double the usual tax were it
now levied. Moreover since the greatest part of the said
population died whilst the plague was raging, now,
through the dearth of servants and labourers, the inhabitants are oppressed and daily are falling most
miserably into greater poverty. Taking into account all
this, the King orders the collector of taxes for Southampton not to require the old amount, but to be content
with only £6 15s. 7¼d."[3] Three years later Hayling
priory, which as one of the alien houses then in the
King's hands had been paying a large rent into the
royal exchequer in place of sending it over to their
foreign mother house, was relieved by the King of the

---

[1] Rot. Claus., 26 Ed. III, m. 12.
[2] *Ibid.*, 25 Ed. III, m. 21.
[3] Originalia Roll, 29 Ed. III, m. 8.

payment of £57, as it was "much oppressed in these days."[1]

Even in Winchester difficulties as to taxation, at this time, led to many people leaving the city. Citizens, as the document relating to it declares, who have long lived there, "because of the taxation and other burdens now pressing on them, are leaving the said city with the property they have made in the place, so as not to contribute to the said taxes. And they, betaking themselves to other localities in the county, are leaving the said city desolate and without inhabitants, to our (*i.e.*, the King's) great hurt."[2]

An *Inquisitio post mortem* for a Hampshire manor, taken in 1350, shows the fall in prices of lands and produce after the mortality. Eighty acres of arable land, which in normal times had been let for two marks (13s. 4d.), now produced only 6s. 8d., or just one-half, being at the rent of 1d. per acre in place of two pence. The same fall is to be seen in the rent of meadow land, which let now at 6d. instead of a shilling, and in the value of woods, 20 acres fetching only 20d., in the place of double that amount, which it used to produce.[3]

In Surrey it is the same story. In the inquiry made as to the lands of William de Hastings, on the 12th March, 1349, it is declared that the tenements let on the manor produce only thirty-six shillings because all the tenants but ten are dead, "and the other houses stand and remain empty for want of tenants, and so are of no value this year." In another case a water-mill is held by

---

[1] Rot. Claus., 26 Ed. III, m. 19. *Cf.* Rot. Pat., 26 Ed. III, pars 1, m. 6.

[2] Rot. Pat., 26 Ed. III, pars 1ª, m. 28d.

[3] Escheator's Inq. p. m., series i, file 90.

the jury to be worthless because "all the tenants who used it were dead." It had remained empty and no one could be found to rent it. Of the land, 300 acres cannot be let. The court of the manor produced nothing, because all are dead, and there are no receipts from the free tenants, which used to amount to £6 a year, "because almost all the tenants on the said manor are dead, and their tenements remain empty for want of some to rent them."[1]

In the absence of any definite information about the institutions of clergy in the county of Gloucester, it may be roughly estimated, from the number of benefices, that between 160 and 170 beneficed clergy in this district perished in the epidemic. Like other religious houses, the abbey of Winchcombe was impoverished by the consequences of the great mortality, and some years after it was unable to support its community and meet its liabilities. "By defect in past administration," as the document puts it, "it is burdened with great debt, and its state, from various causes, is so miserably impoverished that it is necessary to place the custody of the temporalities in the hands of a commission" appointed by the crown.[2]

That this is no exaggerated view of the difficulties which beset the landed proprietors at the time, and that the origin of the misery must be sought for in the great pestilence, a passage in Smyth's *Lives of the Berkeleys* may help to show: "In the 23rd of this King," he writes, "so great was the plague within this lord's manor of Hame (in Gloucestershire) that so many workfolks as amounted to 1,144 days' work were hired to gather in

[1] Escheator's Inq. p. m., 22-23 Ed. III, series i, file 64.
[2] Rot. Pat., 27 Ed. III, m. 17.

the corn of that manor alone, as by their deaths fell into the lord's hands, or else were forsaken by them."[1]

The priory of Lanthony, near Gloucester, was brought to such straits that the community were forced to apply to the Bishop of Hereford to grant them one of the benefices in his diocese. They have been, they say, so situated on the high road as to be obliged to give great hospitality at all times to rich and poor. Their property, in great part, was in Ireland, and it had been much diminished in value by the state of the country. The house was at this time, October 15th, 1351, so impoverished by this and by a great fire, that, without aid, they could not keep up their charity. For " the rents of the priory and the services, which the tenants and natives, or serfs of the said house living on their domain, have been wont yearly, and even daily, to pay and perform for the religious serving God there, now, through the pestilence and unwonted mortality by which the people of the kingdom of England have been afflicted, and, as is known, almost blotted out, are for the greater part irreparably lost."[2]

Some few years after the plague had passed an inquisition held at Gloucester as to the state of the priory of Horsleigh reveals the fact that a great number of the tenants on the estate had died. Horsleigh was at that period a cell of the priory of Bruton, in Somerset, and the question before the jury at this inquiry was as to the dilapidations caused by the prior or minister of the dependent cell. They first found that all revenues from the estates at Horsleigh, after a reasonable amount had been allowed for the support of the prior and his brethren

---

[1] Ed. *Bristol and Gloucester Archaeological Society*, i, 307.
[2] Reg. Heref. Trileck., fol. 102.

living in the cell, should be paid to the head house of Bruton. This the then prior, one Henry de Lyle, had not done. He had, moreover, dissipated the goods of his house by cutting down timber and underwood and selling cattle. Amongst the rest he is declared to have sold "eighty oxen and cows which had come to the house as mortuaries or heriots of tenants who had died in the great pestilence."[1]

Dugdale, in his history of the county, prints some 175 lists of incumbents of Warwickshire livings. In 76 cases there is noted a change at this period, and in several instances more than once is a new incumbent appointed to a living within a short period, so that in all there are some 93 institutions recorded.

A glimpse of the state to which the county generally was reduced is afforded by some *Inquisitiones post mortem*. As soon after the plague as 1350, at Wappenbury in Warwickshire, three houses, three cottages, and 20 acres of land are described as valueless and lying vacant, because of the pestilence late past. At Alcester, on the estate of a man who died June 20th, 1349, rents are not received and tenements are in hand, "for the most part, through the death of the holders." Again, at Wilmacott, an inquiry was held as to the property of Elizabeth, daughter of John de Wyncote, who died 10th August, 1349. It is declared that the mother died on 10th June, and the daughter two months later, whilst the great part of the land is in the hand of the owner "by the death of the tenants in this present pestilence."[2]

---

[1] Bruton Chartulary, f. 121b. Prior Henry appears to have spent the money thus raised in the expense of a journey to Rome and Venice and back. The inquiry was held in June, 29 Ed. III.

[2] Escheator's Inq. p. m., Series i, file 240.

On the estate of one who died in December, 1350, it is certified that there used to be nine villeins, each farming half a virgate of land, for which they paid eight shillings a year. Five of these had died, and their land since had been lying idle and uncultivated. On another portion of the same, two out of four tenants, who had six acres of land each, have been carried off.

On the manor of Whitchurch, owned by Margaret de la Beche, who died in the October of the plague year, 1349, it is noted that there are no court fees, as all the tenements are in hand. And in May, 1351, of another Oxfordshire estate it is said that eight claimants out of eighteen were dead, and no one was forthcoming to take the land; whilst on the same, out of six native tenants, who had each paid 14 shillings, three are gone, and their land has since remained untilled.[1]

One or two examples may be given of the difficulties subsequently experienced by the religious houses. The year after the plague had passed the Cistercian abbey of Bruerne was forced to seek the King's protection against the royal provisors and the quartering of royal servants upon them. This Edward granted, "because it was in such a bad state, that otherwise in a short time there would follow the total destruction of the said abbey, and the dispersal of the monks."[2] Even this protection, however, did not entirely mend matters, for three years later, "to avoid total ruin," the custody of the abbey was handed over to three commissioners."[3]

St. Frideswide's, Oxford, was in much the same case. In May, 1349, as we may suppose from the death of the

[1] Escheator's Inq. p. m., Series i, file 103.
[2] Rot. Pat., 25 Ed. III, pars 1ᵃ, m. 16.
[3] *Ibid.*, 28 Ed. III, m. 10.

superior during the time of the epidemic at Oxford, the plague had visited the monastery, and had, in all probability, carried off many of its inmates. The deaths of many of its tenants, moreover, must have gravely affected its financial condition, and three years later it was found necessary to put the temporalities in the hands of a commission. " By want of good government," it is said, " and through casual misfortunes, coming upon the said priory, both because of the debts by which it is much embarrassed, and for other causes," it is reduced to such a state that it might easily lead to the dispersal of the canons and the total destruction of the house.[1]

Of the tenants of one manor belonging to a religious house in the county of Oxford, it is said " that in the time of the mortality of men or the pestilence, which was in the year 1349, there hardly remained two tenants on the said manor. These would have left had not brother Nicholas de Lipton, then abbot, made new agreements with these and other incoming tenants." [2]

To take but two instances more in other parts of England.

The year after the plague was over, in 1351, the abbey of Barlings had to plead poverty and to beg for the remission of a tax. It is true, they urge the building of their new church, but likewise declare that they have been "impoverished by many other causes." An *Inquisitio post mortem* gives the same picture. Two carucates of land, for example, brought in only forty shillings, on account of the pestilence and general poverty and deaths of the tenants. "For a similar reason," a mill, which used to produce £2 in rent, now yields

[1] Rot. Pat., 28 Ed. III, m. 3.
[2] Quoted in *Saturday Review*, Jan. 16, 1886, " The Manor."

nothing; and so on throughout every particular of the large estate.

In this part of the country, too, the King's officer experienced the greatest difficulties in getting his dues and the Escheator pleads, in mitigation of a small return, that during the whole of 1350 tenements have been standing empty, in Gayton, near Towcester, in Weedon, in Weston, and in Morton, ten miles from Brackley, as tenants cannot be found "by reason of the mortality." He further excuses himself for not levying on the lands and goods of the people "on account of the pestilence."

¹ R. O., L. T. R. Memoranda Roll, 25 Ed. III.

CHAPTER X

SOME CONSEQUENCES OF THE GREAT MORTALITY

IT will be evident to all who have followed the summary of the history of the epidemic of 1349, given in the preceding chapters, that throughout England the mortality must have been very great. Those who, having examined the records themselves, have the best right to form an opinion, are practically unanimous in considering that the disease swept away fully one-half of the entire population of England and Wales.

But whilst it is easy enough to state in general terms the proportion of the entire population which probably perished in the epidemic, any attempt to give even approximate numbers is attended with the greatest difficulty and can hardly be satisfactory. At present we do not possess data sufficient to enable us to form the basis of any calculation worthy of the name. From the Subsidy Roll of 1377—or some 27 years after the great mortality—it has been estimated that the population at the close of the reign of Edward III was about 2,350,000 in England and Wales. The intervening years were marked by several more or less severe outbreaks of Eastern plague; and one year, 1361, would have been accounted most calamitous had not the memory of the fatal year 1349 somewhat overshadowed it. At the same time the French war continued to tax the strength of the country and levy its tithe upon the lives of Englishmen. It may consequently be believed that the losses during the thirty years which followed the plague of 1349 would be sufficient to prevent any actual increase of the population, and that somewhere about two and a half millions of people were left in the country after the epidemic had ceased. If this be so, it is probable that previous to the mortality the entire population of the country consisted of from four to five millions, half of whom perished in the fatal year.[1]

On the other hand, whilst apparently allowing that about one-half of the population perished, so eminent an authority as the late Professor Thorold Rogers held that the population of England in 1349 could hardly have been greater than two-and-a-half millions, and "probably was not more than two millions."[2] The most recent authority, Dr. Cunningham, thinks that "the results (i.e. of an inquiry into the number of the population) which are of a somewhat negative character, may be stated as follows: (i.) that the population was pretty nearly stationary at over two millions from 1377 to the Tudors: (ii.) that circumstances did not favour rapid increase of population between 1350 and 1377; (iii.) that the country was not incapable of sustaining a much larger population in the earlier part of Edward III's reign than it could maintain in the time of Henry VI"[3] Thus the estimate first given, of the population previous to the Black Death, may be taken as substantially the same as

---

[1] Cf. T. Amyot, *Population of English Cities, temp. Ed. III.* (*Archaeologia*, vol. xx, pp. 524-531).

[2] *England before and after the Black Death* (*Fortnightly Review.* vol. viii, p. 191).

[3] W. Cunningham, *Growth of English Industry and Commerce.* p. 304.

that adopted by Dr. Cunningham. Mr. Thorold Rogers, on the other hand, without entering into the question of figures, views the problem altogether from the standpoint of the land, the cultivated portion of which he considers incapable of supporting a larger population than he names.

In the country at large the most striking and immediate effect of the mortality was to bring about nothing less than a complete social revolution. Everywhere, although the well-to-do people were not exempt from the contagion, it was the poor who were the chief sufferers. "It is well known," wrote the late Professor Thorold Rogers, "that the Black Death, in England at least, spared the rich and took the poor. And no wonder. Living as the peasantry did in close, unclean huts, with no rooms above ground, without windows, artificial light, soap, linen; ignorant of certain vegetables, constrained to live half the year on salt meat; scurvy, leprosy, and other diseases, which are engendered by hard living and the neglect of every sanitary precaution, were endemic among the population.[1]

The obvious and undoubted effect of the great mortality among the working classes was to put a premium upon the services of those that survived. From all parts of England comes the same cry for workers to gather in the harvests, to till the ground, and to guard the cattle. For years the same demands are re-echoed until the

[1] *Fortnightly Review*, viii, p. 192. This is, of course, true, but without qualification might give the reader a false impression as to the condition of the English peasant in the Middle Ages. Most of what Mr. Thorold Rogers says is applicable to all classes of society. Dr. Cunningham (*Growth of English Industry and Commerce*, p. 275) takes a truer view: "Life is more than meat, and though badly housed the ordinary villager was better fed and amused."

landowners learnt from experience that the old methods
of cultivation, and the old tenures of land, had been
rendered impossible by the great scourge that had swept
over the land.

It was a hard time for the landowners, who up to this
had had it, roughly speaking, all their own way. With
rents falling to half their value, with thousands of acres
of land lying untilled and valueless, with cottages, mills
and houses without tenants, and orchards, gardens, and
fields waste and desolate, there came a corresponding
rise in the prices of commodities. Everything that the
landowner had to buy rose at once, as Professor Thorold
Rogers pointed out, " 50, 100, and even 200 per cent."
Iron, salt, and clothing doubled in value, and fish—and
in particular herrings, which formed so considerable a
part of the food of that generation—became dear beyond the reach of the multitude. " At that time," writes
William Dene, the contemporary monk of Rochester,
" there was such a dearth and want of fish that people
were obliged to eat meat on the Wednesdays, and a
command was issued that four herrings should be sold
for a penny. But in Lent there was still such a want of
fish that many, who had been wont to live well, had to
content themselves with bread and potage." [1]

Then that which had been specially the scourge of the
people at large began to be looked upon as likely to
prove a blessing in disguise. The landowner's need was
recognised as the labourers' opportunity, upon which
they were not slow to seize. Wages everywhere rose to
double the previous rate and more. In vain did the
King and Council strive to prevent this by legislation,
forbidding either the labourer to demand, or the master

[1] B. Mus. Cott. MS., Faust, B. v, fol. 99b.

to pay, more than the previous wage for work done. From the first the Act was inoperative, and the constant repetition of the royal commands, addressed to all parts of the country, as well as the frequent complaints of non-compliance with the regulations, are evidence, even if none other existed, of the futility of the legislation. Even when the King, taking into consideration "that many towns and hamlets, both through the pestilence and other causes, are so impoverished, and that many others are absolutely desolate," granted, if only the money were paid him in three months, that the fines levied on servants and others for demanding excessive wages, and on masters for giving them, might be allowed to go in relief of the tax of a tenth and fifteenth due to him,[1] the justices appointed to obtain the money plead that they "cannot and have not been able to levy any of these penalties." [2] The truth seems to be that masters generally pleaded the excessive wages they were called upon to pay, as an excuse for not finding money to meet the royal demands, and it was for this reason rather than out of consideration for the pockets of the better classes that Edward issued his proclamations to restrain the rise of wages. But he was quickly forced to understand "that workmen, servants, and labourers publicly disregarded his ordinances" as to wages and payments, and demanded, in spite of them, prices for their services as great as during the pestilence and after it, and even higher. For disobedience to the royal orders regulating wages, the King charged his judges to imprison all whom they might find guilty. Even this coercion was found to be no real remedy, but rather a means of aggravating

---

[1] R. O., Originalia Roll, 26 Ed. III, m. 27.
[2] *Ibid.*, 27 Ed. III, m. 19.

the evil, since districts where his policy was carried out were quickly found to be plunged in greater poverty by the imprisonment of those who could work, and of those who dared to pay the market price for labour.[1]

Knighton thus describes the situation:—" The King sent into each county of the kingdom orders that harvesters and other workmen should not obtain more than they were wont to have, under penalties laid down in the statute made for the purpose. But labourers were so elated and contentious that they did not pay attention to the command of the King; and if anyone wanted to hire them he was forced to pay them what was asked, and so he had his choice either to lose his harvest and crops, or give in to the proud and covetous desire of the workmen. When this became known to the King, he levied heavy fines upon the abbots, priors, and the higher and lesser lords, as well as upon the greater and smaller landowners in the country, because they had not obeyed his orders, and had given higher wages to their labourers; from some he exacted 100*s.*, from some 40*s.*, and from some 20*s.*, and indeed from each as much as he could be made to pay. And he took from every carucate throughout the whole kingdom 20*s.* besides a fifteenth.

" Then the King arrested very many labourers and put them in prison; and many fled and hid themselves in forests and woods for the time, and those who were caught were fined more severely still. And the greater number were sworn not to take higher daily wages than was customary, and were so liberated from prison. In like manner he acted towards the artificers in towns and cities."[2]

[1] R. O., Originalia Roll, 26 Ed. III, m. 25.
[2] Ed. Twysden, col. 2699.

To this account of the labour difficulties which followed on the mortality may be added the relation of the Rochester contemporary, William Dene. "So great was the want of labourers and workmen of every art and craft," in those days, he writes, "that a third part and more of the land throughout the entire kingdom remained uncultivated. Labourers and skilled workmen became so rebellious that neither the King, nor the law, nor the justices, the guardians of the law, were able to punish them."[1] Many instances are to be found in the public documents at the period of combinations of workmen for the purpose of securing higher wages, and of their refusal to work at the old rate of payment customary before the great mortality had made the services of the survivors more valuable. This, in the language of the statute, is called "the malice of servants in husbandry." In the same way tenants who had survived the visitation refused to pay the old rents and threatened to leave their holdings unless substantial reductions were made by their landlords. Thus, in an instance already given, the landowner remitted a third part of the rent of his tenants, "because they would have gone off and left their holdings empty unless they had obtained this reduction."[2]

As a consequence of the great mortality among small tenant farmers and the labouring classes generally, and forced by the failure of legislation to cope practically with the "strike" organised by the survivors, the landowners quickly despaired of carrying on the traditional system of cultivation with their own stock under bailiffs. Professor Thorold Rogers has pointed out that "very

[1] B. Mus. Cott. MS., Faust, B. v, fol. 98b.
[2] R. O., Q. R. Mins. Accts., Bundle 801, No. 1.

speedily after the plague, this system of farming by
bailiff was discontinued, and that of farming on lease
adopted." The difficulty experienced by the tenant of
finding capital to work the farms at first led to the institution of the stock and seed lease, which, after lasting
till about the close of the fourteenth century, gave place
to the ordinary land lease, with, of course, a certain
fixity of tenure, which at this day we do not associate
with that form of lease. Some landowners tried, with
more or less success, to continue the old system; but
these formed the exception, and by the beginning of the
next century the whole tenure of land had been changed
in England by the great mortality of 1349, and by the
operation of the "trades unions," which sprung up at
once among the survivors, and which are designated, in
the statute against them, as "alliances, covines, congre-
gations, chapters, ordinances and oaths."

The people all at once learnt their power, and became
masters of the situation, and although for the next thirty
years the lords and landowners fought against the complete overthrow of the mediaeval system of serfdom,
from the year of the great mortality its fall was inevitable, and practical emancipation was finally won by the
popular rising of 1381. Even to the last, however, the
landowning class appear to have remained in the dark
as to the real issues at stake. They claimed the old
labour rents, by which their manor lands had been
worked, as well as the money payments for which they
had been commuted, and they desired that the old ties
of the tenant in villeinage to the soil of his lord should
be maintained. Even Parliament was apparently at fault
as to the danger which threatened the established
system. It is impossible, however, to read the sermons

of the period without seeing how entirely the clergy were with the people in their determination to secure full and entire liberty for themselves and their posterity, and it is probably to their countenance and advice that the preamble of an Act passed in the first year of Richard II refers, when it says: "Villeins withdraw their services and customs from their lords, by the comfort and procurement of others, their counsellors, maintainers and abettors, which have taken hire and profit of the said villeins and land tenants, by colour of certain exemplifications made out of Domesday, and affirm that they are discharged and will suffer no distress. Hereupon they gather themselves in great routs, and argue by such a confederacy that everyone shall resist their lords by force."

One result of the change of land tenure should be noticed. Previously to the great plague of 1349 the land was divided up into small tenancies. An instance taken by Professor Rogers of a parish, where every man held a greater or less amount of land, is a typical example of thousands of manors all over the country. It shows, he says, "how generally the land was distributed," and that the small farms and portions of land, so remarkable in France at the present day, did prevail in England five hundred years ago. A great portion of this land, however, although held by distinct tenants, lay in common, and it is a very general complaint at this period that, as the fields were undivided, they could not be used except by the multitude of tenants, which had been carried off by the great sickness. To render them profitable, under the condition of things consequent upon the new system of farming, these tracts of country had to be divided up by the plantation of hedges, which form now so distinguishing a mark of the English landscape as compared with that of a foreign country.

The population also having by the operation of the great mortality become already detached from the soil, before the final extinction of serfdom, their liberation resulted not, as in other countries, in the establishment of a large class of peasant proprietors, but in that of a small body of large landowners.

Of course, again, such a phrase must not be interpreted in the modern sense, whereby a " landowner " is an " owner " of land in a way which, in those days of custom and perpetuity of tenure, would not have been even understood. The change then effected rendered possible the character of the land settlement that now prevails.

So terrible a mortality cannot but have had its effect and left its traces upon the education, arts, and architecture of the country. In the first, besides the temporary interference with the education at the Universities, " this pestilence forms," write the authors of the *History of Shrewsbury*, " a remarkable era in the history of our language. Before that time, ever since the Conquest, the nobility and gentry of this country affected to converse in French; children even construed their lessons at school into that language. So, at least, Higden tells us in his *Polychronicon*. But from the time of ' the first Moreyn,' as Trevisa, his translator, terms it, this ' manner ' was ' som del ychaungide.' A school-master, named Cornwall, was the first that introduced English into the instruction of his pupils, and this example was so eagerly followed that by the year 1385, when Trevisa wrote, it had become nearly general. The clergy in all Christian countries are the chief persons by whom the education of youth is conducted, and it is probable that the dreadful scourge of which we have been treating, by carrying off many of those ancient instructors, enabled Mr. Cornwall to work a change in the mode of teaching, which but for that event he would never have been able to effect, and which has operated so mighty a revolution in our national literature."

With regard to architecture, traces of the effects of the great plague are to be seen in many places. In some cases great additions to existing buildings, which had only been partially executed, were put a stop to and never completed. In others they were finished only after a change had been made in the style in vogue when the great mortality swept over the country. Dr. Cox, in his *Notes on the Churches of Derbyshire*, has remarked upon this. " The awful shock," he says, " thus given to the nation and to Europe at large by the Black Death paralysed for a time every art and industry. The science of church architecture, then about at its height, was some years recovering from the blow. In some cases, as with the grand church of St. Nicholas, Yarmouth, where a splendid pair of western towers were being erected, the work was stopped and never resumed. . . . The recollection of this great plague often helps to explain the break that the careful eye not unfrequently notes in church buildings of the 14th century, and accounts for the long period over which the works extended. We believe this to be the secret of the long stretch of years that elapsed before the noble church of Tideswell was completed in that century; and it also affords a clue to much other work interrupted, or suddenly undertaken, in several other fabrics of the country."[1] To this may

[1] Introduction, p. ix.

be added the fact that the history of stained-glass manufacture shows the same break with the past at this
period. Not only just at this time does there appear a
gap in the continuity of manufacture, but the first examples after the great pestilence manifest a change in
the style which had previously existed.

In estimating the mortality among the clergy it has
been already noted that we have, in many instances,
more certain data to work upon than in the case of the
population at large. In each county the number of institutions to benefices during the plague has already been
noticed, and in those cases where the actual figure cannot
be ascertained from documentary evidence, half the total
number of benefices has, in accordance with the general
result where such evidence is available, been taken to
represent the livings rendered vacant during that year.
From this it would appear that in round figures some
5,000 beneficed clergy fell victims to their duty. As
already pointed out this number in reality represents
only a portion of the clerical body; and in any estimate
of the whole, allowance must be made for chaplains,
chantry priests, religious, and others.

It is, of course, possible to come to any conclusion as
to the proportion of the beneficed to the unbeneficed
clergy only by very round numbers. Turning to the
Winchester registers, for example, we find that the
average number of priests ordained in the three years
previous to 1349, was 111.[1] The average number of in-

---

[1] Of course, several of these would be ordained for other dioceses,
but in the same way Winchester priests would be ordained by
letters dimissory elsewhere, so that taking the whole of England
we may assume a practical equalisation. In the diocese of London,
as already stated (p. 203 *ante*), the proportion of non-beneficed to

stitutions to benefices annually during the same period was only twenty-one, so that these figures taken by themselves seem to show that the proportion of bene-ficed to unbeneficed clergy was about one to four. On this basis, and assuming the deaths of beneficed clergy to have been about 5,000, the total death roll in the clerical order would be some 25,000.

This number, although very large, can hardly be con-sidered as excessive, when it is remembered that the peculiar nature of their priestly duties rendered the clergy specially liable to infection; whilst in the case of the religious, the mere fact of their living together in com-munity made the spread of the deadly contagion in their ranks a certainty. The Bishops were strangely spared; although it is certain that they did not shrink from their duty, but according to positive evidence remained at their posts. To their case are applicable the lines of the poet upon the like wonderful escape of the Bishop during the plague in the eighteenth century at Marseilles:

> Why drew Marseilles' good Bishop purer breath
> When nature sickened, and each gale was death?"[1]

On the supposition that five-and-twenty thousand of the clerical body fell victims to the epidemic, and esti-mating that of the entire population of the country one in every hundred belonged to the clergy, and further that the death rate was about equal in both estates, the total mortality in the country would be some 2,500,000. This total is curiously the same as that estimated from the basis of population returns made at the close of the memorable reign of Edward III, evidencing, namely, a

beneficed clergy ordained during 12 years, from 1362 to 1374, was nearly six to one.

[1] Pope, *Essay on Man*, lines 107-8.

total population, before the outbreak of the epidemic, of some five millions.[1]

It remains now briefly to point out some of the un-doubted effects, which followed from this great disaster, upon the Church. It is obvious that the sudden removal of so large a proportion of the clerical body must have caused a breach in the continuity of the best traditions of ecclesiastical usage and teaching. Absolute necessity, moreover, compelled the Bishops to institute young and inexperienced, if not entirely uneducated clerics, to the vacant livings, and this cannot but have had its effect upon succeeding generations. The Archbishop of York sought and obtained permission from the Pope to ordain at any time, and to dispense with the usual intervals between the sacred orders;—Bishop Bateman, of Nor-wich, was allowed by Clement VI to dispense with sixty clerks, who were but twenty-one years of age, " though only shavelings," and to allow them to hold rectories, as otherwise the divine offices of the Church would cease altogether in many places of his diocese.

" At that time," writes Knighton, the sub-contemporary canon of Leicester, " there was everywhere such a dearth of priests that many churches were left without the divine offices, Mass, Matins, Vespers, sacraments, and sacramentals. One could hardly get a chaplain to serve a church for less than £10, or 10 marks. And whereas before the pestilence, when there were plenty of priests, anyone could get a chaplain for 5 or even 4 marks, or

---

[1] Mr. Thorold Rogers' supposition that the population in 1348 was only about 2,500,000 would, on the assumption that the two sexes were about equal in number, lead to the conclusion that one man in every 25 was a priest; a suggestion which seems to bear, on the face of it, its own refutation.

for 2 marks and his board,[1] at this time there was hardly
a soul who would accept a vicarage for £20, or 20 marks.
In a short time after, however, a large number of those
whose wives had died in the pestilence came up to
receive orders. Of these many were illiterate and mere
laics, except in so far as they knew in a way how to read,
although they did not understand " what they read.[2]

One instance of the rapidity of promotion, so that
benefices might not too long remain unfilled, may be
given. In the diocese of Winchester the registers record
at this period very numerous appointments of clerics, not
in sacred orders, to benefices. For example, in 1349 no
fewer than 19 incumbents already appointed to churches
in the city of Winchester came up for ordination, and
eight in the following year. Of these 27 every one took
his various orders of sub-deacon, deacon, and priest at
successive ordinations without the normal interval between each step in the sacred ministry.[3]

[1] Amyot (*Archaeologia*, xx, p. 531) notes that even soldiers appear
to have been better paid than the clergy. A foot soldier had 3d. a
day, or 7 marks a year; a horse soldier 10d. or 12d. a day. Chaucer's
good parson, who was only "rich of holy thought and werk," might
not be remarkable.

[2] Ed. Twysden, col. 2699.

[3] Mr. Baigent's MS. extracts from the Episcopal Registers. It
is of interest to note that in normal times very few were ordained
after their appointment as incumbents. Thus, to take the churches
in the city of Winchester, besides this period and 1361, when again
the mortality among the clergy was very great, only some 8 or 9
were so ordained between 1349 and 1361, as the following table
will show:

1346	1348	1349	1350	1351	1352	1354	1359	1361	1362	1363
1	1	19	8	4	1	2	1	5	1	1

Two examples of the straits to which the Bishops were reduced for priests are to be found in the registers of the diocese of Bath and Wells. The one is the admission of a man to the first step to Orders, in the lifetime of his wife, she giving her consent, and promising to keep chaste, but not, as was usually required under such circumstances, being compelled to enter the cloister, "because she was aged, and could without suspicion remain in the world."[1] The second instance in the same register of a difficulty experienced in filling up vacancies is the case of a permission given to Adam, the rector of Hinton Bluet, to say mass on Sundays and feast days in the chapel of William de Sutton, even although he had before celebrated the solemnities of the mass in his church of Hinton.[2]

Another curious case, which we may suspect really came from the same cause, is noted at an ordination held in December, 1352, at Ely. Of the four then receiving the priesthood two were monks, and from the other two an oath of obedience to the Bishop and his successors was enacted, together with a promise "that they would serve any parish church to which they might be called."[3]

Many instances could be given of the ignorance consequent upon the ordinations being hurried on, and upon laymen, otherwise unfitted for the sacred mission, being too hastily admitted to the vacant cures. To take but two instances, from Winchester, which may serve to illustrate this and at the same time to show the zeal with which the mediaeval Bishops endeavoured to guard

[1] Harl. MS., 6965, fol. 145 (7 Id. Julii, 1349).
[2] *Ibid.*, fol. 146b.
[3] B. Mus. Cole MS., 5824, fol. 23b.

against the evil. On 24th June, 1385, the illustrious William of Wykeham, Bishop of Winchester, caused Sir Roger Dene, Rector of the church of St. Michael, in Jewry Street, Winchester, to swear upon the Holy Gospels that he would learn within twelve months the articles of Faith, the cases reserved to the Bishop, the Ten Commandments, the seven works of mercy, the seven mortal sins, the Sacraments of the Church, and the form of administering and conferring them, and also the form of baptising, etc., as contained in the Constitutions of Archbishop Peckham.[1] The same year, on July 2nd, the Bishop exacted from John Corbet, who on the 2nd of June previous had been instituted to the rectory of Bradley in Hampshire, a similar obligation to learn the same, before the feast of St. Michael then next ensuing. In the former case Roger Dene had been rector of Ryston, in Norfolk, and had been instituted to his living at Winchester by the Bishop of Norwich only on 21st June, 1358, three days before Bishop William of Wykeham required him to enter into the obligation detailed above.[2]

It has been already remarked that one obvious result of the great mortality, so far as the Church is concerned, was the extraordinary decrease in the number of candidates for sacred orders. In the Winchester diocese, for example, the average number of priests ordained in each of the three years preceding 1349 was 111; whilst in the 15 subsequent years, up to 1365, when Bishop Edyndon died, the yearly average was barely 20; and

---

[1] For the real meaning to be attached to learning the *Pater noster*, etc., see my article on *Religious Instruction in England in the 14th and 15th Centuries*, in *Dublin Review*, Oct., 1893, p. 900.

[2] Mr. Baigent's MS. collections.

in the thirty-four years, from 1367 to 1400, even with so
zealous a prelate as William of Wykeham presiding over
the diocese, the annual average number of ordinations
to the sacred priesthood was only 27; a number which
was further decreased during the progress of the fifteenth
century.[1]

The same striking result of the plague, which cannot
but have had a very serious effect upon the Church at
large, is manifested elsewhere. The Ely registers, for
example, show that the average number of all those
ordained, for the seven years before 1349, was 101½;
whilst for the seven years after that date it was but 40½.
In 1349 no ordinations whatever apparently were held,
and the average number of priests ordained yearly, from
1374 to 1394, was only 14. In fact the total number
ordained in that period was only 282, whilst of these
many entered the priesthood for other dioceses, and
more than half, namely 161, were members of the various
religious orders; so that the ranks of the diocesan clergy
of Ely appear to have received but few recruits during
the whole of this time.

In the diocese of Hereford, to take another example,
previously to 1349, there were some very large ordinations. Thus, in 1346, on the 11th of March, 438 people
were ordained to various grades in the sacred ministry.
Of these some 89 received the priesthood, 49 of them
being ordained for the diocese of Hereford. Again, on
the 10th of June in the same year, Bishop Trileck conferred Orders, in the parish church of Ledbury, upon
451 candidates, of whom 148 were made priests; 56
being intended for his own diocese. Altogether, in that

---

[1] From 1400 to 1418 the average was 17, from 1447 to 1467
only 18.

year, some 319 priests were ordained by the Bishop; half of the number being his own clergy.[1] About the same numbers were ordained in the year of the plague itself, 1349, and 371 in the following year. In fact, till 1353 the number remains large, but the greater portion of those ordained were intended for other dioceses. The subjects of the Bishop of Hereford at once show a falling off similar to that noticed in Winchester and Ely. Thus, from 1345 to 1349, the average number of subjects ordained by the Bishop for his own diocese was 72. In the next five years it was only 34, whilst in no subsequent year during Bishop Trileck's pontificate did it rise above 23.

The above three examples will be sufficient to show how seriously the great pestilence affected the supply of clergy. The reason is not difficult to divine. The great dearth of population created a proportionate demand upon the services of the survivors to carry on the business of the nation, and the greater pressure of business thus brought about, and the higher wages to be, in fact, obtained, in spite of royal prohibitions, were not favourable to the development of vocations to the clerical life. The void thus caused by the overwhelming misfortunes of the great mortality was enlarged by the exigencies of the English war with France, whilst popular disturbances, and the subsequent Wars of the Roses, maintained the same causes in operation till far into the reigns of the Tudor sovereigns.

To some extent, the dearth of students at Oxford and Cambridge, which has already been referred to, was brought about by the same causes, and it certainly followed immediately upon the fatal year of 1349. At

[1] Reg. Trileck, fol. 180 *seqq.*

Oxford, no doubt, the serious disturbances, which took place at this time between the students and townsfolk, contributed to aggravate the evil. So serious, indeed, had the state of the great centre of clerical education in England become, in less than six years after the pestilence, that the King was compelled to address the Bishops on the subject. He begs them to help in the task of renewing the University; "knowing," he says, "how the Catholic Faith is chiefly supported by the learning of the clergy, and the State governed by their prudence, we earnestly desire that, particularly in our kingdom of England, the clerical order may be increased in number, morals, and knowledge." But, "in the city of Oxford, in which the fount and source of clerical knowledge" has long existed, owing to the disturbances, students have forsaken the place, and Oxford, once so renowned, has become "like a worthless fig-tree without fruit."[1] It has already been pointed out how, nearly half a century later, the University had not recovered from the great blow it had received at this period.[2]

There seems, indeed, a prevalent misunderstanding in regard to the relation, or proportionate numbers, of secular and regular clergy at this period, and as to the decline in popularity of the regulars, as presumed to be evidenced in the number of those who joined them after the middle of the fourteenth century. It is assumed that up to that period the regular clergy were, both in

[1] Reg. Trileck, fol. 163.
[2] Archbishop Islip founded Canterbury College at Oxford to supply the failing ranks of the clergy and to increase the facilities of learning (Wilkins, iii, p. 52), and William of Wykeham likewise established his schools and colleges with the same object.

numbers and influence, the chief factors in the ecclesiastical system of England, and that after that date they
greatly declined in importance, public estimation, and
numbers. As evidence, not only is an actual diminution
in mere numbers adduced, but also the fact that, after
this time, the new religious institutions took the form of
colleges, not of monasteries. The misconception lies
first of all in this—that there never was a period of the
Middle Ages in England, nor for the matter of that
abroad, when the regular clergy were the great mainstay
of the Church, so far, at least, as numbers, external
work, and the cure of souls are concerned. Writers have
allowed their imaginations to be influenced by the
magnitude of the great monastic houses, or by the
prominent part taken in the government of the Church
by individuals of eminence, belonging to the ranks of
the regular clergy; and have not remembered how comparatively few in fact were these great monastic centres,
and how small a proportion their inmates bore to the
great body of clergy at large.

It is necessary to refer, perhaps, to figures to bring
this home to those who have not devoted special attention to the mediaeval period, or who, having studied it,
still somehow fail to realise facts as distinct from
theories, and to rid themselves of the imaginative pre-
possessions with which they entered upon their investiga-
tions. Thus, even after the institution of the mendicant
orders, and in the flow of their popularity, the ordinations
for the diocese of York, in the year 1344-45, show that
whilst the number of priests ordained was 271, only 44
were regulars. In the same way, the register of Bishop
Stapeldon gives the ordinations in the diocese of Exeter
from 1301 to 1321. During this period 703 seculars were

made priests, against 114 regulars. In both these instances, therefore, more than six seculars were ordained
for every regular.

This has its importance in estimating the change in
the direction given to religious foundations noticed
above. During the course of the thirteenth century,
when so strong a current of intellectual activity and
speculation had set in, the importance of education to
the working clergy—at least to a considerable proportion of them—forced itself upon those who were the
responsible rulers of the Church. The religious houses
were in existence, and, either great or small, were spread
all over the land; indeed, after the pestilence of 1349,
greatly more than sufficed for the number of vocations
in the reduced population. Further, by their foundation
they were not calculated to furnish the means of meeting the new want that was pressing, aggravated as it
was by the sudden diminution of the pastoral clergy in
the sickness. The formation of collegiate institutions,
whether of the University type or of country colleges
for secular priests, such as Stoke-Clare, Arundel, and
the very many others which arose in the century and a
half from 1350 to 1500, is explained by the very circumstances of the case; and there is no need to have re-
course to a supposition as to the wane in popularity of
the religious orders, and the prevalent sense that their
work was over, to explain the diminution in their
numbers, and the absence of new monastic foundations.
If the relative proportion between the numbers of secular
and regular clergy ordained before and after the middle
of the fourteenth century be taken as a test of the truth
of this supposition, the statistics available do not bear it
out. Thus the ordinations to the priesthood, registered

in the registers of the diocese of Bath and Wells, for the 80 years, 1443 to 1523, number 901; of these 679 were those of seculars, and 222 those of regulars. In this instance, consequently, the ordination of seculars to regulars was in the proportion of 8·5 to 2·7, or rather more than three to one.[1]

In common with those in worldly professions and busi-nesses the survivors among the clergy appear to have demanded larger stipends than they had previously obtained for the performance of their ecclesiastical duties. Looking back upon the times, and considering how even the small dues of the clergy had been reduced by the death of a large proportion of their people, till they became wholly inadequate for their support, it is impossible to blame them harshly, and not to see that such a demand must inevitably follow upon a great reduction in numbers. At the time, however, by the direction of King and Parliament, the Archbishops and Bishops sought to restrain them from making these claims, in the same way as the King tried to prevent the labourers from demanding higher wages. In his letter to the Bishops of his province Archbishop Islip refers " to the unbridled cupidity of the human race," which ever

---

[1] In the diocese of London, in the twelve years, from 1362 to 1374, Bishop Sudbury ordained 1,046 seculars and 456 regulars, the proportion consequently being about 2·3 to 1. In the last twenty years of the century, namely, from 1381 to 1401, Bishop Braybroke ordained to the priesthood only 584 seculars, whilst the regulars were 425 during the same period. In other words, during the first period, the average annual number of ordinations to the ranks of the secular clergy in the diocese of London was over 87; during the last twenty years of the century it was only 29·2. The averages of the regulars in the corresponding periods were 35 and 21·2. Similar results appear from the York registers.

requires to be checked by justice, unless "charity is to be driven out of the world." "General complaints have come to me," he writes, "and experience, the best teacher of all things, has shown to me that the priests who still survive, not considering that they are preserved by the Divine will from the dangers of the late pestilence, not for their own sakes, but to perform the ministry committed to them for the people of God, and the public utility," like other workmen, through cupidity, neglect the burdens of curates, and take more profitable offices, for which also they demand more than before. If this be not at once put a stop to " many, and indeed most of the churches, prebends, and chapels of our and your diocese, and indeed of our whole Province, will remain absolutely without priests." To remedy this not only were people urged not to employ such chaplains, but the clergy were to be compelled under ecclesiastical censures to serve the ordinary cures at moderate and usual salaries. It seems not improbable that this measure may have contributed to draw the sympathies of the clergy at large more closely to the people in their struggle for freedom at this period of English history, when both in the civil and ecclesiastical sphere there was the same attempt by public law to impose restraints on natural liberty.

To the great dearth of clergy at this time may, partly at least, be ascribed the great growth of the crying abuse of pluralities. Without taking into account the difficulty experienced on all hands in finding fit, proper, and tried ecclesiastics to fill posts of eminence and responsibility in the Church, it is impossible to account for the great increase in the practice just at this time. The number of benefices, for example, held by William of

Wykeham himself, who entered the Church in consequence of the great mortality among the clergy in 1361, may be explained, if not excused, by the prevalent and in the circumstances inevitable dearth of subjects of training and capacity equal to the arduous and delicate duties devolving on the higher clergy.

Notwithstanding all the great difficulties which beset the Church in England in consequence of the great mortality, there is abundant evidence (which is no part of the present subject) of untiring efforts on the part of the leading ecclesiastics to bring back observance to its normal level. This is evidenced in the institution of so many pious confraternities and guilds, and in a profuse liberality to churches and sacred places.

The consequences of the mortality, so far as the monastic establishments of the country are concerned, have already in the course of the narrative frequently been pointed out. The same reasons which militated against the recruiting for the ranks of the clergy generally after the plague are sufficient explanation of the fact that the religious houses were never able to regain the ground lost in that fatal year. Over and above this, moreover, the sudden change in the tenure of land, brought about chiefly by the deaths of the monastic tenants, so impaired their financial position, at any rate for a long period, that they were unable to support the burden of additional subjects.

To the facts showing how the monasteries were depopulated by the disease already given may be added the following:—In 1235 the abbey of St. Albans is supposed to have counted some 100 monks within its walls. In the plague of 1349 the abbot and some 47 of his monks died at one time, and subsequently one more died whilst at Canterbury, on his way with the newly-elected abbot to the Roman Curia. Assuming, therefore, that the community had remained the same in number as in 1235, St. Albans was at most left with only 51 members. At the close of the century, namely, in 1396, some 60 monks took part in election, and as this number includes the priors of the nine dependent cells, it would seem that the actual community still remained only 51. In 1452 there were only 48 professed monks in the abbey, and at the dissolution of the monastery, nearly a century later, the number was reduced to 39. This instance of the way in which the numbers in the monastic houses were diminished by the sickness, and by its effect on the general population of the country were prevented from ever again increasing to their former proportions, may be strengthened by the case of Glastonbury. This great abbey of the west of England has ever been regarded as in many respects the most important of the English Benedictine houses. It is not too much to suppose that in the period of its greatest prosperity it must have counted probably a hundred members. In 1377 the number, as given on the subsidy-roll, is only 45. In 1456 they stand at 48, and were about the same at the time of the dissolution of the abbey. A similar effect upon the members at Bath has already been pointed out.

It need hardly be said that the scourge must have been most demoralising to discipline, destructive to traditional practice, and fatal to observance. It is a well-ascertained fact, strange though it may seem, that men are not as a rule made better by great and universal visitations of Divine Providence. It has been noticed that this is the evident result of all such scourges, or, as Procopius puts it, speaking of the great plague in the reign of the Emperor Justinian, "whether by chance or Providential design it strictly spared the most wicked."[1] So in this visitation, from Italy to England, the universal testimony of those who lived through it is, that it seemed to rouse up the worst passions of the human heart, and to dull the spiritual senses of the soul. Wadding, the Franciscan annalist, has attributed to this very plague of 1348-9 the decay of fervour evident throughout his own Order at this time. "This evil," he writes, "wrought great destruction to the holy houses of religion, carrying off the masters of regular discipline and the seniors of experience. From this time the monastic Orders, and in particular the mendicants, began to grow tepid and neg-ligent, both in that piety and that learning in which they had up to this time flourished. Then, our illustrious members being carried off, the rigours of discipline re-laxed by these calamities, could not be renewed by the youths received without the necessary training, rather to fill the empty houses than to restore the lost dis-cipline."[2]

We may sum up the results of the great mortality in the words of a reliable writer. "For our purpose," writes Dr. Cunningham, "it is important to notice that the steady progress of the twelfth and thirteenth centuries was suddenly checked in the fourteenth; the strain of the hundred years' war would have been exhausting in

[1] Archbp. Islip at this time (1350) says: "Dum ad memoriam reducimus admirandam pestilentiam que nuper partes istas subito sic invasit, ut nobis multo meliores et digniores subtraxerat."

[2] *Annales Minorum*, viii, p. 22.

any case, but the nation had to bear it when the Black
Death had swept off half the population and the whole
social structure was disorganised." [1]

In dealing with this subject it is difficult to bring
home to the mind the vast range of the great calamity,
and duly to appreciate how deep was the break with
then existing institutions. The plague of 1349 simply
shattered them; and it is, as already pointed out, only
by perpetual reiteration and reconsideration of the same
phenomena that we can bring ourselves to understand
the character of such a social and religious catastrophe.
But it is at the same time of the first importance thoroughly to realise the case if we are to enter into and to
understand the great process of social and religious re-
edification, to which the immediately succeeding generations had to address themselves. The tragedy was too
grave to allow of people being carried over it by mere
enthusiasm. Indeed, the empiric and enthusiast in the
attempts at social reconstruction, as may be found in the
works of Wycliff, could only aggravate the evil. It was
essentially a crisis that had to be met by strenuous
effort and unflagging work in every department of
human activity. And here is manifested a characteristic
of the Middle Ages which constitutes, as the late Professor Freeman has pointed out, their real greatness. In
contradistinction to a day like our own, which abounds
in every facility for achievement, they had to contend
with every material difficulty; but in contradistinction,
too, to that practical pessimism which has to-day gained
only too great a hold upon intelligences otherwise viva-
cious and open, difficulties, in the Middle Ages, called
into existence only a more strenuous and more deter-

[1] *Growth of English Industry and Commerce*, p. 275.

mined resolve to meet and surmount them. And here is
the sense in which the hackneyed, and in a sense untrue,
phrase, "the Ages of Faith," has a real application, for
nothing can be more contrary to the spirit and tone of
mind of the whole epoch than pessimism, nothing more
in harmony with it than hope. In this sense the observa-
tion of a well-known modern writer on art, in noting the
inability of the Middle Ages to see things as they really
are and the tendency to substitute on the parchment or
the canvas conventional for actual forms, has a drift
which, perhaps, he did not perceive. In itself unquestionably this defect is a real one, but in practice it possessed a counterbalancing advantage by supplying the
necessary corrective to that bare literalism and realism
which, in the long run, is fatal no less to sustained effort
than it is to art.

The great mortality, commonly called the Black
Death, was a catastrophe sudden and overwhelming, the
like of which it will be difficult to parallel. Many a
noble aspiration which, could it have been realised, and
many a wise conception which, could it have attained
its true development, would have been most fruitful of
good to humanity, was stricken beyond recovery. Still
no time was wasted in vain laments. What had perished
had perished. Time, however, and the power of effort
and work belonged to those that survived.

Two of the noblest churches in Italy typify the two-
fold aspect of this great visitation—the Cathedral of
Siena and the Cathedral of Milan. The former, the vast
building that crowns the Tuscan Hill, is but a fragment
of what was originally conceived. It was actually in
course of erection, and would have been hardly less in
size than the present St. Peter's had it been completed.

The transepts were already raised, and the foundations of the enormous nave and choir had been laid when the plague fell upon the city. The works were necessarily suspended, and from that day to this have never been resumed.

Little more than a generation had passed from the fatal year when the most glorious Gothic edifice on Italian soil was already rising from the plain of Lombardy—a symbol of new life, new hopes, new greatness, which would surpass the greatness of the buried past. And this, be it observed, was no creation of Prince or Potentate; it was essentially the idea, the work, the achievement of the people of Milan themselves.[1]

What gives, perhaps, the predominant interest to the century and a half which succeeded the overwhelming catastrophe of the Black Death is the fact of the wonderful social and religious recovery from a state almost of dissolution. It is not the place here even to enter upon so interesting and important a subject. It must suffice to have indicated the point of view from which the history of the immediately succeeding generations must be regarded. In spite of wars and civil commotions it was

[1] The *Annali della fabbrica*, published by the Cathedral administration, show in the minutest detail the organisation by which the necessary funds were raised, and enable us to see how it was popular enterprise by which so noble an undertaking was achieved. We can now realise the weekly collections made by willing citizens from door to door, the collections in the churches, the monthly sales of offerings in kind of the most varied nature, jewels, dresses, linen, pots and pans, divers articles of dress and domestic use. Every one, rich and poor alike, felt impelled to join in some way in the work which, as the words of the originators express it, "*was begun by Divine inspiration to the honour of Jesus Christ and His most Spotless Mother.*" Cf. an article by Mr. Edmund Bishop on the subject in the *Downside Review*, July, 1893.

an age of distinct progress, although the very com-
plexity and variety of current and undercurrent is apt at
times to daze the too impatient inquirer, who wishes to
reduce everything to the simple result of the definitely
good, or the definitely bad.

INDEX

ABBOTSBURY abbey, 89, 189.
Abergavenny priory, 138.
Abstinence days, dispensation from, 228.
Aden, trade route to, 4.
Adriatic, coast towns of, 68.
Agatha, St., relics at Catania, 16.
Ages of Faith, meaning of, 253.
Agrarian difficulties, 65, 172, 190-191, *seqq.*
Albans, St., *see* St. Albans.
Alcester, Inq. p.m. at, 221.
Aldgate, Holy Trinity, cemetery at, 108.
Aleppo, 2.
Alexandria and trade with Europe, 4.
Alfonso XI, death of, 67.
Allott, Thomas, 180.
Almeira, 67.
Almsford, 97.
Alnwick abbey, 186.
Alverdiscott, 102.
Amiens, 57.
Amounderness, deanery of, 182.
Andronicus (son of the Emperor Cantacuzene), death of, 14.
Anglada, on nature of the plague, 10.
Anglesey priory, Cambridge, 206.
Anglia, East, plague in, 150; effect on religious houses of, 150.
Animals attacked, 13, 44, 163.

Antioch, patriarch of, archbishop of Catania, 16.
Aragon, Queen of, dies, 67.
Architecture, influence of pestilence on, 235.
Arles, 43.
Armenia, 2.
Arras, decay of, 65.
Arundel college, 246.
Asia, epidemic in, 3; trade route to Europe from, 3; hordes of Tartars in, 3.
Athelney abbey, 98.
Atte Welle, John, 158.
Augustinians of Winchester diocese, 213.
Austria, 70.
Avesbury, Robert of, his account of the pestilence, 85.
Avignon, first reports of plague at, 18; account of plague at, 43, 52, 58, 139; date of epidemic at, 49; extent of mortality in, 49; decrease of population in, 47; new cemeteries at, 44.
Azarius, Peter, notary of Novara, 71.
Azov, otherwise Tana, 6.

Babington, translator of Hecker's *Epidemics*, 3 *note*.
Babington, Somerset, 97.

S

Iron, increased price of, 228.
Islip, Simon, Archbishop of Canterbury, his enthronisation, 123; letter on stipends of clergy, 247.
Istria, 69.
Ivychurch priory, 131, 189.

Jersey, 81.
Jervaulx abbey, 177.
Jessopp, Dr., his account of the plague in East Anglia, ii, 149, 150.
Jews, mortality amongst, 43.
Joan of Burgundy dies, 54.
Joan, daughter of Edward III, dies, 52.
Joan, Queen of Navarre, dies, 54.
John XXI, report as to Eastern commerce to, 3.

Kent, Margaret, Countess of, 159.
Keynsham abbey, 97.
Kidwelly priory, 138.
Kilkenny, 139-140.
Kilkhampton, John de, prior of Bodwin, 104.
Kilmersdon, 97.
King Edward, his compassion seldom manifested, 216; on clerical education, 244.
Kingsmead, prioress of, 171.
Knighton, chronicle by, 84; his account of plague at Bristol, 98; ditto in Leicestershire, 162; on the plague amongst the Scots, 186; his description of labour difficulties, 230; on the scarcity of priests, 238.
Knightsbridge, slaughter place for London at, 110.
Koos, or Chus, a trade station on the Nile, 4.
Kurds, the, attacked by the plague, 2.

Labour, increased cost of, 219-220, 227-228.
Labourers, difficulty of obtaining, 57, 106-107, 122, 163, 197-199, 208, 219; trouble with, 65; feel their power, xxii, 228; get higher wages in spite of legislation, 230-231.
Lagerbring, on plague in Norway, 77.
Lamech, earthquake at, 2.
Lancashire, 180.
Land, depreciation of, 159, 178, 218, 219, 223, 228; rents of, reduced, 123, 167-168, 169, 190 seqq.; cessation of services on, 172-173; a third part of, uncultivated, 231; change of, to large tenures, 233.
Landowners, difficulties of, 227-228; mediaeval meaning of, 234.
Langton, 91.
Language, effect of plague on, 234.
Languedoc, 42.
Langwith, 171.
Lanthony priory, 220.
Laon, abbey of St. John at, 65.
Launceston, appointment of a religious of, as prior of Bodmin, 104.
Laura de Noves, death of, 32-33, 43; announcement of death of, to Petrarch, 33.
Law Courts suspended, 174.
Law suits settled by deaths of parties, 136, 196.
Lay people and clergy, proportion of, 237.
Ledbury, large ordination at, 242.
Leicester, city of, 162.
Leicester, county of, institutions of clergy in, 163-164.
Lesnes monastery, poverty of, 123.
Le Strange, John, 167, 190.

CHISWICK PRESS: PRINTED BY CHARLES WHITTINGHAM AND CO.
TOOKS COURT, CHANCERY LANE, LONDON.